D0948185

Quick Reference to

PEDIATRIC EMERGENCY NURSING

Aspen Series in Emergency and Trauma Nursing
Gail Pisarcik Lenehan, RN, MS, CS, Series Editor
Psychiatric Clinical Nurse Specialist
Emergency Department
Massachusetts General Hospital
Boston, Massachusetts

Clinical Guidelines for Emergency Nursing:
Standardized Nursing Care Plans
Susan Moore
Deborah A. Charlson

Pediatric Trauma Nursing
Connie Joy

Managing Emergency Nursing Services
Iris C. Frank

Quick Reference to
PEDIATRIC EMERGENCY NURSING

Edited by

Donna Ojanen Thomas, RN, MSN, CEN
Director, Emergency Department
Primary Children's Medical Center
Salt Lake City, Utah

Aspen Series in Emergency and Trauma Nursing
Gail Pisarcik Lenehan, Series Editor

AN ASPEN PUBLICATION®
Aspen Publishers, Inc.
Gaithersburg, Maryland
1991

Library of Congress Cataloging-in-Publication Data

Thomas, Donna Ojanen.
Quick reference to pediatric emergency nursing / Donna Ojanen Thomas.
p. cm.
— (Aspen series in emergency and trauma nursing)
Includes bibliographical references.
Includes index.
ISBN 0-8342-0199-2
1. Pediatric nursing— Outlines, syllabi, etc. I. Title. II. Series.
[DNLM: 1. Emergencies— in infancy & childhood— handbooks.
2. Pediatric Nursing— handbooks.
WY 39 T455q]
RJ245.T47 1991
610.73'62-dc20
DNLM/DLC
for Library of Congress
90-14507
CIP

The authors have made every effort to ensure the accuracy of the information herein,
particularly with regard to drug selection and dose. However, appropriate information
sources should be consulted, especially for new or unfamiliar drugs or procedures. It
is the responsibility of every practitioner to evaluate the appropriateness of a particular
opinion in the context of actual clinical situations and with due consideration to new
developments. Authors, editors, and the publishers cannot be held responsible for any
typographical or other errors found in this book.

Editorial Services: Lorna Perkins

Library of Congress Catalog Card Number: 90-14507
ISBN: 0-8342-0199-2

Printed in the United States of America

2 3 4 5

This book is dedicated to the emergency department staff at Primary Children's Medical Center: nurses, physicians, secretaries, and clerks. They are truly special people.

This book is also dedicated to my husband, Bruce Thomas, and my children: Kseniya, William, and Daniel. They gave me much support and encouragement, and sacrificed much time to see me through this project.

Table of Contents

Contributors

John D. Campbell, MD
Orthopedic Surgeon
Wasatch Orthopedic Clinic
Ogden, Utah

Laurel S. Campbell, RN, MSN, CEN
Clinical Specialist, Emergency Department
Primary Children's Medical Center
Salt Lake City, Utah

Bradley Jay Husberg, RN, MSPH, CEN
Former Staff Nurse, Emergency Department
Primary Children's Medical Center
Salt Lake City, Utah

Marilyn K. Johnson, RN, CEN
Coordinator, Child Protection Team
Primary Children's Medical Center
Salt Lake City, Utah

Marina Bishop Larsen, RN, BSN, CEN
Former Staff Nurse, Emergency Department
Primary Children's Medical Center
Salt Lake City, Utah

Louis V. Melini, RN, CEN
Staff Nurse, Emergency Department
Primary Children's Medical Center
Salt Lake City, Utah

Debra Ann Mills, RN, MSN
Pediatric Clinical Specialist
Assistant Professor of Nursing
Salt Lake Community College
Salt Lake City, Utah

Pamela C. Moore, RN
Director, Pediatric LifeFlight
Primary Children's Medical Center
Salt Lake City, Utah

Ramona F. Randolph, RN, BSN, CEN
Staff Nurse, Emergency Department
Primary Children's Medical Center
Salt Lake City, Utah

Donna Ojanen Thomas, RN, MSN, CEN
Director, Emergency Department
Primary Children's Medical Center
Salt Lake City, Utah

Jeanette H. Walker, RN, CEN
Clinical Coordinator, Emergency Department
Primary Children's Medical Center
Salt Lake City, Utah

Preface

The purpose of this book is to provide quick information for emergency department (ED) nurses to help them make decisions when caring for the pediatric patient. ED nurses have long needed a nursing reference book to answer the most commonly asked questions about pediatric emergency care. Pediatric medical reference books cover diseases and treatments, but do not deal with triage, nursing diagnosis, patient and family teaching, nursing documentation, and other areas of nursing care. Although nurses and physicians must and do work collaboratively in the ED setting, emergency nurses often make independent decisions, especially in the area of triage.

The basis for treating children is an understanding of the anatomic and physiological differences between children and adults, as well as the emotional and psychosocial differences. Treating children almost always requires the ability to recognize the needs of the parents or guardian. These needs include teaching, counseling, and sometimes lending support through a major crisis. At times, it may involve talking to a frightened parent in the middle of the night on the telephone.

For accurate triage of the pediatric patient, it is very important to recognize signs and symptoms requiring immediate attention. Each chapter includes triage guidelines: signs and symptoms and questions to ask in making a triage decision, and examples of conditions that are considered emergent, urgent, or nonurgent. Since many nurses handle parent advice calls, guidelines are included for these situations. Nursing diagnoses are included at the end of each chapter.

The emphasis of this book is on life-threatening emergencies, such as cardiopulmonary arrest and shock, as well as common pediatric complaints and their management, such as fever, earaches, and rashes. The book deals with the unique aspects of pediatric emergency nursing; situations that are common to both children and adults and are handled the same way in both situations may be excluded. Parent involvement and teaching are emphasized.

The book is written in an expanded outline form and is intended as a source of information for the ED nurse. Some brief pathophysiology is included. More extensive information can be found in the bibliographic material. The format and content of the book make it a good reference for developing pediatric standards of care for an emergency department.

Acknowledgments

This book would not be possible without the contributions, encouragement, and support of the expert pediatric emergency nurses and physicians with whom I feel honored to work every day. I also thank those nurses and physicians who helped review chapters and offered their knowledge and advice, especially Laurel Campbell, RN, Kris Dalrymple, RN, Dr. Bob Bolte, and Dr. Howard Corneli.

I also thank Amy Monroe for her excellent preparation of the manuscript and for spending many extra Saturdays typing; and Patti Snyder for staying late to do the printing.

Lastly, I must thank my parents, Ray and Georgetta Ojanen, for teaching me to believe that anything is possible, and my husband Bruce for his encouragement and all that he taught me about writing, editing, and getting things done.

Part I

Concepts in Pediatric Emergency Nursing

Chapter 1

Anatomical and Physiological Variables in the Pediatric Patient

Donna Ojanen Thomas

INTRODUCTION

Children are different from adults anatomically, physiologically, and psychologically. These differences are what make pediatric emergency nursing a specialty, and they are an important foundation for understanding and treating pediatric patients. The purpose of this chapter is to outline these important variables and their implications in pediatric emergency care.

HEAD AND NECK

- The head is bigger in proportion to the rest of the body. Therefore, children have a higher incidence of head injuries.
- The bones of the skull are softer and more pliable; children may have fewer skull fractures despite the mechanism of trauma. However, they may have serious brain injury without skull fractures.
- The open fontanelles in a young child allow for expansion of the intracranial contents. The anterior fontanelle is open until 18–24 months of age and can be a good indication of increased intracranial pressure (bulging fontanelle) or dehydration (sunken fontanelle).
- Children have a greater percentage of blood in their heads. Bleeding from a scalp laceration can cause hypovolemia, especially in children less than 1 year old.
- Facial bones resist injury due to underdeveloped sinuses. Direct trauma must be severe to produce fractures. If facial fractures are present, there are often other associated injuries. Because of the underdeveloped sinuses, sinus infections are uncommon in young children.

- The eustachian tube is shorter and straighter; therefore, the child is prone to frequent ear infections due to bacteria entering the inner ear.
- Muscular support of the neck is weak in the young child; cervical fractures as well as bleeding and edema to the cord caused by hyperextension or hyperflexion can occur.

CHEST AND RESPIRATORY SYSTEM

- Infants are obligate nose breathers for the first 2–4 months of life. Anything that causes nasal obstruction can cause respiratory distress.
- The child's tongue is large and can easily obstruct the airway.
- The epiglottis is larger than in an adult and a floppy omega shape. The adult epiglottis is U-shaped.
- The larynx is softer than in an adult and can be compressed, causing airway obstruction, if the neck is hyperflexed or hyperextended.
- The cricoid cartilage is the narrowest portion of the infant's trachea; cuffed endotracheal (ET) tubes in children under 8 years can cause damage to the trachea.
- The airways of a child are smaller with increased resistance; small amounts of mucus can cause major airway obstruction.
- The child's thorax is pliable and resists fractures, but offers little protection to the heart and lungs. Injuries to the chest can cause contusions and lacerations of the heart.
- The lungs have fewer alveoli, although they increase in number as the child grows. There is a greater tendency for the smaller airways to collapse.
- The intercostal muscles are poorly developed. The rib cage moves easily inward or outward. With decreased lung compliance and with greater intrathoracic pressure generated during inspiration, the chest wall moves in instead of out, causing retractions. Retractions indicate increased work of breathing and respiratory distress.
- The accessory muscles are poorly developed, and the child is more dependent on diaphragmatic function in breathing. Anything that compresses the diaphragm (such as a distended abdomen) can cause respiratory distress.

CARDIOVASCULAR SYSTEM

- The heart rate of a child is greater and the stroke volume is less than that of an adult.

- The stroke volume is dependent on the heart rate; if stroke volume decreases due to a loss in blood volume, the heart rate will increase in an attempt to compensate.
- Transient bradycardia may be normal during sleep or vagal stimulation.
- Blood volume is larger per unit of body weight than in an adult, but the absolute blood volume is still relatively small (see Table 1-3).

ABDOMEN

- The liver and spleen are proportionately larger and have poor muscle protection. These organs are often injured by blunt trauma.
- The kidneys are highly vascular and poorly protected in a child.

NEUROLOGICAL SYSTEM

- The central nervous system (CNS) of a young child is immature; reflexes present in an adult may be absent in a baby and vice versa.
- The neurological exam is harder to obtain in a child. The evaluation of the level of consciousness is the most important part of the neurological exam.

MUSCULOSKELETAL SYSTEM

- The bones of a child are soft and pliable, and resist injury. They offer little protection to underlying organs.
- Injuries to the epiphyseal growth plates can arrest or negatively affect future growth.

THERMOREGULATORY SYSTEM

- The temperature-regulating mechanism of an infant is very unstable.
- Infants and young children have a larger surface-area-to-volume ratio and lose more heat to convection and evaporation than adults; therefore, children can become hypothermic very easily.
- Children less than 6 months of age cannot shiver, and they break down fat to conserve heat.

FLUIDS AND CALORIC REQUIREMENTS

Tables 1-1 and 1-2 list maintenance intravenous (IV) fluid rates based on weight and caloric requirements.

- Children require proportionately more fluid daily than adults; children also have greater insensible water loss and increased metabolism which influences fluid requirements.

Table 1-1 Maintenance IV Fluid Rates

"Per Hour" Calculation Method 4 cc/kg/h first 1–10 kg 2 cc/kg/h next 10–20 kg 1 cc/kg/h next 21 kg+		"24 Hour" Calculation Method 100 cc/kg/24 h first 1–10 kg 50 cc/kg/24 h next 10–20 kg 20 cc/kg/24 h next 21 kg+
cc/h	*Weight in kg*	*cc/h*
16	4	16
20	5	21
24	6	25
28	7	29
32	8	32
36	9	38
40	10	42
42	11	44
44	12	46
46	13	48
48	14	50
50	15	52
52	16	54
54	17	56
56	18	58
58	19	60
60	20	62
65	25	67
70	30	71
75	35	75
80	40	79
85	45	83
90	50	88
100	60	96
110	70	104

Source: Courtesy of Marina Larsen, RN, CEN, Primary Children's Medical Center, Salt Lake City, Utah.

Table 1-2 Standard Basal Calories*

Weight in kg	Cal/kg	Cal/24 h
3	40–50	120–150
5	50–70	250–350
10	40–50	400–600
15	40–50	600–750
20	40–50	800–1000
25	35–45	875–1125
30	35 45	1050–1350
40	30–40	1200–1600
50	25–40	1250–2000

*Caloric requirements are increased with fever and with activity. An additional 12% for each degree Centigrade above a rectal temperature of 37.8° C will be needed. Additional fluid will be needed to replace losses due to increased respiratory rate, increased metabolic rate, and excessive diaphoresis.

Source: Courtesy of Marina Larsen, RN, CEN, Primary Children's Medical Center, Salt Lake City, Utah.

- Children have more total body water, and a larger proportion is extracellular, therefore they can become rapidly dehydrated with increased fluid loss from vomiting and diarrhea or decreased intake.
- Children have an increased need for glucose when they are ill; they become hypoglycemic under stress caused by illness or injury.
- The child's kidneys are immature; dehydration and overhydration occur more rapidly. Drug toxicity may develop more frequently because the kidneys cannot excrete toxic substances as readily.

VITAL SIGNS

Table 1-3 lists physiological norms for vital signs and other parameters in children.

- Children have increased heart and respiratory rates, and a decreased blood pressure when compared with an adult (Table 1-3).
- The weight of a child is the "fifth vital sign" as medications are based on the child's weight in kilograms. All children in the emergency department (ED) must be weighed on admission or a weight must be estimated (Table 1-4).
- Because of an unstable temperature-regulating mechanism, infants become hypothermic very rapidly. Hypothermia can lead to acidosis, hypoxemia, and hypoglycemia. Therefore, every attempt must be made to keep infants warm.

Table 1-3 Physiological Norms for Children

Normal Pediatric Blood Pressure Ranges*

Age	Systolic (mm Hg)	Diastolic (mm Hg)
Newborns–12 h (1000 g)	39–59	16–36
Newborns–12 h (3 kg)	50–70	25–45
Newborns–96 h	60–90	20–60
Infants	74–100	50–70
Toddlers	80–112	50–80
Preschoolers	82–110	50–78
School-aged children	84–120	50–78
Adolescents	94–140	62–88

Estimated Blood Volume

Age	Volume
Infants/children	80 cc/kg
Adolescents/adults	65–70 cc/kg

Normal Heart Rate

Age	Beats/min
Infants	120–160
Toddlers	90–140
Preschoolers	80–110
School-aged children	75–100
Adolescents	60–90

Normal Respiratory Rates

Age	Rate (breaths/min)
Infants	30–60
Toddlers	24–40
Preschoolers	22–34
School-aged children	18–30
Adolescents	12–16

Normal Urine Outputs in Children

Age	Urine Output
Newborn	1/2 cc/kg/h
Infants/toddlers	2 cc/kg/h
Preschoolers and school-aged children	1 cc/kg/h

*Ranges are taken from the 10th to 90th percentile ranges determined by the following studies: M. DeSwiet, P. Fayers, and E.A. Shinebourne, "Systolic Blood Pressure in a Population of Infants in the First Year of Life: The Brompton Study," *Pediatrics* 65 (1980): 1028; National Heart, Lung and Blood Institute's Task Force on Blood Pressure Control in Children, 1978; H. Versmold, et al, "Aortic Blood Pressure During the First 12 Hours of Life in Infants with Birthweight 610–4220 gms," *Pediatrics* 67 (1981): 107.

Source: Reprinted from *Advanced Pediatric Life Support Manual* by Primary Children's Medical Center, Salt Lake City, Utah, © 1988.

Table 1-4 Estimated Weight of Children According to Age

Age	Weight (kg)	Weight Estimate
Newborn	4	Under 1 year:
6 months	8	kg = months/2 + 4
12 months	10	
18 months	12	
2–3 years	14	Over 1 year:
5–6 years	20	kg = years × 2 + 15
8 years	25	
10 years	30	
14 years	50	
18 years	65	

Source: Reprinted from *Advanced Pediatric Life Support Manual* by Primary Children's Medical Center, Salt Lake City, Utah, © 1988.

- The blood pressure (BP) in a child in shock is maintained for a much longer time than in an adult. An adequate BP is not an indication that the child is not in shock. Proper equipment must be used to measure the blood pressure: the cuff needs to be two-thirds the width of the upper arm.

BIBLIOGRAPHY

Barness, L.A., "Fluid and Electrolyte Therapy." In *Current Pediatric Therapy,* edited by Sydney S. Gillis and Benjamin M. Kagan, 762. Philadelphia: W.B. Saunders Co., 1986.

Eichelberger, M., and G. Stossel-Pratsch, eds., *Pediatric Emergencies Manual.* Baltimore: University Park Press, 1984.

Hamilton, P.M., *Basic Pediatric Nursing.* St. Louis: C.V. Mosby Co., 1987.

Hayman, L., and E. Sporing, *Handbook of Pediatric Nursing.* Bethany, Conn.: Fleschner Publishing Co., 1985.

Hazinski, M.F., ed., *Nursing Care of the Critically Ill Child.* St. Louis: C.V. Mosby Co., 1984.

Leifer, G., *Principles and Techniques in Pediatric Nursing,* 4th ed. Philadelphia: W.B. Saunders Co., 1982.

Murphy, C., *Quick Reference to Pediatric Nursing.* Philadelphia: J.B. Lippincott Co., 1984.

Primary Children's Medical Center, *Advanced Pediatric Life Support Manual.* Salt Lake City: Primary Children's Medical Center, 1988.

Chapter 2

Psychosocial Concepts in Pediatric Emergency Care

Donna Ojanen Thomas

INTRODUCTION

Children react to illnesses according to their age and developmental level. Understanding the child's developmental level will help the nurse examine the child and prepare him or her for an emergency department (ED) procedure. The following outline suggests ways to deal with children in the ED according to their age and developmental level. These suggestions are intended only as a guideline. All children need to be treated on an individual basis. Circumstances will vary and the approach to the child may have to be modified.

INFANTS

Major considerations for treating this age group include the following:

- fear of separation from parents
- fear of strangers (especially among children older than 9 months)
- poor temperature-regulating mechanism; feel more secure when wrapped

Nursing approach:

- Decrease parents' anxiety; parental emotions are easily transmitted to the infant.
- Allow parents to remain with and hold the infant as much as possible.
- Keep child warm; use warm hands to examine.

TODDLERS

Major considerations for treating this age group include the following:

- fear of separation from parents

11

- fear of loss of control
- fear of pain
- limited verbal ability, although they may understand some concepts

Nursing approach:

- Minimize separation from parents.
- Talk to the child; examine in parent's lap if possible.
- Allow child to make some choices when possible (e.g., what color adhesive bandage to use).
- Prepare a child immediately before a procedure rather than in advance which might heighten anxiety; keep explanations simple.
- Let child touch equipment; invasive procedures such as taking the temperature, looking in ears, etc., evoke a strong reaction more because of fear than actual pain.
- Use restraints only as needed; comfort child throughout the procedure.
- Use finger puppets of cartoon characters to distract child.
- Take a few minutes to play with the child and gain trust.

PRESCHOOLERS

Major considerations for treating this age group include the following:

- fear of bodily injury and mutilation
- fear of loss of control
- fear of unknown, dark, being left alone
- fear of pain and disfigurement
- literal interpretation of terms
- primitive ideas about their bodies (e.g., all of their blood will leak out from a venipuncture)

Nursing approach:

- Prepare in advance for procedure; keep explanations simple and concrete; use pictures or models or actual equipment to explain procedures.
- Encourage participation in exam when possible; use finger puppets to distract the child during the exam.
- Listen to what the child says; be honest; don't say something will not hurt if it will.

- Allow parents to remain during the procedure but don't make them help in restraining the child; they should be there only to provide comfort.

SCHOOL-AGED CHILDREN

Major considerations for treating this age group include the following:

- fear of loss of control
- fear of bodily injury and mutilation
- desire to live up to others' expectations
- increased awareness of death, the significance of illness, hazards of treatment, consequences of injury
- reluctance to ask questions
- modesty about the body

Nursing approach:

- Prepare in advance for procedure; provide explanations to the child to enhance his or her sense of control.
- Have child explain what he or she understands; clear up any misconceptions.
- Give child the choice about parents' presence during procedure.
- Respect child's physical modesty.

ADOLESCENTS

Major considerations for treating this age group include the following:

- fear of loss of autonomy and control
- altered body image
- fear of separation from peer group
- abstract thinking
- may be hyperresponsive to pain; thus reactions to illness and injury may be magnified
- more realistic views of death

Nursing approach:

- Allow choices and control; respect autonomy.

- Prepare in advance for procedure; provide information in a sensitive way because adolescents react not only to what but how they are told.
- Respect adolescents' need to exert independence from parents, including desire to exclude parents during exam; they may alternate between dependency and independence.

A child's development may not always correspond to the chronological age. A seriously ill or injured child may also regress to a previous stage of development. Therefore, children may need to be treated differently depending on the circumstances and their prior experience with illness, injury, and hospitals.

BIBLIOGRAPHY

Fleisher, G., and S. Ludwig, eds., *Textbook of Pediatric Emergency Medicine,* 2d ed. Baltimore: Williams & Wilkins, 1988.

Hazinski, M.F., "Children Are Different." In *Nursing Care of the Critically Ill Child,* edited by M.F. Hazinski, 1–11. St. Louis: C.V. Mosby Co., 1984.

Chapter 3

Parent Teaching and Accident Prevention

Donna Ojanen Thomas

INTRODUCTION

Caring for a child in the emergency department (ED) also involves caring for the parent. The parent knows the child better than anyone else and always needs to be considered in the treatment plan. The following are some suggestions for encouraging family involvement:

- Listen to the parent's ideas about what is wrong with the child.
- Involve the parent in decision making.
- Keep parent and child together as much as possible; parents may remain for most procedures if they feel comfortable doing so and are able to comfort the child without interfering with the procedure.
- Support and respect the family's cultural and religious beliefs; much of how the family reacts to the child's illness or injury will depend on this and previous experience.
- Provide emotional support to the family and realize that all families will have different needs and different ways of coping; assess each family's ability to cope and available resources.
- Provide information about the illness and plan of treatment, as well as follow-up care.
- Anticipate the need for and provide referrals for community resources.

Parent teaching is always part of the care of a child in the ED. Written take-home instructions should be given along with instructions for follow-up.

Follow-up calls can be made by an ED nurse. These calls not only reinforce the teaching given but also serve as a public relations gesture. Many emergency departments have a nurse whose job it is to make follow-up calls to families who have used the ED.

15

ACCIDENT PREVENTION AND SAFETY

Because more than 90% of accidents are preventable, ED nurses should discuss with parents means of preventing common childhood accidents and other safety information. The following are suggestions for parents according to the child's age.

Newborns, 0–6 months:

- Restrain in an approved car seat.
- Buy a crib with slats that are less than 2–3/8 inches apart; keep rails up at all times.
- Never use any type of plastic materials in crib (e.g., to substitute for mattress pad).
- Never leave infant unattended on changing table or in infant seat.
- Never leave the baby alone with his or her bottle "propped up" for feeding.
- Place baby on side or stomach when sleeping.
- Examine all toys for sharp edges and points or detachable pieces; never tie anything around the baby's neck (e.g., a pacifier).
- Don't use heating pads for small babies.
- Never leave child unattended in bathtub.

Age 6–12 months:

- Restrain in an approved car seat.
- Ensure a childproof home: use safety plugs in electrical outlets, latches on drawers and cupboards; keep electrical cords and wires off floors and put them away when not in use.
- Place barriers around open heaters, registers, and fireplaces.
- Keep floors clear of objects that might be swallowed.
- Don't use walkers.
- Use safety strap when baby is in high chair; don't leave unattended.
- Discard houseplants that are poisonous or place them out of reach.
- Keep medications locked up and out of reach; know Poison Control number in area; have syrup of ipecac available and know how to use it.
- Turn down thermostat on water heater to 125º F.
- Never leave child unattended in bathtub.

Age 1–3 years:

- Restrain in approved car seat.
- Provide supervised play areas.

- Don't leave large toys in the crib; child might use them to climb over rails.
- Keep medicines out of reach.
- Never leave child unattended in bathtub or around any type of water.
- Teach the meaning of "hot."
- Teach about outdoor play safety, hazards of streets and automobiles.

Age 3–5 years:

- Use seat belts in car if child weighs more than 40 pounds; otherwise, use booster seat or appropriate car seat.
- Reinforce outdoor safety practices and teach safe use of bicycles and tricycles.
- Check for safety hazards in outdoor play areas.
- Enroll child in swimming class; supervise all water activities.
- Teach fire safety and develop home fire escape plan.
- Keep firearms locked up and unloaded.
- Keep power tools and equipment locked up and out of reach.
- Teach to avoid strange animals.
- Teach never to accept rides with strangers.
- Teach about being "in charge" of own body and right to privacy.
- Teach each child his or her name, address, and phone number.

Age 5–10 years:

- Always use seat belts.
- Teach how to contact police and fire departments.
- Insist on use of a safety helmet when riding a bicycle.
- Review bicycle and traffic safety and laws.
- Continue water safety practices.
- Reinforce concepts of being "in charge" of own body.
- Teach about dangers of fire.
- Begin to educate about the danger of drugs.

Age 10 years to adult:

Make sure that your child

- continues to use seat belts
- knows water safety rules

Table 3-1 Recommended Schedule for Active Immunization of Normal Infants and Children

Recommended Age	Immunization(s)	Comments
2 months	DTP [a], OPV [b]	Can be given as early as 2 weeks of age in areas of high endemicity or during epidemics
4 months	DTP, OPV	2-month interval desired for OPV to avoid interference from previous dose
6 months	DTP	A third dose of OPV is optional (may be given in areas with increased risk of poliovirus exposure)
15 months	Measles, mumps, rubella (MMR) [c]	MMR preferred to individual vaccine. TB testing may be done at the same visit
18 months	DTP [d,e], OPV [e]	
2 years	HBPV [f]	
4–6 years [g]	DTP, OPV	At or before school entry
14–16 years	Td [h]	Repeat every 10 years throughout life

For all products used, consult manufacturer's package insert for instructions for storage, handling, dosage and administration. Biologics prepared by different manufacturers may vary, and those of the same manufacturer may change from time to time.

[a] DTP, Diphtheria and tetanus toxoids with pertussis vaccine

[b] OPV, Oral poliovirus vaccine contains attenuated poliovirus types 1, 2, and 3

[c] MMR, Live measles, mumps, and rubella viruses in a combined vaccine

[d] Should be given 6–12 months after the third dose

[e] May be given simultaneously with MMR at age 15 months

[f] Haemophilus b polysaccharide vaccine

[g] Up to the seventh birthday

[h] Td, Adult tetanus toxoid (full dose) and diphtheria toxoid (reduced dose) in combination

Source: Reprinted from *Report of the Committee on Infectious Diseases,* 21st ed., by Georges Peter (ed.), p. 15, with permission of the American Academy of Pediatrics, © 1988.

- knows and obeys traffic, bicycle, and pedestrian laws
- wears a safety helmet when riding a bicycle
- knows basic first aid, including cardiopulmonary resuscitation (CPR) for kids

- knows the risks of drug abuse
- is exposed to good examples from adults

OTHER RESPONSIBILITIES OF THE EMERGENCY DEPARTMENT NURSE

The ED nurse is in an excellent position to teach preventive health care in the community. This could involve teaching first aid classes to parent groups as well as children. Some emergency departments are involved in classes such as babysitting, bicycle safety, CPR for parents and children, and water safety. Since education may prevent some accidental deaths and serious injuries, these classes should be considered important. They also serve as an excellent source of public relations for emergency departments.

CHILDHOOD IMMUNIZATION SCHEDULE

Table 3-1 lists the suggested schedule for childhood immunizations. Many times children will be seen in the ED who are behind in or have not received their immunizations. Children who have "dirty" injuries may require protection but their

Table 3-2 Guide to Tetanus Prophylaxis in Wound Management

History of Tetanus Immunization (Doses)	Clean, Minor Wounds		All Other Wounds [a]	
	Td [b]	TIG [c]	Td	TIG
Uncertain, or less than three	yes	no	yes	yes
Three or more[d]	no [e]	no	no [f]	no

[a] Including, but not limited to, wounds contaminated with dirt, feces, soil, saliva, etc.; puncture wounds, avulsions; and wounds resulting from missiles, crushing, burns, and frostbite.

[b] Adult type tetanus and diphtheria toxoids. If the patient is less than 7 years old, DT or DTP is given.

[c] Tetanus immune globulin.

[d] If only three doses of fluid tetanus toxoid have been received, a fourth dose of toxoid, preferably an absorbed toxoid, should be given.

[e] Yes, if more than 10 years since the last dose.

[f] Yes, if more than 5 years since last dose.

Source: Reprinted from *Report of the Committee on Infectious Diseases,* 21st ed., by Georges Peter (ed.), p. 412, with permission of the American Academy of Pediatrics, © 1988.

Table 3-3 Reportable Events Following Vaccination

Vaccine/Toxoid	Event	Interval from Vaccination
DTP, P, DTP/polio combined	Anaphylaxis or anaphylactic shock	24 h
	Encephalopathy (or encephalitis)*	7 days
	Shock-collapse or hypotonic-hyporesponsive collapse*	7 days
	Residual seizure disorder*	(See "Aids to Interpretation.")
	Any acute complication or sequela (including death) of above events	No limit
	Events in vaccinees described in manufacturer's package insert as contraindications to additional doses of vaccine* (such as convulsions)	
Measles, mumps, and rubella; DT, Td, tetanus toxoids	Anaphylaxis or anaphylactic shock	24 h
	Encephalopathy (or encephalitis)*	15 days for measles, mumps, and rubella vaccines; 7 days for DT, Td, and tetanus toxoids
	Residual seizure disorder*	(See "Aids to Interpretation.")
	Any acute complication or sequela (including death) of above events	No limit
	Events in vaccinees described in manufacturer's package insert as contraindications to additional doses of vaccine+	(See package insert.)
Oral polio	Paralytic poliomyelitis	
	-in a nonimmunodeficient recipient	30 days
	-in an immunodeficient recipient	6 months
	-in a vaccine-associated community case	No limit

	Any acute complication or sequela (including death) of above events	No limit
	Events in vaccinees described in manufacturer's package insert as contraindications to additional doses of vaccine+	(See package insert.)
Inactivated polio vaccine	Anaphylaxis or anaphylactic shock	24 h
	Any acute complication or sequela (including death) of above event	No limit
	Events in vaccinees described in manufacturer's package insert as contraindications to additional doses of vaccine+	(See package insert)

*Aids to interpretation:

- Shock collapse or hypotonic-hyporesponsive collapse may be evidenced by signs or symptoms such as decrease in or loss of muscle tone, paralysis (partial or complete), hemiplegia, hemiparesis, loss of color or turning pale white or blue, unresponsiveness to environmental stimuli, depression of or loss of consciousness, prolonged sleeping with difficulty arousing, or cardiovascular or respiratory arrest.

- Residual seizure disorder may be considered to have occurred if no other seizure or convulsion unaccompanied by fever or accompanied by a fever of less than 102° F occurred before the first seizure or convulsion after the administration of the vaccine involved and if in the case of measles-, mumps-, or rubella-containing vaccines, the first seizure or convulsion occurred within 15 days after vaccination or in the case of any other vaccine, the first seizure or convulsion occurred within 3 days after vaccination.

- The terms seizure and convulsion include grand mal, petit mal, absence, myoclonic, tonic-clonic, and focal motor seizures and signs. Encephalopathy means any significant acquired abnormality of, injury to, or impairment of function of the brain. Among the frequent manifestations of encephalopathy are focal and diffuse neurologic signs, increased intracranial pressure, or changes lasting at least 6 h in level of consciousness, with or without complete recovery, or they may result in various degrees of permanent impairment. Signs and symptoms such as high-pitched and unusual screaming, persistent unconsolable crying, and bulging fontanel are compatible with an encephalopathy, but in and of themselves are not conclusive evidence of encephalopathy. Encephalopathy usually can be documented by slow wave activity on an electroencephalogram.

+The health care provider must refer to the *contraindications* section of the manufacturer's package insert for each vaccine.

Source: Reprinted from *Report of the Committee on Infectious Diseases*, 21st ed., by Georges Peter (ed.), pp. 23–24, with permission of the American Academy of Pediatrics, © 1988.

current immunization status may be unknown. Table 3-2 lists guidelines for immunization status for wound management.

Other considerations for performing immunizations in the ED are as follows:

- Due to the liability involved in adverse reactions to immunizations, especially the pertussis vaccine, informed consent should be obtained and filed with the patient's chart. Standardized forms are available from local health departments.
- The National Childhood Vaccine Injury Act[1] requires that the following must be recorded on the patient's chart:
  —Date vaccine given
  —Full name of person administering vaccine
  —Manufacturer and lot number of vaccine
- Some types of reactions to immunizations must be reported to the proper authorities, usually the state health department. These are listed in Table 3-3.

NOTES

1. "National Childhood Vaccine Injury Act: Requirements for Reporting of Selected Events After Vaccination," *Morbidity and Mortality Weekly Report* 37 (1988): 197–200.

BIBLIOGRAPHY

American Academy of Pediatrics Committee on Infectious Diseases, *Report of the Committee on Infectious Diseases,* 21st ed. Elk Grove Village, Ill.: American Academy of Pediatrics, 1988.

Leifer, G., *Principles and Techniques in Pediatric Nursing,* 4th ed. Philadelphia: W.B. Saunders Co., 1982.

Murphy, C., *Quick Reference to Pediatric Nursing.* Philadelphia: J.B. Lippincott Co., 1984.

Nelson, J.D., *Current Therapy in Pediatric Infectious Disease,* Vol. 2. Toronto: B.C. Decker, Inc., 1988.

Whaley, L., and D. Wong, *Nursing Care of Infants and Children,* 3d ed. St. Louis: C.V. Mosby Co., 1987.

Part II

Initial Assessment of the Pediatric Patient

Chapter 4

Triage of the Pediatric Patient

Donna Ojanen Thomas

INTRODUCTION

Prompt and accurate triage is one of the most important aspects of pediatric emergency nursing and involves the ability to recognize the sometimes subtle signs and symptoms that suggest that immediate attention is required. The purpose of triage is to immediately assess the child's illness or injury and to assign a priority to the care needed.

Because their condition can change very rapidly and the symptoms of the illness may be subtle, children should be assessed immediately. Depending on the facility, the triage assessment may be brief and include only looking at the child and obtaining a history. Or, the initial assessment may include vital signs and diagnostic tests. Accurate triage assessments of children require practice and an understanding of the anatomic and physiological differences between children and adults. These differences are discussed in Chapter 1.

TRIAGE HISTORY

The history can be obtained while doing other parts of the assessment. The history should include the following:

- current illness (signs and symptoms)
- mechanism of injury
- past medical history including child's baseline condition
- allergies and immunization status
- child's regular source of medical care

25

The "AMPLE" mnemonic is useful to remember in obtaining a complete history

- *Allergies*
- *Medications*
- *Past medical history*
- *Last meal*
- *Events surrounding incident*

PHYSICAL ASSESSMENT

The triage assessment focuses on airway, breathing, circulation (the "ABCs"), and the area of chief complaint. A more thorough assessment is done when the child is taken to a treatment room. More information on a complete pediatric assessment is given in Chapter 5. The triage assessment includes evaluating the following:

- airway (presence or absence of breathing)
- breathing (signs and symptoms of respiratory distress)
- circulation (perfusion and skin turgor, signs and symptoms of dehydration)
- bleeding
- neurologic assessment (level of consciousness)
- vital signs (temperature, pulse, respiration, blood pressure)
- condition of anterior fontanel, if appropriate

NURSING CARE IN THE TRIAGE AREA

In some emergency departments, initial treatment may be done in the triage area. This may include the following:

- basic first aid (ice packs, splints, and bandages)
- administration of antipyretics
- initiation of laboratory studies or x-ray studies

Protocols should exist to guide the nurse in ordering any treatments. Beginning treatment often expedites care while the child is waiting for a room. The physician should be consulted any time a question exists about the child's condition. The triage history assessment, time completed, and any interventions done should be documented.

TRIAGE CATEGORIES

There are many different types of triage categorization systems that can be applied to both children and adults. The easiest is the three-category system.

Emergent: This category represents children who have a condition that may result in loss of life or limb if not treated immediately. Included in this category would be cardiopulmonary arrest, coma, and uncontrolled bleeding.

Urgent: Children in this group require prompt care but will not generally be in danger of death or severe impairment if left untreated for a period of time, usually a few hours. Examples are lacerations with bleeding controlled, possible nondisplaced fractures without neurological impairment, and febrile seizure in a child who is currently active and alert.

Nonurgent: Children with nonurgent complaints require treatment, but time is not a critical factor. Nonurgent conditions include sore throats, mild flu symptoms, and minor sprains.

It is difficult to place pediatric complaints in rigid categories because many variables must be considered. For example, fever may be considered nonurgent, but if it exists in a baby less than 3 months of age, it becomes an urgent condition.

PREHOSPITAL TRIAGE

Prehospital triage involves receiving calls from and giving directions to prehospital care providers such as emergency medical technicians (EMTs) and paramedics. It involves the following:

- an understanding of the medications and equipment carried by the prehospital personnel
- knowledge of the level of training of prehospital personnel
- protocols for treating the pediatric patient that have been approved by the medical director (an example of a protocol for pediatric cardiac arrest is given in Exhibit 4-1)

The duties of the nurse in prehospital triage include the following:

- eliciting a history from prehospital care providers
- deciding if treatment is needed prior to the patient's arrival
- consulting with a physician or following written protocols
- documenting history, any orders given, disposition, and expected time of arrival (ETA) on appropriate patient chart
- alerting emergency department staff of incoming pediatric patient

Exhibit 4-1 Protocol for Pediatric Cardiopulmonary Arrest Prehospital Care

---

All cardiac arrest victims are transported to the nearest facility in the most expeditious manner.

Standing orders:

1. CPR according to current guidelines
2. Endotracheal or nasotracheal intubation
3. Lactated Ringer's intravenous (IV) solution (rate ordered depending on situation, i.e., trauma)
4. Tibial infusion if appropriate and peripheral access unsuccessful
5. MAST (Military Anti-Shock Trousers) if warranted
6. Defibrillation with appropriate watt/second charge (1 joule/kg × 2)
7. Drugs: paramedics may give epinephrine 0.1 cc/kg IV, ET (endotracheal) or through an interosseous line, without an order
8. All other drugs must be ordered by physician or registered nurse

Other drugs that are carried by the paramedics are: atropine, sodium bicarbonate, Isuprel, lidocaine, calcium chloride, dopamine, bretylium, morphine, nitroglycerin, and dextrose 50%.

On all cardiac arrest calls, the ED physician must be in contact with the paramedics to provide additional orders.

Source: Reprinted from *Emergency Department Policy and Procedure Manual,* Primary Children's Medical Center, Salt Lake City, Utah, © 1989.

Pediatric problems encountered in the prehospital triage include:

- major trauma (related to motor vehicle accidents, falls, or drowning)
- respiratory problems (apnea, choking, croup)
- seizures, usually febrile
- sudden infant death syndrome (SIDS)

Children rarely will be transported because of a primary cardiac problem. If a child experiences a cardiac arrest, it is most likely to be caused by trauma or a primary airway obstruction.

Protocols should exist to provide guidance to prehospital care providers when dealing with the pediatric patient. They should be written and approved by the emergency department medical director.

LEGAL IMPLICATIONS OF PEDIATRIC TRIAGE

Because in most hospitals triage is the responsibility of the nurse, the professional liability of the emergency nurse is increased. And because pediatric patients present with special problems that may not be familiar to nurses who deal routinely with adults, triage systems should be developed that incorporate the following concepts:

- physician consultation with the triage nurses on all patients
- structured educational programs for teaching triage nurses how to deal with pediatric patients
- guidelines for setting priorities
- documentation of triage assessment, evaluation, and treatment
- periodic reassessment of the child who is not immediately treated; should be done every 15–30 minutes and should be documented to ensure that any change in condition is noted and acted upon

TELEPHONE TRIAGE

Telephone triage involves giving advice over the telephone to parents who may have a question about their child's condition, and presents legal risks to both the nurse and the hospital. If advice calls are taken, these guidelines should be followed:

- Calls should be handled by an experienced ED nurse who has had formal training. One nurse should be responsible for the calls on each shift.
- Policies and standards of care must be written and approved by the medical director and include who will take the calls, what advice can be given for specific complaints, and who will review the calls.
- Documentation of all calls must be done on a form developed for this purpose (Exhibit 4-2). The documentation should include name, age, phone number, complaint, advice given, and follow-up. This documentation must be kept on file for up to 7 years.
- Advice given must be symptomatic; the nurse should not diagnose or prescribe over the phone. Parents should be encouraged to contact their own physician if they have one.
- Parents should be told that they can bring their child to the ED at any time if they are concerned.

A hospital attorney should also review all policies and protocols for handling parent advice calls. Protocols are highly recommended because they provide the following:

- consistency in the advice given
- accuracy

Exhibit 4-2 Example of a Telephone Log for Documentation of Advice Calls

DATE_____ TIME_____ RN_____ CALLER: MOTHER_____ FATHER_____ OTHER_____

NAME_____ AGE_____ TELEPHONE_____ MD_____

HX/CC/APPEARANCE _____

_____

ADVICE _____

_____

_____FOLLOW-UP: (   ) MD (   ) ED

Source: Reprinted from *Emergency Department Policy and Procedure Manual,* Primary Children's Medical Center, Salt Lake City, Utah, © 1989.

- quality information
- completeness (the nurse will be less likely to leave out important information if guided by protocols)
- ease (guidelines help nurses to think through the process)

BIBLIOGRAPHY

Brown, J. *Telephone Medicine: A Practical Guide to Pediatric Telephone Advice.* St. Louis: C.V. Mosby Co., 1980.

Brown, J. *Pediatric Telephone Medicine: Principles, Triage, and Advice.* Philadelphia: J.B. Lippincott Co., 1989.

Katz, H. *Telephone Manual of Pediatric Care.* New York: John Wiley & Sons, Inc., 1982.

McGear, R., and J. Simms. *Telephone Triage and Management: A Nursing Approach.* Philadelphia: W.B. Saunders Co., 1988.

Rund, D., and T. Rausch. *Triage.* St. Louis: C.V. Mosby Co., 1981.

Schmitt, B. *Pediatric Telephone Advice.* Boston: Little, Brown and Co., 1980.

Thomas, D.O. "The ABCs of Pediatric Triage." *Journal of Emergency Nursing* 14 (1988): 154–59.

Thompson, J., and J. Dains. *Comprehensive Triage: A Manual for Developing and Implementing a Nursing Care System.* Reston, Va.: Reston Publishing Co., 1982.

Chapter 5

Pediatric Physical Assessment in the Emergency Department

Donna Ojanen Thomas

INTRODUCTION

Pediatric physical assessment in the ED involves the following:

- recognizing signs and symptoms of distress
- understanding the medical implications for physiological differences between children and adults
- appreciating the child's developmental level and the effects of the illness or injury at that stage of development
- communicating with both the child and the parents
- listening to the parent, who knows the child better than anyone else

In the ED, two exams are done. The first one is brief and takes place in the triage area. This triage exam is discussed in Chapter 4 and is important because it provides baseline information. The triage nurse should share findings with the primary nurse. The second exam is more detailed and allows the nurse time to focus on all body systems.

The intent of this chapter is to outline a brief approach to the pediatric physical exam. More detail is given in each chapter relating to various illnesses and injuries.

The three components of the pediatric assessment are observation, examination, and communication with the parents. These components are handled simultaneously.

Observation of the child includes:

- general appearance. Does the child look ill? What is the level of consciousness? Does the child appear well-groomed or unkempt?
- activity level for age. Is the child reacting appropriately to a new and strange environment?
- interaction between parent and child. Is the parent supportive or indifferent?

- unusual odor. Foul odors may be the result of poor grooming or may indicate a nasal foreign body.

PRIMARY ASSESSMENT

The pediatric exam begins with the primary assessment: observation; examination of airway, breathing, and circulation; and the neurological exam.

Airway and Breathing

The nurse needs to consider cervical spine precautions when assessing a child's airway and breathing, especially if the child has an injury involving the head, or if the mechanism of injury increases the likelihood of a cervical spine injury. Immobilization of the cervical spine is discussed in Chapter 22.

Observe for signs and symptoms of respiratory distress:

- color of child. Is child pale, mottled, cyanotic (check for cyanosis of nailbeds, mucous membranes)?
- respiratory effort. Use of accessory muscles in neck or chest, presence of nasal flaring or retractions indicates increased effort in breathing.
- noisy breathing. Barking cough or crowing respirations may indicate upper airway obstruction. Wheezing indicates lower airway obstruction.
- level of consciousness. A decreased level of consciousness could be due to hypoxia.

Do the following based on the above assessment:

- Auscultate breath sounds: equal, wheezing, stridor (inspiratory or expiratory), rales, rhonchi.
- Count respiratory rate.
- Check capillary refill time.

Communicate with the parent:

- Investigate past medical history of present illness or mechanism of the injury.
- Inquire about any medications the child is taking.
- Inquire about home treatment.
- Discuss parental perceptions of the child's condition.

Circulation

Observe and **examine** the following:

- skin turgor. Check for "tenting" of the skin when pinched. Tenting indicates dehydration. Are the skin and mucous membranes moist or dry?
- anterior fontanelle (open until about 2 years in most children). Is it bulging or sunken? A bulging anterior fontanelle may indicate increased intracranial pressure while a sunken fontanelle may indicate dehydration.
- skin color and capillary refill time. Capillary refill time is measured by pressing on the child's forehead, or nailbeds of the fingers or toes, and observing for return of the circulation. Normal time is less than 2 seconds.
- peripheral pulses. Check femoral pulses in a newborn. Absent or weak femoral pulses may indicate coarctation of the aorta.
- presence of any bleeding. External bleeding is obvious. Consider possibility of internal bleeding.
- heart rate and blood pressure. A Doppler device may be needed to check blood pressure in neonates.

Communicate with parent (and child, if appropriate):

- Explain purpose of exam.
- Explain significance of abnormal findings.

Neurological Exam

It is not necessary to know all of the normal and abnormal reflexes in infants and children. The history and the level of consciousness are the most important part of the pediatric neurological exam. A more complete exam is done depending on the findings. The following should be noted:

- history of illness or injury
- level of consciousness
- pupillary response
- response to pain
- movement of extremities (both spontaneous movement and movement in response to pain)
- vital signs (temperature, pulse, respiration, blood pressure)

The neurological exam may be focused on one area depending on the chief complaint. For example, the neurological status of the fingers and hand (sensation and movement) would be checked on any injury to the hand, wrist, or arm. Ask family what the child's baseline neurological status is and if any medications are being taken that might affect the exam.

The primary assessment may include appropriate interventions done before the secondary assessment is started, such as the following:

- oxygen and ventilatory support
- interventions to stop active bleeding
- intravenous fluids to support the circulation and deliver medications
- medications to stop seizure activity or to support circulation

SECONDARY ASSESSMENT

The secondary assessment is done next and includes a head-to-toe assessment focusing on the chief complaint. Cervical spine precautions need to be maintained throughout this assessment if indicated. This exam will be more detailed in the trauma patient than in the child with an ear infection. For each category listed below check the following:

Head and Neck

- anterior fontanelle (open or closed)
- injuries (Palpate skull for hematomas or depressions of the skull.)
- tenderness
- nucchal rigidity (stiffness of neck)

Eyes

- pupils (size and reaction to light)
- tearing
- deviation
- drainage or periorbital swelling
- sclera (presence of jaundice)

Ears

- drainage (clear drainage may indicate cerebrospinal fluid (CSF) in the presence of a basilar skull fracture; purulent or bloody drainage may indicate otitis media)
- ecchymosis behind the ear (Battle's sign which might indicate a basilar skull fracture)

Nose

- nasal flaring (indicates increased respiratory effort)
- drainage (clear drainage may indicate CSF in the presence of a basilar skull fracture)
- odor (a foul odor may indicate a retained foreign body)

Throat

- swelling or exudates in pharynx; defer this exam if the child is experiencing severe respiratory distress
- cervical lymph glands (swelling)

Mouth

- color of oral mucosa
- lesions
- moistness of lips and mucous membranes

Chest

- Proceed as listed under "Airway and Breathing" in primary assessment.
- rashes and bruising
- tenderness

Abdomen

- distention (severe abdominal distention in a child can compromise the airway due to pressure on the diaphragm; measure abdominal girth)

- bowel sounds
- tenderness

Extremities

Compare bilaterally:

- swelling
- movement
- deformities
- sensation
- strength
- pulses
- bruises or rashes

Genitalia and Rectum

This exam can be done on younger children while the nurse is doing a rectal temperature. In older children, the exam is not done in the ED unless it relates to the chief complaint. Check for the following:

- diaper rash
- discharge or irritation of genitalia (including foreskin for uncircumcised males)
- rectal bleeding or irritation (if present, may be indicative of sexual abuse in both males and females; see Chapter 31)

OTHER CONSIDERATIONS

- Don't focus on the obvious.
- Consider a chronic condition when performing an evaluation.
- Always listen to the parents and ask for their opinions of the situation.
- Consider child abuse in suspicious circumstances and know your responsibility in reporting abuse (see Chapters 30 and 31).
- If time permits, do a complete exam to assess the physical condition of the child beyond the chief complaint or concern. This will improve your assessment skills in children.

DOCUMENTATION

Documentation in the ED is brief, but must be accurate and complete. Documentation focuses on the chief complaint, all related findings, and interventions. The following are factors that must be documented for all children. Each chapter contains additional information on documentation.

- time of initial exam
- chief complaint
- general appearance
- initial assessment, including vital signs
- interventions done in the ED and child's response
- planned follow-up and teaching given
- condition on discharge from the ED

BIBLIOGRAPHY

Alexander, Mary M., and Marie S. Brown. *Pediatric History Taking and Physical Diagnosis for Nurses*. New York: McGraw-Hill Book Co., 1979.

Bates, B. *A Guide to Physical Examination and History Taking,* 4th ed. Philadelphia: J.B. Lippincott Co., 1987.

Eichelberger, Martin R., and G. Stossel-Pratsch. *Pediatric Emergencies Manual*. Baltimore: University Park Press, 1984.

Emergency Nurses Association. *Trauma Nursing Core Course Provider Manual*. Chicago: Award Printing Corp., 1986.

Ferholt, J.D. *Clinical Assessment of Children: A Comprehensive Approach to Primary Pediatric Care*. Philadelphia: J.B. Lippincott Co., 1980.

Chapter 6

Preparation of the Child for Transport to Another Facility

Pamela C. Moore

INTRODUCTION

If the specialized expertise needed to care for a specific illness or injury is unavailable, transfer of the child to another facility may be necessary. Guidelines for the types of patients and the circumstances under which they are transferred depend on the capabilities of individual referring and receiving hospitals. The primary goal of transporting a child is to provide rapid access to appropriate medical care. If a well-established referral system, protocols for transfer, and transfer agreements are in place, this goal can be accomplished.

Transferring Patients

Reasons for transferring patients include the following:

- availability of pediatric specialists at a pediatric tertiary care center
- potential for child's condition to deteriorate in a hospital that is not capable of caring for the seriously ill child
- social or family factors (knowing that the child will have the benefit of the best pediatric care available will help the family and maintain their coping mechanisms)

PRETRANSFER STABILIZATION

As soon as the decision is made to transfer a child, the referring physician should contact the physician at the receiving hospital. The receiving physician can arrange for the transport team to get under way immediately and assist the referring physician with pretransport stabilization measures, which include the following categories:

1. Airway and breathing

- Maintain an open airway.
- Provide 100% oxygen.
- Intubate prior to transport if airway is unstable in any way.
- Evaluate tube placement by x-ray. Tape securely to avoid inadvertent extubation during transfer.
- Obtain arterial blood gasses (ABGs), especially if transport is longer than a few minutes.
- Insert a gastric tube to remove gastric contents, prevent aspiration, and reduce distention. Severe distention can result in bradycardia and difficulty in ventilation. Unrelieved gastric distention may be aggravated during air transport as gas inside the stomach will expand as atmospheric pressure decreases in flight.

2. Cervical spine

- Immobilize the cervical spine during airway management procedures and keep immobilized if there is any suspicion of neck injury. Transport necessitates that the child be moved several times (from ED to helicopter, to another ED).
- Obtain lateral neck film, showing all seven cervical vertebrae, but don't rely on a normal film; cervical spine injury may still be present even with good alignment and no evidence of bone injury.

3. Circulation

- Place at least one large-bore intravenous (IV) line; two lines if the child is a trauma victim or unstable medical patient.
- Secure the line without obscuring the IV site; transport personnel will need to observe for infiltrations.
- Use plastic containers for any IV solutions, drips, and "piggyback" medications to decrease the possibility of breakage during transfer.

4. Bleeding

- Control external bleeding.
- Type and cross-match child's blood. If blood is available, it may be given during transport if necessary.

5. Baseline neurological exam

- Assess level of consciousness.
- Monitor pupillary responses to light.
- Check extraocular movements.

- Check motor functions.
- Watch vital sign trends. Decreasing heart rate, widening pulse pressure, and decreasing level of consciousness indicate increasing intracranial pressure.

6. Miscellaneous

- Insert urinary catheter (except in cases of suspected pelvic fracture or urethral injury) to prevent overdistention of bladder during transport.
- Splint and pad all suspected or known fractures; may include use of femur traction device or MAST.
- Send complete copies of child's medical record including physician and nursing notes, original x-rays, and laboratory values. These will be necessary for the receiving physician to evaluate care already given.

The key to pretransfer stabilization is to avoid delay. Do the evaluation and treatment necessary to stabilize the child for transfer, but reconsider laboratory tests, x-rays, and procedures not immediately necessary for care. To determine how extensive the pretransfer stabilization should be, consider the following:

- .What are the capabilities and level of expertise of the team that will be transporting the child?
- What kinds of procedures are they able to perform during transfer?
- What type of equipment do they have to monitor the child?
- What medications are immediately available?
- What is the total time that the child will be out of a hospital setting during transfer?

AIR VERSUS GROUND TRANSPORT

The critical issue in transport is not how long it takes the child to arrive at the receiving hospital but how long it takes for the expert care to be delivered. The delivery of expert care begins when the referring and receiving physicians begin talking to one another as the transport team is mobilized and en route. It continues as the mobile intensive care unit arrives at the referring hospital, readies the child to go, and maintains delivery of critical care throughout the transport.

The following considerations need to be reviewed when deciding on the method of transfer of a child to a tertiary care facility.

1. Time

- Ground transport allows the child to leave the referring hospital more quickly, but out-of-hospital time is much longer.

- Air transport allows less out-of-hospital time. The child remains in a controlled environment until the air transport team arrives.

2. **Skills of transport personnel and available equipment**

- Ground ambulance personnel are generally emergency medical technicians who are well trained as first responders but do not have advanced skills in pediatrics.
- Available equipment on ground ambulances is usually basic life support and not geared to pediatrics.
- Air transport crews have advanced skills and are used to working in an environment with limited space and lighting.
- Available equipment on air transport is designed especially for transport and capable of providing advanced life support and monitoring.

3. **Weather**

- Weather can limit both air and ground transport; helicopters can usually fly even if road conditions are poor.
- Fixed-wing aircraft may be able to fly around or above storms or other poor weather conditions.
- Fixed- and rotor-wing aircraft are limited by fog, heavy snow, freezing rain, and thunderstorms, making ground transport the only option.

The majority of air transport programs isolate their pilots from patient information. The decision to go or not go is made by the pilot, based only on his or her evaluation of the weather conditions and other safety factors.

4. **Expense**

Air transport is much more expensive than ground transport, but the expense may be well justified if the child is critically ill or injured, has the potential to deteriorate rapidly, or is located in an area that is inaccessible by other means.

DEVELOPING A RELATIONSHIP WITH THE PEDIATRIC REFERRAL CENTER

Transfer of a patient from one care facility to another is simplified if there is a good working relationship already in place between the two institutions. Preparation for transfer includes the following:

- Know capabilities of various receiving hospitals for caring for special problems such as trauma, burns, cardiac bypass.
- Have phone numbers of each institution readily available, including direct numbers to physicians or departments that can be contacted initially for consultation.

- Use the expertise of the receiving facilities to provide inservices and develop standards of care for the types of patients that will be transferred to them. Take advantage of the person-to-person contact that inservices can provide. Just knowing the expectations, personalities, and pressures on each side can help the transfer go more smoothly.

BIBLIOGRAPHY

American Academy of Pediatrics Committee on Hospital Care. "Guidelines for Air and Ground Transportation of Pediatric Patients." *Pediatrics* 78 (1986): 943–50.

Black, R.E., et al. "Air Transport of Pediatric Emergency Cases." *New England Journal of Medicine* 307 (1982): 1465–68.

Mayer, T. "Transportation of the Injured Child." In *Emergency Management of Pediatric Trauma*, edited by T. Mayer, 508–23. Philadelphia: W.B. Saunders Co., 1985.

Ochsenschlager, D., and B. Klein. "Transport of the Injured Child." In *Pediatric Trauma Care*, edited by M. Eichelberger and G. Pratsch, 209–12. Gaithersburg, Md.: Aspen Publishers, Inc., 1988.

Worthington, T. "Transporting the Critically Injured Child." In *Pediatric Trauma Nursing*, edited by C. Joy, 143–154. Gaithersburg, Md.: Aspen Publishers, Inc., 1989.

Part III

Cardiovascular Problems

Chapter 7

Cardiopulmonary Arrest

Bradley Jay Husberg

INTRODUCTION

The majority of cardiac arrests in children occur secondary to a primary respiratory problem, or shock. The ED nurse must be able to recognize signs and symptoms of impending respiratory and cardiac arrest and intervene to prevent further deterioration of the child's condition. Recognition of the child in distress requires pediatric assessment skills and an understanding of the conditions that might precipitate arrest. The ED nurse must also be familiar with pediatric advanced life support procedures.

PATHOPHYSIOLOGY

In a child, cardiac arrest is usually preceded by respiratory distress, leading to failure. Initially, the body compensates by increasing the heart rate in an attempt to increase cardiac output. As the child becomes more hypoxic, this mechanism fails, and the child becomes bradycardic. If no interventions occur at this stage, cardiac arrest follows.

Volume depletion can also lead to circulatory collapse. Although the blood is adequately oxygenated, blood flow to vital organs is insufficient to meet metabolic demands.

Cardiac arrest results in circulatory collapse, which leads to loss of perfusion to vital organs such as the brain, lungs, and kidneys. Irreversible damage occurs to these organs if circulation and oxygenation are not restored immediately.

Cardiopulmonary arrest may be manifested in three ways:

1. asystole. No electrical activity shown on electrocardiogram (ECG). This is the most common manifestation in children.
2. ventricular fibrillation. This is rare in children.

3. electromechanical dissociation (EMD). Usually associated with trauma resulting in pericardial tamponade, tension pneumothorax, and hypovolemia. A normal sinus rhythm (NSR) may be evident on the monitor. Blood pressure and pulses will be absent.

CAUSES OF PEDIATRIC ARRESTS

In an adult, the primary cause of cardiac arrest is coronary artery disease. In children, cardiopulmonary arrest is most commonly preceded by a respiratory event that leads to hypoxia, bradycardia, and asystole. Causes that may precipitate an arrest in children include:

1. Respiratory (most common)
   - aspiration
   - bronchiolitis
   - asthma
   - croup
   - drowning
   - bronchopulmonary dysplasia
   - botulism
   - epiglottitis
   - respiratory distress syndrome
2. Cardiovascular
   - congenital heart disease
   - septic shock
   - severe dehydration
   - pericarditis
   - myocarditis
   - congestive heart failure
3. Central nervous system (CNS)
   - hydrocephalus (ventricular shunt failure)
   - meningitis
   - seizures
   - tumor
   - head trauma
4. Other
   - Sudden infant death syndrome (SIDS)

- multiple trauma
- poisonings

TRIAGE ASSESSMENT

A rapid cardiopulmonary assessment should be performed on all children with the following signs and symptoms:[1]

- respiratory rate greater than 60
- heart rate greater than 180 (under 5 years)
- heart rate greater than 150 (over 5 years)
- respiratory distress
- trauma
- burns
- cyanosis
- failure to recognize parents
- diminished level of consciousness
- seizures
- fever with petechiae

The rapid cardiopulmonary assessment is shown in Table 7-1.

TRIAGE HISTORY

A child who is in respiratory distress and has a decreased level of consciousness or has signs and symptoms of shock should be taken immediately to the treatment area. While treatment is being given, the parents should be questioned about the following:

- pre-existing medical conditions
- medications the child may be taking (or may have ingested accidentally)
- history of illness (signs and symptoms, duration of symptoms)
- known trauma
- known allergies
- treatment done prior to arrival (e.g., cardiopulmonary resuscitation [CPR])

Table 7-1 Rapid Cardiopulmonary Assessment

Respiratory Assessment	Cardiovascular Assessment
Airway patency	Circulation
Breathing	Heart rate
Rate	Blood pressure
Air entry	Peripheral pulses
Chest rise	Present/absent
Breath sounds	Volume
Stridor	Skin perfusion
Wheezing	Capillary refill time
Mechanics	Temperature
Retractions	Color
Grunting	Mottling
Color	CNS perfusion
	Recognition of parents
	Reaction to pain
	Muscle tone
	Pupil size

Source: Reproduced with permission. *Textbook of Advanced Cardiac Life Support,* 1985. Copyright © American Heart Association.

TELEPHONE TRIAGE GUIDELINES

A child with any of the signs and symptoms listed under "Triage Assessment" should be seen by a physician immediately. In most cases, the parents should be instructed to call the emergency medical service (EMS) for assistance. For a child who is reported to be in cardiopulmonary arrest, the nurse may need to give basic life support instructions over the phone while another nurse in the ED calls the EMS.

PRIORITY RATING

Emergent: Children who are experiencing cardiopulmonary arrest or who have any of the symptoms requiring a rapid cardiopulmonary assessment should be treated immediately. Immediate intervention in a child with respiratory distress may prevent further hypoxia leading to cardiac arrest. A child with bradycardia should be considered to be in a prearrest state.

TREATMENT AND NURSING CARE

I. Basic Life Support[2]
  A. Airway
    1. Determine unresponsiveness or respiratory difficulty.
       • Maintain cervical spine precautions if there is a possibility of head or neck trauma.
       • If child is breathing with difficulty, allow to maintain position of comfort.
    2. Call for help.
    3. Position the child.
       • Place child on backboard on bed.
       • Maintain cervical spine precautions as indicated.
    4. Open the airway (this maneuver may be all that is necessary for the child to begin breathing again).
       • Place child in "sniffing position" with tip of nose pointing up.
       • Use head tilt and chin lift maneuver. Be careful not to close mouth completely or apply pressure to the soft tissue under the chin.
       • Use jaw thrust maneuver. Use the jaw thrust without the head tilt if cervical spine injury is suspected.
  B. Breathing
    1. Assess whether the child is breathing.
    2. Breathe for the child if child is not breathing.
       • For infant, use mouth-to-mouth and nose.
       • For child, use mouth-to-mouth seal.
       • Deliver two slow breaths with a pause between to allow the rescuer to take a breath. An appropriate volume of air is one that causes the chest to rise.
  C. Circulation
    1. Assess the pulse.
       • For children over 1 year, use carotid pulse.
       • For children less than 1 year, use femoral or brachial pulse.
       • If pulse is present but no spontaneous respirations, continue ventilations (20 breaths/minute for an infant; 15 breaths/minute for a child).
    2. Activate the EMS.
    3. Perform chest compressions. Indications for performing chest compressions include:
       • asystole
       • bradycardia (less than 60 beats/minute) that is unresponsive to ventilation and oxygenation

Table 7-2 describes the proper positioning, rate, and depth for chest compressions in the infant and child.

II. Advanced Life Support

A. Airway

1. Oropharyngeal airway keeps tongue from obstructing the airway. Correct size needs to be used; improper size can cause obstruction.

2. Endotracheal tube (ETT). (Table 7-3 lists proper sizes for ETT and suction tubes. One smaller and one larger than the recommended sizes should be available.) Cuffed ETTs are not used in children less than 8 years of age.

3. Nasogastric (NG) tube should be inserted to decompress the stomach and prevent aspiration.

4. Esophageal obturator airways are not recommended for use in children.

B. Breathing

1. Mouth to mask: Because of the threat of infection, mouth-to-mouth should be avoided in the hospital setting. All emergency departments should have bag and mask equipment available. Pocket masks with a one-way valve to prevent spread of infection are available and should be kept in the triage area.

2. Bag and mask

3. Bag and ETT/tracheostomy

C. Circulation

1. Intravenous access (see Chapter 15).

2. Fluid of choice is lactated Ringer's solution or normal saline solution.

3. A bolus of fluid (20–40 cc/kg) may be given since pediatric arrests are often caused by hypovolemia.

4. Dextrose 5% and water is not an appropriate solution in an arrest situation because it is not an isotonic solution and will not replace lost volume.

D. Drugs

Drugs used in pediatric cardiopulmonary resuscitation and in the postresuscitation stabilization are listed in Table 7-4. A chart such as this one should be posted in the resuscitation room. Nurses need to be familiar with the drugs and doses used in children. The following are the main drugs used in cardiopulmomary resuscitation:

1. Oxygen: Indicated for hypoxemia; highest available concentration should be used.

2. Epinephrine: Has both α- and β-adrenergic effects. Epinephrine should not be added to a bicarbonate infusion because it will be inactivated by

Table 7-2 Chest Compressions in Infants and Children

	Infants (less than 1 year)	Children (more than 1 year)
Position	Lower third of the sternum: Place index finger of hand farthest away from infant's head under intermammary line where it intersects the sternum. Area of compression is one finger width below this intersection.	Lower third of the sternum: Locate lower margin of rib cage with middle finger to notch where the ribs and sternum meet. Place middle finger on notch, index finger next to middle finger. The heel of the same hand is placed next to the previous location of index finger, with the long axis of the heel parallel to the sternum.
Compress with	Two fingers or Hand encircling	Heel of one hand One or two hands (older children)
Depth	0.5–1 in	1.0–1.5 in 1.5–2.0 in (older children)
Rate	100–120/min	80–100/min
Compression/ ventilation ratio	5:1 (pause for ventilation)	5:1 (pause for ventilation)

Source: Reproduced with permission. © *Textbook of Pediatric Advanced Life Support*, 1988. American Heart Association.

Table 7-3 Suggested Sizes for Endotracheal Tubes, Laryngoscope Blades, and Suction Catheters*

Age	Internal Diameter of Tube (mm)	Laryngoscope Blade Sizes	Suction Catheters
Newborn	3.0	0-1	6 F
6 months	3.5	1	8 F
3 years	4.5	2	8 F
5 years	5.0	2	10 F
6 years	5.5	2	10 F
8 years	6.0	2	10 F
12 years	6.5	2	10 F
16 years	7.0	3	10 F
Adult (F)	7.5–8.0	3	12 F
Adult (M)	8.0–8.5	3	14 F

*Have available one size larger and one size smaller to allow for individual variations in the child's size.

Source: Reprinted from *Advanced Pediatric Life Support,* p. 5, with permission of the American Academy of Pediatrics and the American College of Emergency Physicians, © 1989.

the alkaline solution. It can be given via ETT or via intraosseous infusion. Effects of epinephrine include the following:

- It elevates perfusion pressure generated during chest compressions.
- It improves contractile state.
- It stimulates spontaneous contraction.

3. Sodium bicarbonate
- It can be used when airway maneuvers (intubation and hyperventilation), chest compression, and epinephrine fail to improve the child's condition.
- It is used to correct acidosis.
- It cannot be given via ETT as it is hyperosmolar and will produce a chemical burn.

4. Atropine
- It can be given via ETT or IV.
- It is used for bradycardia when accompanied by poor perfusion and hypotension.
- Since bradycardia is most often the result of hypoxia, treatment should be initially directed at ventilation and oxygenation.

Table 7-4 Drugs Used in Pediatric Advanced Life Support

Drug	Dose	How Supplied	Remarks
Atropine sulfate	0.02 mg/kg/dose (1.0 mL)	0.1 mg/mL	Minimum dose of 0.1 mg
Calcium chloride	20 mg/kg/dose	100 mg/mL (10%)	Give slowly.
Dopamine hydrochloride	2–20 µg/kg/min	40 mg/mL	α-Adrenergic action dominates at 15–20 µg/kg/min.
Dobutamine hydrochloride	5–20 µg/kg/min	250 mg/vial lyophilized	Titrate to desired effect.
Epinephrine hydrochloride	0.1 mL/kg (0.01 mg/kg)	1:10,000 (0.1 mg/mL)	1:1,000 must be diluted.
Epinephrine infusion	Start at 0.1 µg/kg/min	1:1,000 (1 mg/mL)	Titrate to desired effect (0.1–1.0 µg/kg/min).
Isoproterenol hydrochloride	Start at 0.1 µg/kg/min	1 mg/5 mL	Titrate to desired effect (0.1–1.0 µg/kg/min).
Lidocaine	1 mg/kg/dose	10 mg/mL (1%) 20 mg/mL (2%) 40 mg/mL (4%)	
Lidocaine infusion	20–50 µg/kg/min	1 mg/mL	Titrate to desired effect (0.1–1.0 µg/kg/min).
Norepinephrine infusion	Start at 0.1 µg/kg/min		
Sodium bicarbonate	1 mEq/kg/dose or 0.3 × kg × base deficit	1 mEq/mL (8.4%)	Infuse slowly and only if ventilation is adequate.

Source: Reprinted from *Journal of American Medical Association,* Vol. 255, No. 21, p. 2966, with permission of the American Medical Association, © 1986.

5. Glucose: given because infants and ill children rapidly use up glycogen stores. Signs and symptoms of hypoglycemia may mimic hypoxemia. Glucose is hyperosmolar and may be sclerosing to peripheral veins; 25% dextrose should be used or 50% dextrose may be diluted.
   - Give glucose after obtaining bedside glucose test.
   - Give to infants who fail to respond to initial resuscitation measures.
6. Calcium: controversial as a first-line arrest drug.
   - Use if hypocalcemia is documented or suspected.
   - Use if hyperkalemia is present.
   - Use if hypermagnesemia and calcium channel blocker overdose exist.
7. Lidocaine
   - Use for ventricular fibrillation (rare in children).
   - Use for ventricular tachycardia.
8. Bretylium: not currently used extensively in children; in adults, used for ventricular fibrillation that is not responsive to lidocaine.

   Postresuscitation drugs are used to help stabilize a child with unstable perfusion and blood pressure. Many of these drugs are given as a continuous infusion. They are listed in Table 7-4. Table 7-5 illustrates a method of mixing continuous infusions and a chart with the appropriate doses per body weight.

E. Equipment

All emergency departments should keep a separate pediatric cart that includes equipment necessary to treat pediatric emergencies. Chapter 21 discusses recommended equipment.

F. Diagnostic Studies
   1. chest x-ray to check tube placement
   2. arterial blood gasses (ABGs)
   3. complete blood count (CBC)
   4. electrolytes (sodium, potassium, glucose)
   5. creatinine and blood urea nitrogen (BUN)
   6. toxicological screen if poisoning is suspected

PARENT TEACHING AND SUPPORT

All parents should be encouraged to learn basic life support techniques and how to access the EMS in their area. Many of the causes of pediatric arrest are preventable and parents need to be taught safety measures (use of car seats, water safety, etc.) listed in Chapter 3.

Table 7-5 Infusion Medications by Weight and Age for Infants and Children 0–10 Years

Add 0.6 mg (3 mL)* of **isoproterenol**
   0.6 mg (0.6 mL)* of **epinephrine** **To** 100 mL of diluent
   60.0 mg (1.5 mL)* of **dopamine**
   60.0 mg (2.4 mL)* of **dobutamine**

Infuse at 1 mL/kg/h or according to following table in order

To give 0.1 μg/kg/min isoproterenol
    0.1 μg/kg/min epinephrine
    10 μg/kg/min dopamine
    10 μg/kg/min dobutamine

Age	50th Percentile Weight (kg)	Infusion Rate (mL/h)+
Newborn	3.0	3.0
1 month	4.0	4.0
3 months	5.5	5.5
6 months	7.0	7.0
1 year	10.0	10.0
2 years	12.0	12.0
3 years	14.0	14.0
4 years	16.0	16.0
5 years	18.0	18.0
6 years	20.0	20.0
7 years	22.0	22.0
8 years	25.0	25.0
9 years	28.0	28.0
10 years	34.0	34.0

*Based on the following concentrations:
 isoproterenol = 0.2 mg/mL
 epinephrine = 1:1000 (1 mg/mL)
 dopamine = 40 mg/mL
 dobutamine = 25 mg/mL
+These are starting doses. Adjust concentration to dose and fluid tolerance.

Source: Reproduced with permission. © *Textbook of Pediatric Advanced Life Support*, 1988. American Heart Association.

The parents need to be supported while the child is in the ED. A nurse or social worker should

- keep the family updated on what is being done
- contact any other family members or other support, such as clergy
- allow the family to see the child after the condition is stabilized or during the resuscitation, if appropriate

NURSING DOCUMENTATION

- history
- prehospital care (CPR, medications, etc.)
- frequent vital signs: temperature, pulse, respiration, and blood pressure
- ED interventions and child's response: medications, fluids, CPR
- laboratory tests and results
- time CPR was discontinued
- disposition of child (including intensive care unit, morgue)

NURSING DIAGNOSES

- ineffective airway clearance related to partial or complete airway obstruction
- ineffective breathing patterns related to respiratory arrest
- alteration in cardiac output related to decreased volume
- alteration in tissue perfusion related to decreased cardiac output
- impaired gas exchange related to hypoxia and respiratory arrest
- anticipatory grieving of parents related to seriousness of child's condition
- ineffective family coping

NOTES

1. Leon Chameides, ed., *Textbook of Pediatric Advanced Life Support* (Dallas: American Heart Association, 1988), 3.

2. American Heart Association, "Standards and Guidelines for Cardiopulmonary Resuscitation (CPR) and Emergency Cardiac Care (ECC)," *Journal of the American Medical Association* 255 (1986): 2954–60.

BIBLIOGRAPHY

American Heart Association. "Standards and Guidelines for Cardiopulmonary Resuscitation (CPR) and Emergency Cardiac Care (ECC)." *Journal of the American Medical Association* 255 (1986): 2841–3044.

American Heart Association. *Textbook of Advanced Cardiac Life Support.* Dallas: American Heart Association, 1985.

Baker, D.M. "Arrest Team Management of Pediatric Cardiopulmonary Arrest." *American Journal of Emergency Medicine* 5 (1987): 149–52.

Bass, E. "Cardiopulmonary Arrest Pathophysiology and Neurologic Complications." *Annals of Internal Medicine* 103 (1985): 920–27.

Carpenito, L.J., ed. *Nursing Diagnosis Application to Clinical Practice*, 2d ed. Philadelphia: J.B. Lippincott Co., 1987.

Chameides, Leon, ed. *Textbook of Pediatric Advanced Life Support*. Dallas: American Heart Association, 1988.

Fisher, D.H., and V. Wrape. "Outcome of Cardiopulmonary Resuscitation in Children." *Pediatric Emergency Care* 3 (1987): 235–38.

Fredrickson, J.M. "Basic Pediatric Cardiopulmonary Resuscitation (CPR) Update." *Journal of Emergency Nursing* 14 (1988): 76–81.

Gildea, J. "A Crisis Plan for Pediatric Code." *American Journal of Nursing* 86 (1986): 557–65.

Kelley, S.J. "Cardiopulmonary Resuscitation of Infants and Children." In *Pediatric Emergency Nursing*, edited by S.J. Kelley, 103–22. Norwalk, Conn.: Appleton & Lange, 1987.

Ludwig, S., and G. Fleisher. "Pediatric Cardiopulmonary Resuscitation: A Review and a Proposal." *Pediatric Emergency Care* 1 (1985): 40–44.

Manley, L., K. Haley, and M. Dick. "Intraosseous Infusion: Rapid Vascular Access for Critically Ill or Injured Infants and Children." *Journal of Emergency Nursing* 14 (1988): 63–69.

Nichols, D.G., et al. "Factors Influencing Outcome of Cardiopulmonary Resuscitation in Children." *Pediatric Emergency Care* 2 (1986): 1-5.

Orlowski, J.P. "Optimum Position for External Cardiac Compression in Infants and Young Children." *Annals of Emergency Medicine* 15 (1986): 667–73.

Redding, J.S. "Cardiopulmonary Resuscitation: An Algorithm and Some Common Pitfalls." *American Heart Journal* 98 (1979): 788–97.

Riddle, K., et al. "Pediatric Code Team Response to the Emergency Department: A Collaborative Effort." *Journal of Emergency Nursing* 14 (1988): 342–45.

Sherar, K.V., and L.T. Cooper. "Systematic Orientation of Emergency Nurses to Pediatric Arrests." *Journal of Emergency Nursing* 14 (1988): 346–51.

Thomas, D.O. "The ABCs of Pediatric Triage." *Journal of Emergency Nursing* 14 (1988): 154–59.

Wayland, B., and M. Rowland. "Pediatric Immediate Care Cart." *Journal of Emergency Nursing* 14 (1988): 91–95.

Zaritsky, A., et al. "CPR in Children." *Annals of Emergency Medicine* 16 (1987): 1107–11.

Chapter 8

Dysrhythmias

Bradley Jay Husberg

INTRODUCTION

Dysrhythmias, disturbances in the normal rhythm or conduction pattern of the heart, are rare in children. When they do occur, the hemodynamic effects can be serious.

The majority of life-threatening pediatric dysrhythmias can be prevented if conditions leading to the dysrhythmia are recognized and treated. An understanding of pediatric anatomy, physiology, and assessment techniques is essential for the prevention, detection, and treatment of dysrhythmias.

PATHOPHYSIOLOGY

Dysrhythmias in children result from an abnormal coronary artery blood flow. In adults, they usually occur because of abnormal coronary arteries, arterial blood flow, and ischemia. In newborns and infants, they occur because of the immaturity of the conduction system. Dysrhythmias often occur in pediatric patients with normal hearts but they are seldom primary events, occurring rather as the result of an abnormal quality of the blood being delivered to the heart.

Some common causes of pediatric dysrhythmias include the following:

- hypoxia (the most common cause of bradycardia in children)
- hypercapnia
- acidosis
- electrolyte disturbances
- hyperthermia
- hypothermia
- drug ingestion

- congenital heart disease (CHD)
- acquired heart disease (e.g., myocarditis)
- trauma
- hypovolemia

Specific Dysrhythmias

Cardiac dysrhythmias in children can be simplified into four groups—fast, slow, wide, and narrow—depending on heart rate and duration of the QRS complex.[1] Table 8-1 summarizes these four groups. The specific dysrhythmias in each group include the following:

1. **Fast heart rates:** Faster-than-normal rates (tachycardia) account for the majority of pediatric dysrhythmias. Table 8-2 lists approximate normal ranges for heart rates, respiratory rate, and blood pressure according to age. Included in the fast group are
   - ventricular tachycardia (most serious)
   - supraventricular tachycardia (SVT) (the most common dysrhythmia in children[2])
   - sinus tachycardia
   Common causes of tachycardia in children include the following:
   - hypovolemia
   - anxiety
   - fear
   - fever
   Prolonged periods of tachycardia can lead to myocardial exhaustion and congestive heart failure.
2. **Slow heart rates (bradycardia):** Slower than normal heart rates in children are most often caused by systemic hypoxia. Prolonged bradycardia will lead

---

Table 8-1 Basic Pediatric Dysrhythmia Recognition

	Fast Heart Rate for the Age of the Child	Slow Heart Rate for the Age of the Child
Wide QRS complex (> 0.09)	Ventricular tachycardia	Agonal/idioventricular
Narrow QRS complex (< 0.09)	Supraventricular tachycardia, sinus tachycardia	Bradycardia, second- or third-degree heart blocks

Table 8-2 Approximate Range of Vital Signs for Children

	Infant	*Toddler*	*School-Age*
Heart rate	110–180	80–150	60–130
Respiratory rate	30–40	24–30	16–20
Blood pressure	76/50–106/68	106/68–110/70	112/70–120/80

to decreased cerebral perfusion resulting in lethargy and confusion. If untreated, bradycardia can progress to cardiac arrest. Dysrhythmias included in this group are

- sinus bradycardia
- atrioventricular (AV) blocks
- agonal rhythms

Other causes of slower-than-normal heart rates in children include increased intracranial pressure, digitalis overdose, other drug ingestions, and vagal stimulation in the newborn.

3. **Wide QRS complex:** A wide QRS complex (greater than 0.09) implies electrical conduction outside of the normal conduction pathways. This condition is usually the result of a discharge from an ectopic irritable focus in the ventricles and can lead to inadequate cardiac output due to inadequate filling times. Dysrhythmias in this group can be further divided into wide and fast rhythms (ventricular tachycardia), or wide and slow rhythms (agonal or idioventricular rhythms).

The most common causes of wide QRS rhythms in children include the following:

- hypoxia
- myocardial damage
- hypovolemia
- tricyclic antidepressant ingestion (see Chapter 26)

4. **Narrow QRS complex:** A QRS complex that is narrow (less than 0.09) is usually normal. No adverse effects occur unless the heart rate is affected (either too slow or too fast for age).

TRIAGE ASSESSMENT

As in all children, airway, breathing, and circulation (the ABCs) must be assessed first. The triage assessment includes the rapid cardiopulmonary assessment listed in Chapter 7.

TRIAGE HISTORY

- previous history, especially of CHD or recent heart surgery
- signs and symptoms (duration)
- history of recent trauma or illness
- current medications; possibility of accidental overdose

TELEPHONE TRIAGE GUIDELINES

Parents of any child with a history of CHD or recent cardiac surgery who is having chest pain, respiratory difficulty, or poor color should be told to call the emergency medical service or come to the emergency department immediately. If the child is not judged to be in any immediate danger, the parents should be advised to contact their cardiologist. Often the ED nurse can and should contact the cardiologist and have him or her call the parents. No advice should be given by the nurse concerning medications or treatment other than to come to the ED.

PRIORITY RATING

Emergent: Any child with signs and symptoms of decreased cardiac output, decreased level of consciousness, especially those with history of CHD or prior dysrhythmias, or bradycardia.

Urgent: History of SVT without signs of decreased cardiac output; these children should be seen as soon as possible, but a short delay will not be harmful.

Because children may not be outwardly symptomatic, the triage nurse needs to assess vital signs and get a good history. Children in the waiting room should be assessed frequently for changes.

TREATMENT AND NURSING CARE

Care that is common to all dysrhythmias includes the following:

1. airway management. Give oxygen. Hypoxia is a common cause of dysrhythmias in children. Intubation and mechanical ventilation may be necessary.
2. breathing assessment. Check rate, breath sounds. Evaluate color.
3. circulation assessment. Place on cardiac monitor to evaluate rhythm, check heart rate, blood pressure, and capillary refill time. Insert IV for possible medications.

4. disability assessment. Do neurological evaluation and check temperature.

5. interventions for specific dysrhythmia. The nurse needs to know specific medications including dosages and actions, according to the American Heart Association guidelines. Consult an advanced pediatric life support manual for specific treatment of specific dysrhythmias.

6. emotional support to both the parents and the child

PARENT TEACHING

- Explain child's condition.
- Explain medications prescribed.
- Outline precipitating factors that may lead to dysrhythmia.
- Discuss signs and symptoms of dysrhythmia.
- Make referral to cardiologist as indicated.
- Discuss any activity restrictions.
- Refer parents to the American Heart Association or the American Red Cross for basic life support classes if classes are unavailable in the hospital.

NURSING DOCUMENTATION

- initial assessment and interventions
- rhythm strip and 12-lead ECG
- medications given and response to medications
- condition on discharge
- follow-up planned and parent teaching

NURSING DIAGNOSES

- alteration in tissue perfusion and cardiopulmonary function related to decreased cardiac output
- potential for alteration in respiratory function
- fear (of child) related to ED procedures and environment
- alteration in comfort, pain related to ED procedures
- knowledge deficit (family) of child's condition
- anticipatory grieving (family) related to severity of child's condition

NOTES

1. Leon Chameides, ed., *Textbook of Pediatric Advanced Life Support* (Dallas: The American Heart Association, 1988), 63–67.

2. A. Garson, P. Gillette, and D. McNamara, "Supraventricular Tachycardia in Children: Clinical Features, Response to Treatment, and Long-term Follow-up in 217 Patients," *Journal of Pediatrics* 98 (1981): 875–82.

BIBLIOGRAPHY

American Academy of Pediatrics and American College of Emergency Physicians. *Advanced Pediatric Life Support*. Elk Grove Village, Ill., and Dallas: American Academy of Pediatrics and the American College of Emergency Physicians, 1989.

American Heart Association. "Standards and Guidelines for Cardiopulmonary Resuscitation and Emergency Cardiac Care." *Journal of the American Medical Association* 255 (1986): 2841–3044.

Carpenito, L.J., ed. *Nursing Diagnosis Application to Clinical Practice*, 2d ed. Philadelphia: J.B. Lippincott Co., 1987.

Chameides, L. "Reading a Child's ECG." *Emergency Medicine* 16 (1984): 78–111.

Chameides, Leon, ed. *Textbook of Pediatric Advanced Life Support,* Dallas: American Heart Association, 1988.

Curley, M.A.Q. "Cardiac Dysrhythmias." In *Pediatric Emergency Nursing,* edited by S. Kelley, 252–75. Norwalk, Conn.: Appleton & Lange, 1988.

Gillette, P.C., and A. Garson. *Pediatric Cardiac Arrhythmias*. New York: Grune & Stratton, 1981.

Lanros, N.E. "Section A: Cardiac Emergencies and Advanced Cardiac Life Support (ACLS) Guidelines." In *Assessment and Intervention in Emergency Nursing,* 3d ed., edited by N. Lanros, 163–201. Norwalk, Conn.: Appleton & Lange, 1988.

Manley, L., K. Haley, and M. Dick. "Intraosseous Infusion: Rapid Vascular Access for Critically Ill or Injured Infants and Children." *Journal of Emergency Nursing* 14 (1988): 63–69.

Chapter 9

Resuscitation of the Newborn in the Emergency Department

Laurel S. Campbell

INTRODUCTION

Neonatal resuscitation involves life support measures necessary to restore cardiopulmonary function in the neonate. A neonate is usually defined as any infant from birth to 1 month of age. Neonatal resuscitation may be required in the ED setting if any of the following situations exist:

- emergency delivery of a neonate in the ED
- transfer of a neonate to the ED following birth in a nontraditional (out-of-hospital) setting
- onset of neonatal distress during the first month of life

PATHOPHYSIOLOGY

A number of prenatal, perinatal, and neonatal factors can precipitate neonatal distress[1].

Prenatal Factors

- maternal drug/alcohol abuse
- lack of prenatal care
- maternal metabolic disorders (diabetes, heart disease, lung disease, hypertension, preeclampsia, eclampsia)
- maternal infection
- maternal age (less than 16 years or more than 35 years)

67

Perinatal Factors

- abnormal fetal position/presentation
- prolapsed cord
- placenta previa, abruptio placenta
- maternal cardiopulmonary distress, arrest, seizures
- meconium-stained amniotic fluid
- multiple birth (more than one fetus)

Neonatal Factors

- respiratory: mucous plug, asphyxia due to cord compression or strangulation (cord around the neck), meconium aspiration, congenital anomalies, immature respiratory system, hyaline membrane disease, respiratory arrest
- cardiac: congenital anomalies, persistent fetal circulation, cardiac dysrhythmias, hypovolemia
- metabolic: hypoglycemia, sepsis, hypothermia

These factors can result in impaired neonatal cardiopulmonary function. Ineffective oxygenation leads to tissue hypoxia, anaerobic metabolism, and alterations in cardiac contractility. Decreased cardiac perfusion and contractility eventually are manifested in cardiac dysrhythmias, most commonly bradycardia and asystole.[2]

TRIAGE ASSESSMENT

Impending childbirth is categorized as an emergent problem due to the threat of morbidity and mortality to two lives (mother and fetus). Therefore, assessment in the triage area should be limited only to recognition of impending childbirth as a potentially life-threatening situation. Initial stabilization and assessment should be done in the treatment area.

Initial triage assessment of a neonate brought to the ED after an out-of-hospital birth or at any time during the first month of life should follow the same parameters as for the assessment of the neonate delivered in the ED. These include:

- airway
- breathing
- circulation (pulse, blood pressure, skin color)
- muscle tone

- reflex irritability to stimuli (nasal/oral suctioning)
- temperature

An Apgar score at 1 and 5 minutes after delivery should be calculated and recorded (Table 9-1).

TRIAGE HISTORY

The following arc clements of the triage history:

- gestational age of neonate
- maternal drug use (recreational or therapeutic)
- account of events during labor and delivery
- maternal medical conditions (diabetes, hypertension, toxemia)

TELEPHONE TRIAGE GUIDELINES

Any neonate born in an out-of-hospital setting should be evaluated by a physician as soon as possible. Telephone triage may include "talking the parents through" with infant cardiopulmonary resuscitation (CPR) instructions until trained medical personnel arrive on the scene to transport the neonate to the ED. The triage nurse should be prepared for this scenario by periodically reviewing current guidelines for infant CPR (see Exhibit 9-1) and by including a copy of these guidelines in the telephone triage protocols. The ED nurse can direct another personnel member to call the local

Table 9-1 The Apgar Scoring System

Sign	0	1	2
Heart rate	Absent	Slow (<100/min)	>100/min
Respirations	Absent	Slow, irregular	Good, crying
Muscle tone	Limp	Some flexion	Active motion
Reflex irritability	No response	Grimace	Cough, sneeze
Color	Blue or pale	Pink body with blue extremities	Completely pink

Source: Reprinted from *Journal of the American Medical Association*, Vol. 255, No. 21, p. 2971, with permission of the American Medical Association, © 1986.

Exhibit 9-1 Guidelines for Neonatal/Infant Cardiopulmonary Resuscitation

---

AIRWAY
1. Determine unresponsiveness.
2. Position infant. Turn on back as unit, supporting head and neck. Place on firm, hard surface.
3. Position the infant. Use the head-tilt/chin-lift maneuver or the sniffing or neutral position. Do not overextend the head. If the infant has just been delivered, place on back in a slight Trendelenburg position, turn head to one side if copious secretions are present.

BREATHING
1. Determine breathlessness. Place ear over mouth; observe chest; look, listen, and feel for breathing.
2. Ventilate twice. Make tight seal on infant's mouth and nose, observe chest rise, and allow deflation between breaths.

CIRCULATION
1. Determine pulselessness. Feel for brachial pulse while maintaining head-tilt/chin-lift with other hand.
2. Activate EMS.
3. Begin chest compressions. Place two or three fingers on sternum, one finger's width below intermammary line. Compress 1/2 to 3/4 inches (1/2 to 1 inch for the older infant) equal compression-relaxation. Compression rate is 120/min for the neonate and 100/min for the older infant. Compression/ventilation ratio is five compressions to one slow ventilation per cycle.
4. Reassess after 10 cycles. Check brachial pulse and continue CPR.

Source: Reproduced with permission. © *Textbook of Pediatric Advanced Life Support*, 1988. American Heart Association.

---

emergency medical services number with the parents' address and details of the situation if the parents must maintain phone contact with the nurse for instructions.

PRIORITY RATING

The birth of a neonate should be considered an emergent situation until the initial assessment and stabilization are completed. Priority rating for care of any neonate transported to the emergency department should be based on the following guidelines:

Emergent: Any child experiencing cardiopulmonary distress or arrest; heart rate less than 100 beats/minute; slow, irregular, or absent respirations; pale or cyanotic skin.

Urgent: Child with acrocyanosis, grunting respirations, poor muscle tone.

Nonurgent: Child with heart rate greater than 100 beats/minute; spontaneous, nonlabored respirations; skin pink and warm; good muscle tone; active, healthy cry.

TREATMENT AND NURSING CARE

Treatment of the neonate in cardiopulmonary distress or arrest is primarily focused on stabilization and support of cardiac and respiratory functions. Diagnostic interventions such as laboratory and radiological procedures are appropriate only after initial stabilization has been accomplished.

The success of the resuscitation is dependent on having the proper equipment. Exhibit 9-2 lists recommended equipment that all emergency departments should have available.

Exhibit 9-2 Suggested Neonatal Resuscitation Equipment for the Emergency Department

AIRWAY/BREATHING
Resuscitation bag (250–500 mL)
Face masks (newborn and premature sizes)
Laryngoscope and blades (straight 0 and 1)
Endotracheal tubes (2.5, 3.0, and 3.5)
Endotracheal tube stylet
Suction catheters (one 5 F and two 8 F taped to the appropriate ET tubes)
Suction with manometer
Bulb syringe
DeLee suction trap

CIRCULATION
Umbilical catheter (5 F)
Dilators
Syringes and three-way stopcocks
Feeding tube (5 and 8 F)

DRUGS
Neonatal Narcan, .02 mg/mL
Epinephrine 1:10,000
Sodium bicarbonate 4.2% (Can dilute adult solution [8.4%] 1:1 with sterile water.)

MISCELLANEOUS
OB kit containing cord-cutting materials, cord clamp, and sterile towels
Doppler device
Pulse oximeter
Radiant warmer
Volume expanders

Note: Most of this equipment can be kept on a newborn resuscitation tray. This tray should be checked routinely and restocked as necessary. Emergency departments should also keep current guidelines and drug doses for neonatal resuscitation posted in the resuscitation area. Resuscitations should be practiced using mock megacodes.

Nursing care includes the following:

1. Assessment of airway status, respirations: Assess for spontaneous respirations, chest expansion, presence and quality of breath sounds.
   - Respirations should be spontaneous after brief stimulation of the infant (slapping or flicking soles of feet, rubbing infant's back, suctioning).
   - If respirations are shallow, slow, or absent, respiratory support should be initiated with bag mask ventilations using a small-tidal-volume, self-inflating resuscitation bag, neonatal mask, and 100% oxygen at a rate of 40–60/minute.[3]
   - If respiratory depression is thought to be induced by maternal narcotic use, naloxone hydrochloride should be given using a neonatal solution. The dose is 0.01 mg/kg.[4]
   - If initial ventilations with a bag mask system do not produce adequate respiratory response, the nurse may need to assist with intubation.
2. Assessment of circulatory status: Assess skin color, heart rate, femoral and brachial pulses.
   - If the heart rate is less than 100 or absent, and skin color is pale or cyanotic, ventilation and oxygenation should be supported with positive pressure ventilations using a bag mask system.[5]
   - If the heart rate is less than 60–80 beats/minute despite adequate ventilation with 100% oxygen, chest compressions should be initiated.[6] Exhibit 9-1 describes one method of doing chest compressions. Another method (not taught to the layperson) is the chest encirclement technique (Figure 9-1).
3. Temperature control: Resuscitation measures may be ineffective if the neonate is hypothermic.
   - Completely dry the neonate after delivery; wrap in warm towels or blanket if resuscitation measures are not indicated.
   - Place the infant under a radiant warmer if resuscitation measures are necessary.
   - Minimize heat loss from the neonate's head by using a cap (can be made from a length of stockinette knotted at one end).
4. Intravenous access: IV access should be initiated for administration of fluids and as an access route for medications.
   - Peripheral venous cannulation is difficult in the neonate due to vasoconstriction and poor peripheral circulation.
   - Cannulation of the umbilical vein with an umbilical catheter may be more effective due to accessibility and size of the umbilical vein.
   - Umbilical artery cannulation can be initiated for arterial pressure monitoring and as an access for arterial blood samples.

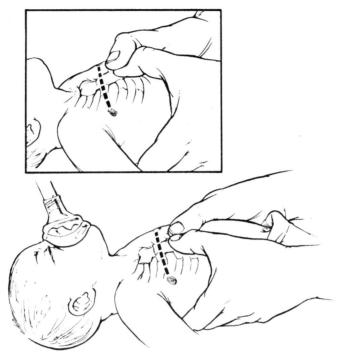

Figure 9-1 Hand Position for Chest Encirclement Technique for External Chest Compressions in Neonates. Thumbs are side by side over the midsternum. In the small newborn, thumbs may need to be superimposed. The xiphoid portion of the sternum should not be compressed due to the danger of damaging abdominal organs. *Source:* Reproduced with permission. © *Textbook of Pediatric Advanced Life Support,* 1988. American Heart Association.

5. Administration of fluids and medications: IV fluids are indicated if the neonate exhibits signs of noncardiogenic shock indicated by weak peripheral pulses, cool diaphoretic skin, and pallor despite adequate oxygenation.
   - Volume expanders such as 10 mL/kg of type O-negative blood (cross-matched with the mother's blood), albumin, or normal saline can be used to increase preload in the hypovolemic infant.[7]
   - Fluids should be administered over a 5- to 10-minute period, followed by assessment for signs of circulatory improvement.

Table 9-2 lists drugs and doses used in neonatal resuscitations, as well as guidelines for sizes of endotracheal tubes, suction catheters, and laryngoscope blades.

Table 9-2 A Review of Neonatal Resuscitation Drugs and Airway Equipment

Ventilation rate: 40–60/min
Compression rate: 120/min
Medications: Heart rate < 80/min despite adequate ventilations with 100% O_2 and chest compressions

Medication	Concentration to Administer	Preparation	Dosage/Route*	Total Dose/Infant		Rate/Precautions
				Weight	Total	
Epinephrine	1:10,000	1 mL	0.1–0.3 mL/kg IV or ET	1 kg 2 kg 3 kg 4 kg	0.1–0.3 mL 0.2–0.6 mL 0.3–0.9 mL 0.4–1.2 mL	Give rapidly.
Volume expanders	Whole blood 5% albumin Normal saline Ringer's lactate	40 mL	10 mL/kg IV	1 kg 2 kg 3 kg 4 kg	10 mL 20 mL 30 mL 40 mL	Give over 5–10 min.
Narcan neonatal (naloxone)	0.02 mg/mL	2 mL	0.5 mL/kg IV, IM, SQ, ET	1 kg 2 kg 3 kg 4 kg	0.5 mL 1.0 mL 1.5 mL 2.0 mL	Give rapidly.
Dopamine	$\dfrac{6 \times \text{wt(kg)} \times \text{desired dose (μg/kg/min)}}{\text{desired fluid (mL/h)}}$ = mg of dopamine/100mL of solution		Begin at 5 μg/kg/min (may increase to 20 μg/kg/min if necessary) IV	1 kg 2 kg 3 kg 4 kg	5–20 μg/min 10–40 μg/min 15–60 μg/min 20–80 μg/min	Give as an infusion using an infusion pump. Monitor heart rate and blood pressure closely. Seek consultation.

| Sodium bicarbonate | 0.5 mEq/mL (4.2% solution) | 20 mL or two 10-mL prefilled syringes | 2 mEq/kg IV | 1 kg — 4 mL (2 mEq); 2 kg — 8 mL (4 mEq); 3 kg — 12 mL (6 mEq); 4 kg — 16 mL (8 mEq) | Give slowly over at least 2 min. Give only if infant being effectively ventilated. |

Equipment	Weight	ET/Suction Catheter	Laryngeal Blade
ET/suction catheter	1 kg	2.5/5F	0
	2 kg	3.0/6F	0
	3 kg	3.5/8F	0–1
	4 kg	3.5/8F	1

*IM = intramuscular; ET = endotracheal tube; IV = intravenous; SQ = subcutaneous

Source: Reproduced with permission. © *Textbook of Pediatric Advanced Life Support*, 1988. American Heart Association.

PARENT TEACHING

Parents who have spent months preparing for the events associated with a "normal" labor and delivery will be extremely anxious if their baby requires resuscitation. Often during the resuscitation phase, the parents are separated from the baby and receive little information on his or her condition. The parents need support during this time. Hospital patient–family service representatives, chaplain support services, and members of the parents' families may be helpful. Parent teaching should include what is being done to support the baby as well as any plans to transfer or admit the baby to a neonatal intensive care unit for further management.

NURSING DOCUMENTATION

- antepartum history (maternal drug use, including narcotics; eclampsia; gestational age of neonate)
- intrapartum history (cord compression/asphyxia, presence of meconium, time of rupture of membranes, maternal bleeding)
- Apgar score at 1 and 5 minutes (See Table 9-1)
- temperature, pulse, blood pressure, respirations
- airway/ventilatory support measures initiated, size of ET tube, amount of oxygen used, type of secretions
- circulatory support, time chest compressions initiated, intravenous access routes, fluids used
- medications given
- neonate's response to all interventions
- presence of neonatal resuscitation support members (neonatologist, neonatal intensive care nurse, respiratory therapist, and psychosocial support services)
- disposition of baby (admit to newborn intensive care, transport to another facility, etc.)

NURSING DIAGNOSES

- ineffective airway clearance related to incomplete expulsion of fetal lung fluids and aspiration
- impaired gas exchange related to ineffective breathing patterns, incomplete expulsion of fetal lung fluids and aspiration
- actual or potential fluid volume deficit related to intrapartum complications (maternal hypotension, hemorrhage, and/or cord occlusion)

- alteration in temperature related to heat loss from evaporation and convection
- alteration in cardiac output related to hypoxia and persistent fetal circulation
- altered family process related to separation during initial parent–infant bonding period
- anticipatory grieving of family

NOTES

1. Susan Pasternack, "Resuscitation of the Newborn," in *Pediatric Emergency Nursing,* ed. S. Kelley (Norwalk, Conn.: Appleton & Lange, 1988), 81–102.

2. American Heart Association, "Standards for Cardiopulmonary Resuscitation and Emergency Cardiac Care," *Journal of the American Medical Association* 255 (1986): 2969–73.

3. Ibid.

4. Ibid.

5. Ibid.

6. Ibid.

7. Ibid.

BIBLIOGRAPHY

Chameides, Leon, ed. *Textbook of Pediatric Advanced Life Support.* Dallas: The American Heart Association, 1988.

Hazinski, M.F. "New Guidelines for Pediatric and Neonatal Cardiopulmonary Resuscitation and Advanced Life Support." *Pediatric Nursing* 13 (1987): 57–59.

Pasternack, S. "Resuscitation of the Newborn." In *Pediatric Emergency Nursing,* edited by S. Kelley, 81–102. Norwalk, Conn.: Appleton & Lange, 1988.

"Standards for Cardiopulmonary Resuscitation and Emergency Cardiac Care." *Journal of the American Medical Association* 255 (1986): 2905–84.

Stephenson, D., L. Frankel, and W. Benitz. "Immediate Management of the Asphyxiated Infant." *Journal of Perinatology* 7 (1987): 221–25.

Chapter 10

Shock

Donna Ojanen Thomas

INTRODUCTION

Shock is a clinical syndrome of circulatory dysfunction that results in an acute failure to perfuse tissues with oxygen and other nutrients. Shock is classified in many ways, but commonly into three main types:

1. **hypovolemic:** caused by acute blood, plasma, or fluid loss. This is the most common type of shock in the child and is discussed in the most detail.
2. **distributive:** caused by loss of sympathetic tone, which results in peripheral vasodilation. Septic shock and neurogenic shock are included in this category.
3. **cardiogenic:** caused by abnormalities in cardiac function resulting in failure of the cardiovascular system to meet metabolic needs. Obstructive shock is included in this category and results in decreased cardiac output due to inflow and outflow obstructions.

PATHOPHYSIOLOGY

As in an adult, cardiac output in a child is determined by heart rate and stroke volume ($CO = HR \times SV$). When heart rate and stroke volume decrease, cardiac output decreases. In children, shock is usually a result of a decrease in stroke volume caused by decreased circulating volume.

When cardiac output drops, compensatory mechanisms take over. These compensatory mechanisms are manifested in the signs and symptoms of shock. Depending on these signs and symptoms, shock can be classified in three stages: compensated (early), uncompensated (progressive), and late (irreversible). These stages and their signs and symptoms are defined and described in Table 10-1.

Table 10-1 Stages of Shock: Signs and Symptoms in the Pediatric Patient

Stage	Signs and Symptoms	Comments
Compensated (early)	Tachycardia. Other vital signs usually normal. Possible fever in early septic shock	Usually the earliest sign of shock in a child, indicating an attempt to increase cardiac output by increasing rate of contractions. In neurogenic shock, hypotension may be present without tachycardia.
	Increased capillary refill time	Blood shunted away from skin to heart and brain.
	Cool, pale extremities; thready, weak pulses	In early septic shock and neurogenic shock, extremities may be warm and dry, due to vasodilation.
	Anxiety, irritability	Due to increasing hypoxia.
Uncompensated (progressive)	Signs and symptoms as above plus tachypnea	May appear earlier in septic shock due to fever. Results from metabolic acidosis—attempts to blow off excess CO_2.
	Confusion, stupor	Due to increasing hypoxia.
Late (irreversible)	Hypotension	Hypotension is a late sign of shock. It may indicate a loss of 30–50% of blood volume.
	Coma	Some children may maintain CNS function or "talking shock."
	Marked tachypnea or dysfunctional respirations	May require mechanical ventilation.

Table 10-2 Causes of Shock in the Pediatric Patient

Type of Shock	*Causes*
Hypovolemic	Blood loss due to external or internal trauma Fluid loss due to vomiting and diarrhea, diabetic ketoacidosis, heat stroke Plasma loss due to burns, sepsis acidosis, hypoxia, hypothermia
Distributive	Loss of sympathetic tone due to: Sepsis (early), usually gram-negative bacteria Anaphylaxis: drugs, bites, and stings Drug ingestions: phenobarbital, antihypertensives Spinal cord or major brainstem injury Toxic shock syndrome—wound infections, tampon use in adolescent females
Cardiogenic	Congenital heart disease Myocarditis Cardiomyopathy Drugs Myocardial infarction (rare in children) Chronic anemia Pulmonary embolism Tension pneumothorax Pericarditis Tamponade

Severe shock results in altered cellular metabolism and energy production, which result in altered cellular function and structure. Cells die, releasing proteolytic enzymes and other toxic products that further alter cellular function in other tissue beds. As shock progresses, the brain, heart, and other major organs are damaged and may not recover.

Causes of shock in the pediatric patient are listed in Table 10-2.

TRIAGE ASSESSMENT

Since recognition of shock is the most important factor in the treatment, initial assessment must be focused on early signs and symptoms that are listed in Table 10-1. The initial triage assessment should include the following:

- *vital signs:* temperature, pulse, respiration, and blood pressure (TPR, BP). Tachycardia may be the earliest sign of shock. Decreased BP is a late finding.

- *general appearance:* level of consciousness, skin color, presence of rashes.
- *extremities:* temperature, capillary refill time (CRT).* In hypovolemic shock and late septic shock, extremities will be cold and clammy with increased capillary refill time. In early septic shock, they will be warm and dry.

TRIAGE HISTORY

- history of trauma or burns
- history of illness, especially fever, diarrhea, and vomiting
- current medications
- past medical history including diabetes, heart disease, chronic infection, anemia
- allergies
- menstrual history and use of tampons

TELEPHONE TRIAGE GUIDELINES

Any child with a history of significant trauma with possible increased blood loss or with vomiting and diarrhea with decreased fluid intake and urine output should be evaluated immediately. The nurse should follow the guideline that any child who has a decreased level of consciousness should be viewed as emergent. The nurse needs to consider the possibility of anaphylactic shock when discussing insect bites or stings, or in a child with multiple allergies.

PRIORITY RATING

Emergent: Any child who is suspected of being in early shock either by history or by appearance should be seen and treated immediately.

TREATMENT AND NURSING CARE

The treatment of all types of shock is aimed at restoring cellular and organ perfusion, and treating the underlying cause. Nursing care includes:

---

*Capillary refill time is measured by pressing on the forehead or nailbeds of the fingers or toes and timing the return of circulation. Normal is less than 2 seconds.

1. Recognition
   - Evaluate history for fluid or blood loss, trauma, sepsis.
   - Check vital signs: presence of tachycardia, prolonged capillary refill time. Remember that a decreased blood pressure is a late sign of shock, except in neurogenic shock.
2. Airway
   - Provide 100% oxygen.
   - Prepare to assist with intubation.
3. Bleeding
   - Apply direct pressure.
   - Consider use of MAST (controversial in pediatrics).
4. Intravenous access/fluids
   - Insert two large-bore IV lines.
   - Consider intraosseous infusion as a temporary route if peripheral access is unsuccessful because it is quicker and easier than central lines or cutdowns. (See Chapter 15.)
   - Administer fluids: initial IV bolus of 20 cc/kg of lactated Ringer's solution. May need to repeat. Whole blood may be indicated.

     Note: D5W should never be used to treat shock as it is a hypotonic solution and will not increase circulating volume.
5. Monitoring the following:
   - response to fluid boluses: urine output, improving CRT, level of consciousness. Insert Foley catheter.
   - oxygen saturation with pulse oximeter or arterial blood gasses (ABGs).
   - ECG. Remember that bradycardia is often caused by hypoxia.
   - temperature. Use warmed fluids and bloods, warmed humidified oxygen.
   - lab work. Obtain ABGs, electrolytes, complete blood count (CBC), blood and urine cultures, urinalysis, BUN, and creatinine.
6. Drugs
   - Fluids are the "drug" of choice in hypovolemic shock.
   - Dextrose may be necessary (2 cc/kg D25); hypoglycemia is common in septic shock, and infants have limited glucose reserves.
   - Vasopressors are contraindicated in hypovolemic shock. "Don't give pressors on an empty tank." Dopamine or Isuprel may be indicated in distributive shock (see Chapter 7).
   - Antibiotics are indicated in septic shock.
   - Naloxone may reverse hypotension in septic shock.

- Steroids are of questionable use in septic shock.
- Epinephrine may be used in cases of anaphylactic shock.

Other interventions may be done to treat the cause of shock. The child may require immediate surgery or other invasive procedures that are described in Chapters 21 to 23.

PARENT TEACHING

Since shock is a life-threatening condition, the parents will have many concerns, mostly about the outcome of the child. The ED nurse can help by

- explaining all equipment and procedures
- answering all questions
- allowing parents to be with child after stabilization
- providing a hospital social worker to support family
- preparing parents and child for admission

NURSING DOCUMENTATION

- initial assessment and history
- vital signs
- interventions: fluids, oxygen, medications
- response to interventions
- disposition of child

NURSING DIAGNOSES

- potential alteration in body temperature (hypo- or hyperthermia) related to infection and/or shock state
- fluid volume deficit related to increased metabolic needs, increased losses, and decreased intake
- alteration in cerebral and cardiopulmonary tissue perfusion related to decreased cardiac ouput
- decreased cardiac output related to hypovolemia, relative or absolute
- fear (child's) related to injuries and ED procedures
- knowledge deficit (of parents) related to disease process and hospital care
- anticipatory grieving of parents related to seriousness of child's condition

BIBLIOGRAPHY

Anderton, B., et al. *Advanced Pediatric Life Support*. Salt Lake City: Primary Children's Medical Center, 1987.

Bone, R., et al. "A Controlled Clinical Trial of High Dose Methylprednisone in the Treatment of Severe Sepsis and Septic Shock." *New England Journal of Medicine* 17 (1988) 175–76.

Budassi, S., J. Marvin, and C. Jimmerson. *Manual of Clinical Trauma Care: The First Hour*. St. Louis: C.V. Mosby Co., 1989.

Perkin, R., and D. Levin. "Shock in the Pediatric Patient, Part I." *Journal of Pediatrics* 101 (1982): 163–69.

Perkin, R., and D. Levin. "Shock in the Pediatric Patient, Part II." *Journal of Pediatrics* 101 (1982): 319–32.

Perry, A., and P. Potter. *Shock: Comprehensive Nursing Management*. St. Louis: C.V. Mosby Co., 1983.

Selbst, S., and S. Torrey. *Pediatric Emergency Medicine for the House Officer*. Baltimore: Williams & Wilkins, 1988.

Part IV

Respiratory Problems

Chapter 11

Upper Airway Emergencies

Laurel S. Campbell

INTRODUCTION

The upper airway in the child consists of the oropharynx, nasopharynx, supraglottic structures, subglottic structures, larynx, and trachea. Upper airway problems are more common in children than adults due to several factors:

- Children have a smaller diameter in the airways and more soft tissue; therefore, they have an increased likelihood of obstruction and edema.
- Children have a tendency to put small objects in the mouth to explore them, and therefore an increased likelihood of aspiration leading to airway obstruction.
- Children have a higher incidence of viral and bacterial infections that affect the respiratory tract.

Although there are other causes of upper airway obstruction in children, this chapter discusses three of the more common conditions seen in the emergency department:

1. foreign body obstruction
2. laryngotracheobronchitis (croup)
3. epiglottitis

PATHOPHYSIOLOGY

1. *Foreign body obstruction.* Airway obstruction caused by foreign objects results in about 200 deaths annually in children less than 5 years.[1] Causes of obstruction include:

- food: hot dogs, popcorn, nuts, beans, seeds
- coins
- small toys or parts of toys
- small batteries found in hearing aids and watches

2. *Croup*. Croup is a viral illness resulting in inflammation and edema of the area around the vocal cords and trachea. Characteristics include the following:

- It is most common in children under 3 years.
- It occurs during late fall/early winter or during cold weather.
- Its most common causes are parainfluenza viruses.

3. *Epiglottitis*. Epiglottitis is a bacterial infection of the epiglottis resulting in swelling and inflammation of the epiglottis and surrounding area. It is considered a life-threatening emergency that requires prompt recognition and treatment because of the potential for complete airway obstruction by the inflamed epiglottis. Characteristics include the following:

- It is most common in children between 2 and 6 years.
- It can occur at any time of year.
- Its most common cause is *Haemophilus influenzae* type B.

TRIAGE ASSESSMENT

Prompt recognition and treatment are important to the outcome of a child with upper airway obstruction. The triage nurse should assess for the following:

- inspiratory and expiratory stridor
- retractions (suprasternal, supraclavicular, intercostal, subcostal)
- cyanosis or pallor
- lethargy or agitation
- chest wall movement with respirations
- posture of the child (sitting up or leaning forward)
- nasal flaring
- presence of drooling

One method of giving a standard measurement to the evaluation of the patient with upper airway obstruction is to use a recognized scoring system as shown in Table 11-1.

Table 11-1 Upper Airway Obstruction (UAO) Score

Indicator	0	1	2
Stridor	None	Inspiratory	Inspiratory and expiratory
Cough	None	Hoarse cry	Bark
Retractions and nasal flaring	None	Flaring and suprasternal retractions	Flaring and suprasternal, intercostal and subcostal retractions
Cyanosis	None	In air	In 40% oxygen
Inspiratory breath sounds	Normal	Harsh, with wheezing or rhonchi	Delayed

Interpretation:
A score of 4 or more indicates moderately severe airway obstruction.
A score of 7 or more, despite therapy, indicates the need for intubation.

Source: Reprinted from *Anesthesiology,* Vol. 43, No. 2, p. 242, with permission of J.B. Lippincott, © 1975.

TRIAGE HISTORY

- past medical history
- time of onset, duration of symptoms
- possibility of foreign body aspiration
- presence of upper respiratory infection (URI) symptoms: runny nose, cough, sore throat
- fever: time of onset, how high
- medications, treatments given at home and when

Since croup, epiglottitis, and foreign body aspiration may have similar signs and symptoms, the nurse needs to incorporate the triage assessment findings with the history to help in the differential diagnosis of upper respiratory disease or obstruction. Table 11-2 compares the three forms of upper airway obstruction discussed in this chapter.

Table 11-2 Differentiation of Upper Airway Obstruction Etiologies

Parameter	Foreign Body	Croup	Epiglottitis
Etiology	Mechanical	Viral	Bacterial
Onset of symptoms	Acute	Over 1–2 days	Over a few hours
Fever	Absent*	Low grade	Infant: low; child: high
Cough	With partial obstruction: present; with complete obstruction: absent	Barking	Usually absent
Inspiratory stridor	Present	Present	Present
URI symptoms	Absent*	Present	Usually absent until onset of distress
Drooling	Possible	Absent	Usually present

*Usually absent unless child also has an underlying upper respiratory illness.

TELEPHONE TRIAGE GUIDELINES

Based on the information received from the caller, the triage nurse may have to give the parents instruction on how to access the emergency medical services (EMS) as well as how to relieve an upper airway obstruction due to a foreign object. Even if the parents are successful in relieving the obstruction, the child should be evaluated by a physician for possible airway damage.

If epiglottitis is suspected based on history and symptoms, the child should be evaluated immediately at the nearest medical facility.

If the information obtained is consistent with croup, the nurse should give the following advice if the child is not in severe distress:[2]

- Encourage consumption of PO liquids to aid in liquefying secretions.
- Turn the shower on and fill the bathroom with warm, misty air. Stay with the child for at least 15 minutes or until his or her condition improves.
- If symptoms worsen at night, dress child warmly and take outside in cold air for 10–15 minutes.
- If symptoms worsen or do not improve, child should be evaluated by a physician immediately.

PRIORITY RATING

Emergent: Any child with partial or complete airway obstruction, cyanosis, severe retractions, lethargy, stridor; UAO score greater than 5.

Urgent: Mild retractions, color pink, taking oral fluids, active; UAO score 2–5.

Nonurgent: No retractions, color pink, taking oral fluids, playful; UAO score 0–1.

TREATMENT AND NURSING CARE

Foreign Body Obstruction

For the child who has a completely obstructed airway, follow the American Heart Association guidelines for an obstructed airway in an infant or child. These guidelines are summarized in Exhibit 11-1. Attempts at clearing the airway should be made when[3]

- aspiration of a foreign body is witnessed or strongly suspected
- the child is unconscious, nonbreathing, and the airway remains obstructed despite the usual attempts to open it (Figures 11-1 to 11-5)

If the airway is only partially obstructed and the child is moving air, attempts should not be made to remove the obstruction. The following guidelines should be followed:

- Allow the child to maintain a position of comfort.
- Don't attempt to visualize the obstruction.
- Don't upset the child in any way by attempting to take vital signs or examine.
- Have the ED physician immediately evaluate the child.
- Remain with the child.

Objects in the upper airway that are not completely obstructing breathing may require surgical removal.

Croup

- Give oxygen by mask if oxygen saturation is less than 90% (measured by pulse oximetry) and child will tolerate it. Exhibit 11-2 lists tips on administering oxygen to children.
- Give racemic epinephrine by aerosol, as ordered by physician.
- Assess child's respirations and heart rate, and UAO score before and after racemic epinephrine treatments.

Exhibit 11-1 Guidelines for Airway Obstruction Management

INFANT
1. Deliver four back blows with the heel of the hand between the infant's shoulder blades (Figure 11-1).
2. Supporting the head and neck, turn the infant and deliver four chest thrusts (Figure 11-2).

CHILD
Heimlich maneuver with child standing or sitting (conscious):
1. Stand behind child and wrap arms around waist with one hand made into a fist (Figure 11-3).
2. Grasp fist with other hand and press into child's abdomen with a quick upward thrust. Repeat 10 times or until foreign body is expelled.

Heimlich maneuver with child lying (unconscious):
1. Position the child face up on back and kneel at child's feet (Figure 11-4). Use the astride position if the child is too large.
2. Place the heel of one hand on the child's abdomen in the midline slightly above the navel and below the rib cage. Place the other hand on top of the first.
3. Press into the abdomen with a quick upward thrust: six to ten thrusts are performed.

MANUAL REMOVAL OF FOREIGN BODIES
1. Avoid blind finger sweeps of the throat in infants and children since the foreign body may be pushed back into the airway and cause further obstruction.
2. In the unconscious, nonbreathing child, following the chest or subdiaphragmatic thrusts, open the mouth by grasping both the tongue and lower jaw between the thumb and finger and lift (Figure 11-5).
3. If the foreign body is visualized, it can be removed.

Source: Reproduced with permission. © *Textbook of Pediatric Advanced Life Support,* 1988. American Heart Association.

- Give oral fluids if tolerated; IV fluids if severely dehydrated.
- X-ray of lateral neck may be ordered if epiglottitis is suspected.

Note: Administration of racemic epinephrine is usually followed by airway improvement within 5 to 15 minutes after treatment. However, a "rebound effect" may occur up to 4 hours after treatment, and the airway inflammation may be as bad as or worse than before the treatment. For this reason, a child receiving a racemic epinephrine treatment should remain in the ED for observation for 3–4 hours after the treatment[4] or should be admitted to the hospital.

Epiglottitis

- Allow parent to remain with child at all times.
- Administer oxygen by mask only if tolerated.

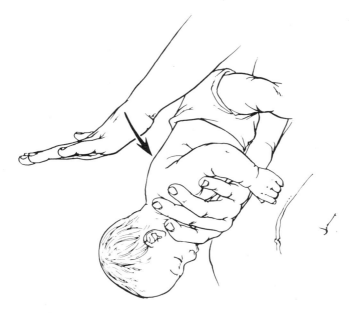

Figure 11-1 Positioning an Infant for Back Blows. *Source:* Reproduced with permission. *Textbook of Pediatric Advanced Life Support*, 1988. Copyright © American Heart Association.

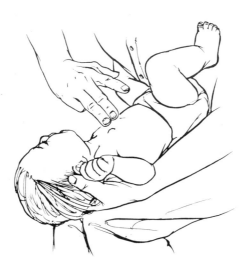

Figure 11-2 Positioning an Infant for Chest Thrusts. *Source:* Reproduced with permission. *Textbook of Pediatric Advanced Life Support*, 1988. Copyright © American Heart Association.

Figure 11-3 Heimlich Maneuver—Child Standing or Sitting (Conscious). *Source:* Reproduced with permission. *Textbook of Pediatric Advanced Life Support,* 1988. Copyright © American Heart Association.

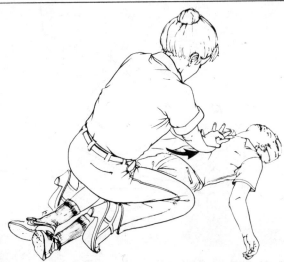

Figure 11-4 Heimlich Maneuver—Child Lying (Unconscious). *Source:* Reproduced with permission. *Textbook of Pediatric Advanced Life Support,* 1988. Copyright © American Heart Association.

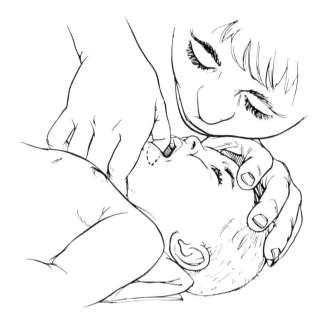

Figure 11-5 Tongue-Jaw Lift. *Source:* Reproduced with permission. *Textbook of Pediatric Advanced Life Support,* 1988. Copyright © American Heart Association.

- Prepare equipment for emergency airway management.
- Avoid any invasive procedures: IV infusions, lab work, vital signs.
- Do not attempt an oral exam with a tongue blade (may result in spasm, airway occlusion).
- Take x-rays only if attended by nurse, physician, or anesthesiologist with airway equipment on hand.
- Assist with controlled intubation (preferably in an operating room).
- Give IV antibiotics only after airway is stabilized.
- After intubation, restrain child to prevent accidental extubation.

Medications

Medications used in the treatment of croup and epiglottitis are listed in Table 11-3.

Exhibit 11-2 Tips on Administering Oxygen to Children

NASAL CANNULA
This apparatus can supply up to 50% oxygen concentration and is tolerated better by older children. A high flow rate (> 6 L/min) is irritating to the nasopharynx.

- To avoid nasal irritation, cut off the nasal cannula prongs and position the holes of the cannula below the nares.
- Instead of taping to the face, position the nasal cannula and cover the sections lateral to the nares with transparent occlusive dressings.

MASK
The mask can supply 35–60% oxygen concentration with a flow rate of 6–10 L/min. If the child will not tolerate wearing a mask

- Hold the mask (or have the parent hold) near the nose and mouth. This method is called the "blow by" technique. A bag-valve-mask device can also be used for blow-by.
- Describe the mask as a "space mask" to a preschool child and integrate it into an astronaut role play.

PAPER CUP METHOD
This method can be used for children who resist the conventional method. Oxygen concentration delivery will vary. Cut a hole the size of the oxygen tubing into the bottom of a paper cup. Thread the oxygen tubing through the hole and have the child breathe from the cup.

Note: These methods should be used for the child who needs minimal oxygen supplementation. The nurse should monitor oxygen saturation by oximeter to gauge effectiveness of treatment. The delivery device chosen should be dependent on the child's age and his or her acceptance of the device.

Diagnostic X-Ray Findings

- foreign body aspiration: inspiration/expiration views; air trapping on expiration views. Foreign object may be visible.
- croup: "Steeple sign" (narrowing at the subglottic area) on anterior/posterior (AP) view
- epiglottitis: edema of aryepiglottic folds, epiglottis on lateral neck view (must obtain lateral neck films for x-ray diagnosis; cannot assess on AP film)

PARENT TEACHING

1. Foreign body obstruction
   - Observe for fever related to airway damage or infection.
   - Discuss making the home environment "childproof."
   - Encourage parents to learn the American Heart Association guidelines for obstructed airway management.

Table 11-3 Medications Commonly Used in the Treatment of Croup and Epiglottitis

	Drug	Dose*	Route	Nursing Considerations
Epiglottitis	Ampicillin	200–400 mg/kg/day Divided in q 6 h doses	IV	Venipuncture and drugs *only* after airway management completed.
	Chloramphenicol	Loading: 20 mg/kg Maintenance: 50–100 mg/kg/day Divided in q 6 h doses	IV	Give until culture and sensitivity results are available.
	Cefotaxime	50–180 mg/kg/day Divided in q 6 h doses	IV	May cause reaction in patients who are penicillin-allergic.
Croup	Racemic epinephrine	0.05 ml/kg/dose of 2.25% solution diluted to 3 mL with normal saline or distilled water	Aerosol	See statement on rebound effect under "Treatment and Nursing Care."
	Dexamethasone	0.25–0.5 mg/kg q 6 h PRN	PO, IM, IV	PO, IM routes preferred unless in shock or acutely ill.

*Dosages from: Peter C. Rowe, ed., *The Harriet Lane Handbook* (Chicago: Year Book Medical Publishers, Inc., 1987), 136, 142, 144, 150, 157.

- Instruct parents to avoid foods and objects that commonly cause airway obstruction.
2. Croup. See information under "Telephone Triage Guidelines."
3. Epiglottitis. Most parent teaching should deal with the immediate treatment need and information on the plan of care during the hospitalization. Siblings and other close contacts may be treated with antibiotics prophylactically if the organism is *Haemophilus influenzae*. (See Chapter 18 for more information on treatment of *Haemophilus* infections.)

NURSING DOCUMENTATION

- vital signs (temperature, pulse, respirations, blood pressure)
- UAO score before and after treatment
- general appearance (level of consciousness, color)
- signs and symptoms of hypoxia or increased respiratory effort
- oxygen saturation level (measured by pulse oximetry)
- first aid measures or treatments done at home
- interventions done and child's response

NURSING DIAGNOSES

- impaired gas exchange related to obstructed airway and inadequate oxygenation
- ineffective airway clearance related to edema from viral or bacterial inflammation
- ineffective breathing patterns related to obstruction of airway by inflammatory or mechanical means
- potential or actual altered body temperature; fever
- potential or actual fluid volume deficit related to insensible fluid losses and/or decreased intake
- alteration in comfort related to respiratory distress
- fear (child's) related to hospitalization, nurses, and medical interventions
- knowledge deficit (parents') related to preventative measures, disease process, and treatment

NOTES

1. National Safety Council, *Accident Facts,* 1988 ed. (Chicago: National Safety Council, 1988), 7.
2. R. Behrman and V. Vaughan, eds., *Nelson Textbook of Pediatrics,* 13th ed. (Philadelphia: W.B. Saunders Co., 1987), 869, 887, 889–90, 893.
3. R. Wood, et al., *Pediatrics* (Philadelphia: J.B. Lippincott Co., 1989), 66.
4. Ibid.

BIBLIOGRAPHY

Boat, T., et al. "Upper Respiratory Tract." In *Nelson Textbook of Pediatrics,* 13th ed., edited by R. Behrman and V. Vaughan, 868–93. Philadelphia: W.B. Saunders Co., 1987.

Brilli, R., G. Benzing, and D. Cotcamp. "Epiglottitis in Infants Less Than Two Years of Age." *Pediatric Emergency Care* 5 (1989): 16–21.

Butt, W., et al. "Acute Epiglottitis: A Different Approach to Management." *Critical Care Medicine* 16 (1988): 43–47.

Gershan, W., et al. "Acute Airway Obstruction in a Seven Month Old Infant with Epiglottitis." *Pediatric Emergency Care* 4 (1988): 197–99.

Kissoon, N., and M. Walia. "The Critically Ill Child in the Pediatric Emergency Department." *Annals of Emergency Medicine* 18 (1989): 30–33.

Kulick, R., et al. "Thermal Epiglottitis After Swallowing Hot Beverages." *Pediatrics* 81 (1988): 441–44.

Laks, Y., and Z. Barzilay. "Foreign Body Aspiration in Children." *Pediatric Emergency Care* 4 (1988): 102–06.

Marcus, M., and L. Semsl. "An Unusual Case of Epiglottitis in a Patient with Asthma." *Pediatric Emergency Care* 4 (1988): 124–26.

Mauro, R., S. Poole, and C. Lockhart. "Differentiation of Epiglottitis from Laryngotracheitis in the Child with Stridor." *American Journal of Diseases of Children* 142 (1988): 679–82.

"Respiratory Disorders." In *Pediatrics,* edited by R. Wood et al., 65–71. Philadelphia: J.B. Lippincott Co., 1989.

Schuh, S., A. Huang, and J. Fallis. "Atypical Epiglottitis." *Annals of Emergency Medicine* 17 (1988): 168–70.

Stool, S. "Croup Syndrome: Historical Perspective." *Pediatric Infectious Disease Journal* 7 (1988): S157–61.

Chapter 12

Lower Airway Emergencies

Donna Ojanen Thomas

INTRODUCTION

The lower airways consist of bronchi, bronchioles, and alveoli. Major causes of lower airway emergencies in children discussed in this chapter include:

1. asthma
2. bronchiolitis
3. pneumonia
4. foreign body aspiration

Lower airway problems occur in children for the following reasons:

- Children have narrow airways that can easily become occluded by secretions caused by infection or mechanical obstruction (foreign bodies).
- Younger children have less immunity.
- The small size of the airways allows for rapid spreading of infection to all areas of the respiratory tract.

PATHOPHYSIOLOGY

Asthma

Asthma is a disease characterized by a hyperreactive airway associated with reversible obstruction of that airway and is the most common chronic disease in children.[1] Asthma attacks have been shown to be initiated by the following:

- allergies: inhalation of a substance that the child is allergic to
- exercise: thought to be caused by loss of heat in the airway during exercise

103

- infections: upper respiratory infections, especially viral infections, by increasing inflammation, mucus production, and airway reactivity
- irritants: sulfur dioxide, cigarette smoke, and ozone
- weather changes: reasons for increased exacerbation of asthma during weather changes not clearly understood
- emotions: may be secondary to CNS stimulation
- drugs: aspirin, nonsteroidal anti-inflammatory agents

Smooth muscle hypertrophy, bronchospasm, mucous gland hypertrophy, and mucous plugging all contribute to the obstruction seen in the asthmatic child.

Bronchiolitis

Bronchiolitis is a viral infection of the lower respiratory tract most commonly caused by the respiratory syncytial virus (RSV). Children under 1 year of age are commonly affected. Airway obstruction is caused by edema and secretions.

Pneumonia

Pneumonia can be caused by a virus or a bacterium. Viral agents account for 60–90% of all cases, but bacteria, especially *S. pneumoniae,* play a major role.[2]
The types of bacteria that cause pneumonia vary with the age of the child. Usually the pathogens reach the lung by aspiration (the main cause) or by spread from the blood. Viral pneumonia usually occurs secondary to spreading of the virus from the upper airway to the lungs. A few viruses may reach the lungs through dissemination from the blood.

Foreign Body Aspiration

Foreign bodies in the lower respiratory tract do not present an acute condition such as those that lodge in the upper airways. The right mainstem bronchus is often the site of lodging of a foreign body, due to its shorter length and straight angle, but objects can be lodged elsewhere. Usually the object causes irritation, inflammation, or varying degrees of obstruction. Objects commonly aspirated are:

- peanuts
- popcorn
- beans and other small uncooked vegetables
- small toys or parts of toys

Other forms of lower respiratory diseases such as pertussis and tuberculosis must be kept in mind. Although the cases of pertussis have decreased due to use of the vaccine, several thousand cases occur yearly in the United States.[3] Tuberculosis is unusual, but it is seen occasionally.

TRIAGE ASSESSMENT

As with all respiratory illnesses in the child, prompt evaluation is important to recognize impending respiratory failure. If not recognized and treated, it can lead to severe hypoxia, bradycardia, and cardiac arrest. Signs and symptoms that the triage nurse should look for include the following:

- wheezing (often the most common symptom of a lower airway problem); not always a sign of asthma and possibly absent despite severe distress
- presence and type of retractions
- presence of cough
- level of consciousness. The child in impending respiratory failure may be lethargic or agitated.
- breath sounds (equal, decreased bilaterally or unilaterally)
- color of child. Cyanosis is a late sign and always requires prompt treatment.
- vital signs: temperature, pulse, respiration, and blood pressure (TPR, BP). Tachypnea and tachycardia are signs of respiratory distress.

Table 12-1 shows an asthma scoring system that was developed to help identify the severely ill child or child with impending respiratory failure.

Another method of evaluating respiratory distress is based on clinical signs and symptoms. This method should serve only as a guide in evaluating the degree of distress.

1. The signs and symptoms indicating mild distress are
   - wheezing
   - tachypnea and tachycardia
   - good air movement on auscultation
2. The signs and symptoms indicating moderate distress are
   - anxiety
   - respiratory grunting
   - nasal flaring
   - use of accessory muscles
   - decreased breath sounds bilaterally

Table 12-1 An Asthma Scoring System

	0	1	2
Cyanosis (PaO$_2$)	None (70–100 mm Hg)	In air (<70 mm Hg)	In 40% O$_2$ (<70 mm Hg)
Inspiratory breath sounds	Normal	Unequal	Decreased or absent
Use of accessory muscles	None	Moderate	Maximal
Expiratory wheezing	None	Moderate	Marked
Cerebral function	Normal	Depressed or agitated	Coma

Interpretation of Score:
0–4   No immediate danger
5–6   Impending respiratory failure
7 or greater   Respiratory failure

Source: Reprinted from *Anesthesiology,* Vol. 43, No. 2, p. 242, with permission of J.B. Lippincott, © 1975.

3. The signs and symptoms indicating severe distress are
   - decreasing level of consciousness compared with prior examinations
   - restlessness or agitation
   - somnolence
   - cyanosis
   - distant or absent breath sounds (wheezing may be absent)

TRIAGE HISTORY

- time of onset, duration of symptoms
- presence of fever
- pre-existing conditions: asthma, other chronic lung or cardiac disease
- medications taken and times
- immunizations (pertussis should be considered in the unimmunized child)

Table 12-2 compares the four types of lower respiratory emergencies discussed in this chapter.

Table 12-2 Comparison of Lower Respiratory Conditions in Children

Condition	Age of Onset	Cause	History and Presenting Signs and Symptoms	Emergency Department Treatment
Asthma	> 1 year	Allergies, infections	Dyspnea, wheezing (may be absent), prolonged expiratory phase Fever (present if underlying infection exists)	Oxygen, nebulized adrenergic agents, aminophylline.* Child should be placed on a cardiac monitor and pulse oximeter. Fever control measures
Bronchiolitis	< 1 year	Usually RSV (respiratory syncytial virus)	Coryza, progression to cough, fever may be present. Gradual onset of respiratory distress: tachypnea, wheezing. May progress to apnea spells in infants	Oxygen (may require intubation in severe cases) Bronchodilators (nebulized) may be helpful. Cardiac monitor and pulse oximeter. Ribavirin aerosol may be given in severe cases (usually done in the intensive care unit).
Pneumonia	All ages	Varies with age: majority caused by viruses	Viral: gradual onset, cough, coryza, low-grade fever, tachypnea	Viral: supportive care, fluids. Infants may require hospitalization.

continues

Table 12-2 continued

Condition	Age of Onset	Cause	History and Presenting Signs and Symptoms	Emergency Department Treatment
		Most common bacteria: *S. pneumoniae* *H. influenzae*	Bacterial: abrupt onset, tachypnea, fever, and chills, chest pain	Bacterial: penicillin preparations
Foreign body aspiration	Any age; most commonly less than 5 years	Peanuts, popcorn, raw vegetables, small toys	History of choking or coughing. Abrupt onset of respiratory distress, unilateral wheezing, and decreased breath sounds	Surgical consult and bronchoscopy for removal. Antibiotics may be ordered for infection.

*See Table 12-3 for more information on drugs used in the treatment of asthma.

TELEPHONE TRIAGE GUIDELINES

Usually the parent will call the ED with the complaint of "difficulty breathing." This term can mean many things, from nasal congestion to severe respiratory distress. The nurse should ask the age of the child and questions listed under triage history.

The following should be seen immediately:[4]

- A child less than 3 months old who has been wheezing for more than an hour; such children may need to be admitted because they often become dehydrated due to decreased fluid intake and increased insensible water loss.
- A child who is wheezing and has to work hard to get air in and out even after prescribed medications.
- A child who has poor skin color.
- A child who looks sick.
- A child whose wheezing is associated with fever and coughing.

Parents whose child has had symptoms for more than 8 hours and is not in acute distress should be told to call their physician for an appointment. The parents should be told that they can come to the ED at any time.

Often the parents will have questions concerning various asthma medications their child is taking. The parents should be instructed to call their pediatrician. If he or she is not available, the ED physician should be consulted.

The following symptomatic care can be recommended if the child is not in acute distress:

- clear liquids to help loosen secretions
- vaporizer to humidify the air
- medications as ordered by the child's pediatrician
- keeping child in sitting or semisitting position

PRIORITY RATING

Emergent: Child with signs and symptoms of impending respiratory failure: cyanosis, lethargy or agitation, decreased or diminished breath sounds (wheezing may be absent), tachypnea and tachycardia (asthma score greater than 5), wheezing in a child less than 3 months of age.

Urgent: Decreased breath sounds, fever but moving air well, history of chronic asthma, color pink, alert, asthma score 1–4.

Nonurgent: Minimal distress, no use of accessory muscles, breath sounds normal, asthma score 0–1.

TREATMENT AND NURSING CARE

Specific treatment for the various conditions is listed in Table 12-2. General treatment of children with any type of respiratory distress includes the following:

- evaluation of degree of distress; clinical signs and symptoms (as listed under "Triage Assessment")
- oxygen by mask or nasal cannula
- cardiac monitor and pulse oximeter to measure oxygen saturation. A cardiac monitor should be used any time the asthmatic patient is receiving intravenous bronchodilators such as aminophylline.
- medications (see Table 12-3 for drugs used in the ED to treat asthma). Nebulized agents are currently recommended as the first-line drugs of choice due to decreased side effects and longer duration of action over subcutaneous injections of epinephrine.[5]
- chest x-ray. This may be ordered to aid in diagnosis, not routinely done on known asthmatic patients.
- laboratory tests. Arterial blood gasses may be necessary to evaluate therapy especially if the child does not improve. Pulse oximetry is preferred as a noninvasive method for measuring oxygen saturation.

A complete blood count (CBC) may be useful to help diagnose underlying bacterial infection (if epinephrine is given, a falsely high white blood count may be obtained). Blood cultures may be done to rule out bacteremia.

A child in severe respiratory distress may require intubation and mechanical ventilation. Rapid sequence intubation is recommended to make the intubation easier and less stressful to perform. Protocols should exist that include IV access, preoxygenation, cardiac monitoring, and pulse oximetry. The nurse and physician need to be familiar with the drugs used, their contraindications, and side effects.

Table 12-4 lists types of medications that may be used prior to intubation. The child requiring intubation may need to be transported to a pediatric facility if the treating hospital does not have a pediatric intensive care unit.

PARENT TEACHING

- pathophysiology of asthma. Explain what triggers an attack and how this can be avoided.
- treatment. Discuss medications prescribed for asthma, as well as any antibiotics; provide written instructions.

Table 12-3 Drugs Used in the Treatment of Asthma in the Emergency Department

Drug/Concentration	Dose/Route	Comments and Nursing Considerations
Nebulized Agents Albuterol (Proventil) 0.5% respirator solution, 5 mg/mL	< 2 years—0.2 mL 2–9 years—0.4 mL > 9 years—0.6 mL	These drugs are all selective β-2 agents with fewer side effects than non-selective agents such as epinephrine.
Terbutaline (Brethine) 0.1% parenteral ampule, 1 mg/mL	< 2 years—0.5 mL 2–9 years—1.0 mL > 9 years—1.5 mL	These drugs are diluted to a total of 3 cc with normal saline and delivered by nebulizer with a continuous oxygen low, usually given by respiratory therapist and well tolerated by most children.
Metaproterenol (Alupent) 5% inhalant solution 50 mg/ml	< 2 years—0.1 mL 2-9 years—0.2 mL > 9 years—0.3 mL	Dose may be repeated every 20 min up to three times. If no improvement occurs after three treatments, other interventions are needed. The nurse should document child's response after each treatment.
Subcutaneous Injections Epinephrine* 1:1000 solution	0.01 mL/kg up to 0.3 cc. May be repeated for three doses, 20 min apart	Subcutaneous epinephrine has been replaced in most facilities as a first-line drug for the treatment of asthma due to its adverse effects (nausea, vomiting, palpatations, tremors, and headache) and also due to the pain experienced by the child.
Sus-Phrine 1:200 solution (long-acting epinephrine)	0.005 mL/kg up to 0.15 mL	These drugs may be used in children who will not tolerate nebulized administration or if using nebulized medications would significantly delay treatment. Sus-Phrine is usually given 20 min after last epinephrine dose to prolong bronchodilation.

continues

Table 12-3 continued

Drug/Concentration	Dose/Route	Comments and Nursing Considerations
Aminophylline	Loading dose 5-6 mg/kg IV (bolus); continuous 1.0 mg/kg/h infusion	Blood levels should be done on patients receiving oral theophylline prior to a loading dose of aminophylline. Give loading dose over 30 min (dose may be less for the child taking oral theophylline preparations). Cardiac monitor should be used on all patients receiving IV aminophylline to observe for dysrhythmias.
Methylprednisolone	1–2 mg/kg IV bolus	Steroids are being used more frequently for prolonged or severe asthma attacks (to reduce mucosal edema). A short oral course may be prescribed on discharge.

*Sus-Phrine given alone may be as effective in treating an acute asthma attack as repeated injections of epinephrine.

Source: Robert G. Bolte, "Nebulized Beta-Adrenergic Agents in the Treatment of Pediatric Asthma," *Pediatric Emergency Care* 2 (1986): 250–53; Meyer Katlan, "An Evaluation of Repeated Injections of Epinephrine for the Initial Treatment of Acute Asthma," *American Review of Respiratory Disease* 127 (1983): 101–05.

Table 12-4 Types of Medications Used for Rapid Sequence Intubation

Type	Comments
Adjunctive agents	Used to block vagal stimulation. Atropine is commonly used to prevent bradycardia and decrease secretions. Lidocaine may be used to lower intracranial pressure and suppress the cough reflex.
Sedation drugs	Used to induce unconsciousness. Valium, versed, or other barbiturates and narcotics with rapid onset and short duration are often used. These drugs also help to prevent increased intracranial pressure.
Muscle relaxants	Used to cause complete muscle paralysis. Succinylcholine, pancuronium, vecuronium, and atracurium are all drugs that may be used. Succinylcholine has many side effects, which need to be considered.

- supportive care. Encourage fluids to loosen secretions (see "Telephone Triage Guidelines").
- signs and symptoms. Worsening condition is evidenced by increased lethargy or agitation, cyanosis, increased work of breathing.

NURSING DOCUMENTATION

- history of present condition, home care including prescribed medications child is taking
- general appearance: level of consciousness, color, respiratory effort
- vital signs (temperature, pulse, respiration, and blood pressure)
- asthma score before and after any interventions (not universally used)
- oxygen saturation level (by pulse oximetry)
- interventions and response to interventions in the ED
- discharge instructions and follow-up

NURSING DIAGNOSES

The nursing diagnoses for the child who has a lower airway emergency are the same as those listed in Chapter 11.

NOTES

1. Gerald B. Kolski, "Allergic Emergencies," in *Textbook of Pediatric Emergency Medicine*, eds. Gary Fleisher and Steven Ludwig (Baltimore: Williams & Wilkins, 1988), 648.

2. Gary R. Fleisher, "Infectious Disease Emergencies," in *Textbook of Pediatric Emergency Medicine*, eds. Gary Fleisher and Steven Ludwig (Baltimore: Williams & Wilkins, 1988), 439, 444.

3. Ibid.

4. Jeffrey L. Brown, *Pediatric Telephone Medicine. Principles, Triage, and Advice* (Philadelphia: J.B. Lippincott Co., 1989), 97.

5. Robert G. Bolte, "Nebulized Beta-Adrenergic Agents in the Treatment of Pediatric Asthma," *Pediatric Emergency Care* 2 (1986): 250–53.

BIBLIOGRAPHY

Anas, N., and R. Perkin. "Resuscitation and Stabilization of the Child with Respiratory Disease." *Pediatric Annals* 15 (1986): 43–57.

Downes, J., and R. Raphaely. "Pediatric Intensive Care." *Anesthesiology* 43 (1975): 238–50.

Grossman, L. "Clinical, Laboratory, and Radiological Information in the Diagnosis of Pneumonia in Children." *Annals of Emergency Medicine* 17 (1988): 43–46.

"Immunity, Allergy, and Related Diseases: Allergic Disorders." In *Nelson Textbook of Pediatrics,* 13th ed., edited by R. Behrman and V. Vaughan, 494–501. Philadelphia: W.B. Saunders Co., 1987.

Nederhand, K., J. Solon, J. Sweet, and S. Conner. "Respiratory Syncytial Virus: A Nursing Perspective." *Pediatric Nursing* 15 (1989): 342–45.

Ogle, K. "Problems in the Management of Respiratory Distress." In *Problems in Pediatric Emergency Medicine,* edited by R. Luten, 219–40. New York: Churchill Livingstone, 1988.

Phelan, A. "Respiratory Emergencies." In *Pediatric Emergency Nursing,* edited by Susan J. Kelley, 310–48. Norwalk, Conn.: Appleton & Lange, 1988.

Smith, D., and J. Dean. "Lower Airway Obstruction." In *Handbook of Pediatric Emergencies,* edited by G. Baldwin, 69–75. Boston: Little, Brown, and Co., 1989.

Welliver, R., and J. Cherry. "Bronchiolitis and Infectious Asthma." In *Textbook of Pediatric Infectious Diseases,* edited by R. Feigin and J. Cherry, 278–85. Philadelphia: W.B. Saunders Co., 1987.

Yamamoro, L., G. Yim, and G. Britten. "Rapid Sequence Anesthesia Induction for Emergency Intubation." *Pediatric Emergency Care* 6 (1990): 200–13.

Chapter 13

Near-Drowning

Donna Ojanen Thomas

INTRODUCTION

Drowning is the second most common cause of accidental death in children and the third leading cause of death from all causes in children between the ages of 1 and 13.[1] Toddlers and teenage boys are the two age groups mostly at risk.

Drowning is defined as death by suffocation after submersion in liquid. Near-drowning refers to survival or temporary survival greater than 24 hours after a submersion episode. A new category of drowning that has recently been added is ice-water drowning or near-drowning. Children in this category have been reported to survive with intact neurological status after prolonged submersions in extremely cold water.[2]

PATHOPHYSIOLOGY

Although the physiological response to submersion in salt water versus fresh water is theoretically different, the end result is the same. Aspiration of either salt water or fresh water produces a significant alveolar-arterial oxygen difference and decreased lung compliance, resulting in hypoxemia. Salt water is hypertonic and, when it is aspirated, disrupts the alveolar capillary membrane and promotes rapid movement of water and plasma proteins into the interstitium and parenchymal air spaces. Alveolar flooding and diffuse pulmonary edema are the result. Hypotonic freshwater aspiration inactivates surfactant and produces microatelectasis.

Morbidity and mortality associated with submersion injuries occur from damage to the central nervous system due to hypoxia. The final outcome of the child depends on:

- age of the child
- pre-existing health

- water temperature
- duration of submersion
- resuscitation attempts immediately after submersion

Drowning can occur any time an infant or child is left unsupervised around any type of water. Toddlers can and do drown in bathtubs, buckets of water, and toilets, as well as in swimming pools and hot tubs. Supervised swimming events account for only a small percentage of near-drowning accidents.

Teenagers often drown when they take risks that exceed their swimming ability. Alcohol also plays a role in accidental drowning in this age group.

TRIAGE ASSESSMENT

Initial presentation of the near-drowning victim can be classified as follows:[3]

1. *Category A (awake):* alert, minimal injury
2. *Category B (blunted):* unconscious, normal respirations, normal pupillary response, purposeful response to pain
3. *Category C (comatose):* comatose, respirations impaired; category C can be further divided as follows:
   - C1: comatose, nonpurposeful response to pain, all reflexes intact
   - C2: comatose, no withdrawal to pain, most reflexes intact
   - C3: comatose, most or all reflexes absent
   - C4: comatose, reflexes absent, apneic, asystolic

TRIAGE HISTORY

- length of submersion
- temperature of water
- circumstances (need to be concerned about cervical spine injury with diving accidents)
- condition at scene and resuscitative measures attempted (how soon after incident)
- pre-existing conditions (seizures, developmental problems)

TELEPHONE TRIAGE GUIDELINES

Any child who has had a submersion incident should be evaluated by a physician even if he or she appears asymptomatic. Severe respiratory distress can develop later on, and may occur rapidly. Even asymptomatic children are usually admitted and observed for 24 hours.

PRIORITY RATING

Emergent: all children in categories B and C (as defined under "Triage Assessment")
Urgent: all children in category A

TREATMENT AND NURSING CARE

The goals of nursing and medical care include the following:

1. Support airway, breathing, circulation (ABCs).
   - Basic and advanced life support: Provide supplemental oxygen (including possible need for mechanical ventilation).
   - Consider cervical spine (C-spine) injury in diving accidents; stabilize neck.
   - Start IV infusion; infuse warmed fluids.
   - Monitor vital signs (temperature, pulse, respirations, blood pressure (TPR, BP). Cardiac monitor and continuous temperature readings are necessary. A thermometer that can measure low body temperatures is needed to obtain accurate readings.
   - Assess for other life-threatening injuries based on history of accident.
2. Prevent increased intracranial pressure (ICP).
   - Monitor neurological status.
   - Hyperventilate as ordered by physician.
   - Observe for hypoxic seizures.
   - Monitor IV fluid intake.
     Other measures to prevent increased ICP may be done in the intensive care unit (ICU). These include steroids (controversial) and diuretics. Invasive ICP monitoring techniques may also be done.
3. Prevent aspiration.
   - Insert nasogastric (NG) tube.
   - Apply suction as necessary.
   - Elevate head of bed.
4. Rewarm the child.
   - Give warmed IV fluids.
   - Administer peritoneal or gastric lavage with warmed fluids.

- Give warmed, humidified oxygen.
- Use heat lamps carefully; may cause external burns if used in the severely hypothermic child.

Because of reports of survival after prolonged submersions in ice water, the following dictum should be followed: "No patient is considered dead until he or she is warm and dead." Basic life support measures should be continued until the child's temperature is near normal and he or she is still unresponsive to CPR.

Warming by cardiopulmonary bypass has been done with success in some cases of severe hypothermia.[4] For this reason, emergency departments should know of the nearest facility that has this capability and be able to arrange transport of the patient if necessary.

5. Obtain diagnostic studies.
   - arterial blood gases. Continuously monitor oxygen saturation by pulse oximeter.
   - chest x-ray. Consider C-spine films based on history.
   - drug and alcohol levels. Consider based on history.

PARENT TEACHING

- Provide support for family (social worker, clergy, etc.); prepare them for possible negative outcome.
- Provide teaching to families whose children arrive in ED awake. This includes:
  1. water safety. Advise them to enroll children in swimming lessons.
  2. supervision. Toddlers should never be left unattended near any water sources or bathtubs. Children should be supervised when swimming regardless of their ability.
  3. fences. All pools should be fenced.
  4. children with special problems. Children with seizure disorders should never be left unattended in bathtubs or pools, despite their age. They should routinely take showers instead of baths when old enough.

NURSING DOCUMENTATION

- history of incident
- initial presentation
- resuscitative efforts—prehospital and in emergency department (ED), and child's response

- interventions (ABCs, vital signs, rewarming) and child's response
- disposition of child

NURSING DIAGNOSES

- ineffective breathing pattern related to decreased lung compliance caused by pulmonary edema
- alteration in tissue perfusion, cerebral and cardiopulmonary, related to prolonged hypoxia
- potential for aspiration related to submersion
- hypothermia related to prolonged submersion
- potential for injury related to accident (cervical spine or head injury)
- anticipatory grieving of parents related to possible loss of child's functioning or life

---

NOTES

1. American Safety Council, *Accident Facts* (Chicago: American Safety Council, 1988), 6–9.

2. Robert G. Bolte et al., "The Use of Extracorporeal Rewarming in a Child Submerged for 66 Minutes," *Journal of the American Medical Association* 260 (1988): 377–79.

3. A.W. Conn, J.F. Edmonds, and G.A. Barker, "Cerebral Resuscitation in Near Drowning," *Pediatric Clinics of North America* 26 (1979): 691–701.

4. Bolte, et al., "The Use of Extracorporeal Rewarming," 377–79.

BIBLIOGRAPHY

Gonzalez-Rothi, R. "Near Drowning: Consensus and Controversies in Pulmonary and Cerebral Resuscitation." *Heart and Lung* 16:5 (1987), 474–81.

Henderson, D. "Submersion Injuries." In *Pediatric Trauma Nursing,* edited by Connie Joy. Gaithersburg, Md.: Aspen Publishers, Inc., 1989.

Orlowski, J. "Drowning, Near-Drowning, and Ice-Water Submersions." *Pediatric Clinics of North America* 34 (1987): 75–92.

Selbst, S., and S. Torrey. *Pediatric Emergency Medicine for the House Officer.* Baltimore: Williams & Wilkins, 1988.

Part V

Fluid and Electrolyte Problems

Chapter 14

Dehydration

Marina Bishop Larsen

INTRODUCTION

Dehydration occurs when total output of fluids and electrolytes exceeds intake. Dehydration is frequently classified as mild, moderate, or severe, depending on estimated percentage of body fluid lost.

PATHOPHYSIOLOGY

Dehydration develops when intake of food and water are limited or stopped, or when output of body fluids is increased such as with diarrhea and vomiting. Increased fluid losses also occur with the following:

- fever
- anxiety
- tachypnea

Dehydration resulting from these losses is primarily due to a reduction in extracellular fluid (ECF). These losses are significant in a child because

- Total body water (TBW) in an infant represents about 75% of body weight compared with 60% in an adult.
- The percentage of ECF is greater in a child than in an adult.
- Infants have a higher metabolic rate and a proportionally greater surface area than adults, and can develop fluid losses quickly.

Dehydration can be classified into three types, based on the child's level of serum sodium. These are defined in Table 14-1.

Table 14-1 Types of Dehydration

Types	Serum Sodium (mEq/L)	Causes
Isotonic	130–150	Equal sodium and water losses. Occurs with 70% of dehydrated patients
Hyponatremic	<130	Loss of sodium in excess of water. Losses are replaced with free water. Increased sodium losses as with cystic fibrosis. Occurs in 10% of patients
Hypernatremic	>150	Loss of water in excess of sodium. Occurs in 20–25% of dehydrated patients

Source: L. Finberg, et al., *Water and Electrolytes in Pediatrics: Physiology, Pathophysiology and Treatment* (Philadelphia: W.B. Saunders Co., 1982), 77.

The most common causes of dehydration in pediatrics are diarrhea, vomiting, and inadequate fluid intake. Because diarrhea and vomiting are common complaints in an emergency department (ED), they are discussed in detail in this chapter.

Other causes of dehydration include the following:

- burns (Chapter 24)
- polyuria
- poisonings (Chapter 25)
- diabetic ketoacidosis (Chapter 16), or diabetes insipidus
- intussusception
- bowel obstruction
- necrotizing enterocolitis
- pyloric stenosis
- inappropriate diet or incorrect mixing of infant formula
- child abuse or neglect
- asthma
- environmental heat and exercise

Diarrhea

Diarrhea is a frequent complaint encountered in the emergency department, and is defined as an increase in frequency, fluidity, and volume of stool. During the first

3 years of life a child will experience an estimated one to three acute severe episodes of diarrhea; most episodes subside within 72 hours with fluid administration and dietary changes.[1] Some causes of diarrhea are listed in Exhibit 14-1.

Exhibit 14-1 Causes of Diarrhea

VIRAL INFECTIONS
Rotaviruses (leading cause)
Parvoviruses
Adenoviruses

INVASIVE BACTERIAL INFECTIONS
Shigella
Salmonella

BACTERIAL TOXIN INFECTIONS
Cholera
E. coli (second to rotavirus as a cause of diarrhea in infants)
S. aureus (associated with food poisoning)

PARASITIC DISEASES
Giardia lamblia

PARENTERAL INFECTION
Upper respiratory infection
Urinary tract infection
Otitis media

NONINFECTIOUS
Congenital chloride diarrhea
Hormone-secreting tumors
Intestinal lesions occurring after an enteritis has damaged the gut
Immune deficiencies
Hepatic and pancreatic disorders
Hirschsprung's disease
Hemolytic-uremic syndrome
Intussusception
Use of antibiotics

DIETARY
Overfeeding
New foods
Food sensitivities

Source: L. Finberg, et al., *Water and Electrolytes in Pediatrics: Physiology, Pathophysiology and Treatment* (Philadelphia: W.B. Saunders Co., 1982), 148–51; L. Whaley and D. Wong, *Nursing Care of Infants and Children,* 3d ed. (St. Louis: C.V. Mosby Co., 1987), 1189–90.

Vomiting

Diseases in almost any system, particularly the brain, can cause vomiting. Common causes of vomiting are listed in Exhibit 14-2. Increased intracranial pressure due to infection or trauma should also be considered as a cause for persistent vomiting.

TRIAGE ASSESSMENT

- general appearance, including level of consciousness
- signs and symptoms of dehydration (Table 14-2)
- associated signs and symptoms (signs and symptoms of increased intracranial pressure, diseases other than gastrointestinal)
- appearance of vomitus or diarrhea
- vital signs

Exhibit 14-2 Common Causes of Vomiting

NEWBORN (BIRTH TO 2 WEEKS)
Normal variations ("spitting up")
Gastroesophageal reflux
Gastrointestinal (GI) obstruction—congenital anomalies
Necrotizing enterocolitis (premature birth)
Infections—meningitis, sepsis

OLDER INFANT (2 WEEKS TO 12 MONTHS)
Normal variations
Gastroesophageal reflux
GI obstruction—especially pyloric stenosis, intussusception, incarcerated hernia
Gastroenteritis
Infections—sepsis, meningitis, urinary tract infection, otitis media, pertussis, encephalitis
Drug overdose—aspirin, theophylline

OLDER CHILD (OVER 12 MONTHS)
Gastrointestinal obstruction—incarcerated hernia, intussusception
Other gastrointestinal causes—gastroenteritis, gastroesophageal reflux, appendicitis
Infections—meningitis, urinary tract infection, upper respiratory infection, encephalitis
Reye's syndrome
Metabolic—diabetic ketoacidosis
Toxins/drugs—aspirin, theophylline, iron, lead
Pregnancy

Source: Reprinted from *Textbook of Pediatric Emergency Medicine* by G. Fleisher and S. Ludwig, p. 334, with permission of the Williams & Wilkins Company, © 1988.

Table 14-2 Signs and Symptoms of Dehydration

Physical Finding		Mild	Moderate	Severe
Weight loss		5%	10%	15%
Urine output	< 2 yrs	One wet diaper in 8 h	One wet diaper in 12 h	One wet diaper in 24 h
	> 2 yrs	Voiding once in 12 h	Voiding once in 18–24 h	24 h without urine
Mucous membranes		Sticky	Dry	Parched
Skin elasticity (skin pinch test) (symptom usually seen only in infants)		Skin snaps back to normal tautness	Pinch returns slowly to normal	Pinch stands in folds ("tenting")
Skin color		Pale	Gray	Mottled
Eyes		Glazed	Glazed, slightly sunken	Sunken
Tears		Decreased	Scant or absent	Absent
Blood pressure		Normal or + orthostatic	Normal or low	Low
Pulse		Normal or slightly elevated	Tachycardic	Tachycardic
Temperature		Normal or slightly elevated	Febrile	Febrile
Respiratory rate		Normal	Slightly elevated	Tachypneic
Level of consciousness		Normal to listless	Lethargic	Very lethargic, difficult to arouse
Anterior fontanelle		Flat	Slightly sunken	Sunken
Perfusion (capillary refill time)		Normal to slightly delayed	Slightly delayed	Delayed
Ph		7.40–7.30	7.30–7.10	< 7.10
Urine specific gravity		≤ 1.020	> 1.030	> 1.035
BUN		Normal	Slightly elevated	Very elevated

Source: Louis V. Melini, RN, unpublished, used with permission; R. Barkin, *Emergency Pediatrics,* 2d edition (St. Louis: C.V. Mosby Co., 1990), 52.

TRIAGE HISTORY

- age of the child
- symptoms and duration: number of stools, number of times vomited
- appearance of vomitus or diarrhea
- diet: oral intake and urine output (number of wet diapers)
- pre-existing conditions, medications taken
- recent exposure to illnesses

TELEPHONE TRIAGE

Ask questions as listed under "Triage Assessment" and "Triage History." A child with the following signs and symptoms should be seen immediately in the ED or by a private physician:[2]

- Child looks acutely ill.
- Infant has significant dehydration (no urine output, no tears), especially with a history of both vomiting and diarrhea.
- Child has extreme abdominal pain.
- Parents are uncomfortable and want the child to be seen, despite how mild the symptoms are reported to be over the phone.

A child with mild to moderate diarrhea that has lasted longer than 3 days, with an associated fever, should be seen by a pediatrician if the symptoms continue and do not resolve with dietary modifications.

PRIORITY RATING

Emergent: Child with decreased level of consciousness, seizure activity, poor perfusion, history of significant fluid losses, signs and symptoms of shock (Chapter 10), 10–15% dehydration.

Urgent: Child with chronic condition (diabetes, asthma, congenital heart disease), 5–10% dehydration.

Nonurgent: Alert, happy child, 0–5% dehydration, taking and retaining oral fluids.

TREATMENT AND NURSING CARE

1. Airway, breathing, and circulation (the ABCs): The severely dehydrated child may require treatment for shock.
2. Fluids: The treatment for dehydration is oral or intravenous fluids, depending on the severity of the child's condition and ability to retain fluids.
   A. Oral rehydration therapy (ORT)
      - Pedialyte, apple juice, half-strength Jell-O water, Gatorade, and 7-Up or similar sodas
      - fluids containing 50–90 mmol/L sodium in a 2% glucose solution, if the child is more than 5% dehydrated[3]
      - commercial preparations and conventional clear liquids (Gatorade, 7-Up) if child is less than 5% dehydrated

   Table 14-3 lists the contents of frequently used clear liquids and commercial solutions. Exhibit 14-3 lists the method for using ORT in the treatment of dehydration.
   B. Intravenous (IV) therapy
      - 20 cc/kg bolus of either normal saline (NS) or lactated Ringer's (LR) solution
      - additional fluid boluses for signs and symptoms of hypovolemic shock (see Chapter 10)
      - dextrose-containing solutions are not used in fluid bolus; for glucose, 1–2 cc/kg of 25% dextrose by IV push may be ordered

---

Table 14-3 Contents of Frequently Used Clear Liquids and Commercial Solutions

Product	Sodium (mmol/L)	Potassium (mmol/L)	Carbohydrate
Pedialyte	30	20	5% glucose
Pedialyte RS	75	20	2.5% dextrose
Apple juice	2.0	28	10.7%
Gatorade	20	3.0	4.6%
7-Up	5.2	1.5	7.4%

Source: Adapted from *The Emergently Ill Child: Dilemmas in Assessment and Management* by R.M. Barkin, pp. 248–49, Aspen Publishers, Inc., © 1987.

Exhibit 14-3 Oral Rehydration Therapy Guidelines

1. Vomiting is not a contraindication for using ORT.
2. Withhold all fluids for 20–30 min after last episode of vomiting.
3. Begin giving fluids slowly and in small amounts (1/2 oz.) every 10–20 min.
4. Increase the amount of fluids given for an older child.
5. If this method is unsuccessful, the child may need intravenous therapy.

- After electrolyte results are obtained, additional treatment for isotonic, hypotonic, or hypertonic dehydration may be started. Deficits will usually be replaced over the next 24–48 hours depending on the type of dehydration.

3. Laboratory tests
   - electrolytes
   - glucose
   - blood urea nitrogen (BUN)
   - creatinine
   - urinalysis
   - stool for ova and parasites, white blood cells and culture

   Other diagnostic tests such as x-rays may be done based on the child's signs and symptoms.

4. Medications
   - antibiotics if a specific bacterial infection is isolated
   - antiemetics or antidiarrhea agents (not routinely used in children due to potential side effects)

PARENT TEACHING

- Give clear liquid diet for 24 hours, or clear liquids in addition to breast milk or half-strength formula.
- Avoid apple juice if diarrhea is present.
- As stool output decreases, use half-strength formula the second 24 hours.
- Use full-strength formula on the third day.
- If a child has diarrhea for more than 3 days, a soy formula may be used.
- Watch for signs and symptoms of dehydration (lethargy, decreased urine output).
- Use medications as prescribed.
- Keep diaper area clean and dry to prevent rash from excessive diarrhea.
- Follow up with private physician.

NURSING DOCUMENTATION

- general appearance
- vital signs: temperature, pulse, respiration, blood pressure, weight
- signs and symptoms of dehydration (as listed in Table 14-2)
- history of present illness
- interventions and child's response
- follow-up care: child's condition on discharge

NURSING DIAGNOSES

- fluid volume deficit related to decreased intake or increased losses
- alteration in nutrition: less than body requirement related to decreased intake
- potential for infection
- potential for transmission of infection
- alteration in oral mucous membranes
- impaired tissue integrity due to excessive diarrhea
- alteration in bowel elimination, diarrhea
- alteration in comfort related to vomiting and diarrhea
- knowledge deficit of parents concerning treatment of diarrhea and vomiting

---

NOTES

1. R. Behrman and V. Vaughan, eds., *Nelson Textbook of Pediatrics* (Philadelphia: W.B. Saunders Co., 1987), 553.

2. Jeffrey L. Brown, *Pediatric Telephone Medicine: Principles, Triage and Advice* (Philadelphia: J.B. Lippincott Co., 1989), 58.

3. Dawn L. Martin, "Oral Rehydration Therapy," in *The Emergently Ill Child: Dilemmas in Assessment and Management,* ed. Roger M. Barkin (Gaithersburg, Md.: Aspen Publishers, Inc., 1987), 245–52.

BIBLIOGRAPHY

Barkin, R.M., ed. *Emergency Pediatrics,* 2d ed. St. Louis: C.V. Mosby Co., 1990.

Finberg, L., R.E. Kravath, and A.R. Fleischman. *Water and Electrolytes in Pediatrics: Physiology, Pathophysiology and Treatment.* Philadelphia: W.B. Saunders Co., 1982.

Fleisher, G., and S. Ludwig, eds. *Textbook of Pediatric Emergency Medicine.* Baltimore: Williams & Wilkins Co., 1988.

Martin, D.L. "Oral Rehydration Therapy." In *The Emergently Ill Child: Dilemmas in Assessment and Management,* edited by R.M. Barkin, 245–52. Gaithersburg, Md.: Aspen Publishers, Inc., 1987.

Whaley, L.F., and D.L. Wong, eds. *Nursing Care of Infants and Children,* 3d ed. St. Louis: C.V. Mosby Co., 1987.

Chapter 15

Intravenous Access

Marina Bishop Larsen

INTRODUCTION

Starting an IV in a pediatric patient can be challenging. The keys to success are a gentle approach, a positive attitude, and practice.

GENERAL GUIDELINES

1. Avoid placing IV over joints such as in the wrist; these veins are more elastic and likely to roll.
2. To increase venous distention and visibility of extremity veins
   - place a warm pack over the site, or wrap a diaper moistened with warm tap water around the hand and foot
   - use the double tourniquet method; tie the first tourniquet midway on the arm or leg. Milk the extremity, moving distally, then tie a second tourniquet midway between the first tourniquet and the IV site.
3. Do not use butterfly-type needles for long-term infusions as they have a tendency to infiltrate sooner than the catheter types.
4. As a general rule, after three failed attempts to start an IV, someone else should try.
5. Tape the IV securely without obscuring the site; the IV is only as good as it is taped.
6. Pediatric IVs should be placed on infusion pumps at all times to prevent inadvertent fluid overload (unless massive amounts of fluid are being infused rapidly).

CHOOSING THE SITE

Hands and Arms

- metacarpal vein: between fourth and fifth metacarpals on the back of the hand
- cephalic vein: along the radial border just above the wrist joint—usually a stable site and larger than the metacarpal vein
- antecubital fossa: usually accessible and large but with limited longevity and hard to secure

Feet

- saphenous vein: located approximately 1 cm anterior and superior to the medial malleolus; usually used for a cutdown site
- lateral aspect of the foot: these veins usually straight but small

Figures 15-1 and 15-2 show IV sites in children.

Scalp

Scalp veins can be very useful in infants if other veins are not accessible. Parents find this site disturbing and need reassurance that it is not any more painful than other areas. The following procedure is recommended for scalp veins:

1. Use a rubber band as a tourniquet and place around infant's head.
2. Shave site, using "light hand" with the razor. Save shaved hair for family as they often want it as a memento.
3. Differentiate between vein and artery.
   - An artery will have a pulse, blood will flow forcefully into the IV tubing, and the site will blanch when fluid is infused.
   - Veins have no pulse and will not blanch with infusion of fluids.
   - For absolute identification, send a sample to the laboratory for blood gas analysis.
4. Secure the IV.
   - Use tincture of benzoin or a like preparation to help glue tape down.
   - Assure the parent that adhesive remover will be used to remove tape when IV is discontinued.

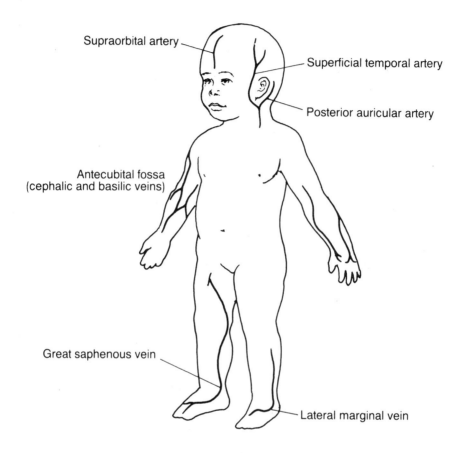

Figure 15-1 Possible Sites for Intravenous Infusion in the Pediatric Patient. *Source:* Courtesy of Wendy A. Bishop, Primary Children's Medical Center, Salt Lake City, Utah.

- An alternative method is to use paper tape and a water-soluble lubricant. Tape the catheter with paper tape, then apply a thin film of lubricant over the tape. The tape will harden, but will loosen easily when moistened with water.

- Clip around the rim of a paper cup to make tabs and spread the tabs out. Cut a hole in the bottom of the cup, invert, and place over the site and catheter. Tape over the tabs.

- Secure the IV tubing to the infant's upper back with a single piece of tape.

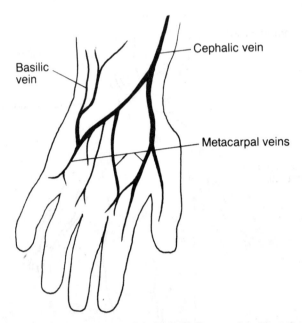

Figure 15-2 Possible Sites for Intravenous Infusion in the Dorsum of the Hand. *Source:* Courtesy of Wendy A. Bishop, Primary Children's Medical Center, Salt Lake City, Utah.

PREPARATION OF PARENTS AND CHILD

Explain the procedure to the parents and the child. Make the explanation appropriate to the child's age and understanding. Refer to the IV catheter as a "straw" to give the vein a "drink." Be honest with the child, letting him or her know that the procedure does hurt but doesn't take long. Let the child know that it is okay to cry, but that he or she needs to hold very still. Having the older child count while the procedure is done is often useful. Be sure to have enough help to restrain the child without making the parents do this. The parents' role should be to comfort the child.

EQUIPMENT

- pediatric catheter sizes: 24-, 22-, or 20-gauge needles
- sterile normal saline (NS)
- extension tubing (T tubing)

- 3-cc syringe filled with NS
- arm boards
- tape
- cotton balls
- cups (paper and plastic medicine cups)

PROCEDURE

1. Flush the catheter with the NS.
   - This assures catheter patency.
   - It also aids in "flashback" of blood into tubing and helps prevent puncturing back wall of vein.
2. Connect the syringe to the connecting tubing and flush.
   - This gives extra stability to the IV.
   - Connect and disconnect tubing from the T connector, not from catheter.
3. Pierce the skin with a needle larger than the IV catheter (optional). This prevents shredding of the catheter and plugging of the stylet.
4. With flushed catheter in hand, aim on top of selected vein rather than to the side, keeping angle low.
5. Once vein is punctured and flashback obtained, rotate catheter 180º; this repositions bevel of stylet to help prevent puncturing vein.
6. Slowly insert catheter and stylet as a unit another 1/8–1/4 inch into the vein.
7. Remove stylet while advancing catheter.
8. Connect the connecting tubing to attached flush syringe.
9. Gently infuse saline flush to assure patency of IV.
10. Secure catheter with tape.
11. Restrain the extremity on a padded arm board.
12. Don't wrap with bandages; this obscures site.
13. When taping child's hand to an arm board, place fingers well around the end of the board as if they were gripping the board, and tape them in place, leaving thumb free.
14. Cut a paper cup in half lengthwise (or a plastic cup for a small infant) and tape it in place over catheter. Remove flush syringe and connect IV tubing directly to T tubing.
15. Tape tubing to arm board.

ALTERNATE SITES

1. Intraosseous access: An intraosseous (IO) line is indicated in the critically ill or injured child when IV access is unsuccessful. Its indications for use are if an IV is unable to be started after 2 minutes of CPR or 5 minutes of trauma resuscitation.[1] Advantages are as follows:
   - Good for quick placement (generally a minute or less).
   - IO can be used in children less than 5 years of age.
   - All fluids, blood, and medications can be given in large volume and infused rapidly.
   - Placement does not interfere with CPR.

   The IO line is a temporary one and should be discontinued as soon as an intravenous line is established. Equipment needed for an IO includes the following:
   - 16- to 20-gauge spinal needle or 15-gauge bone marrow needle
   - syringe
   - antiseptic solution

   The preferred site for the IO is the anterior tibia, 1 to 2 cm (or two finger widths) below the tibial tuberosity and slightly medial. Figure 15-3 shows the correct site for insertion of IO.

   With training, the IO route can be established quickly by nurses, doctors, and paramedics. Valuable time may be wasted trying to start a peripheral IV or even a venous cutdown in the ill child. If the child is less than 5 years old, an IO line should be initiated when a peripheral or central line cannot be started quickly. The procedure is as follows:
   - Place the needle at a 90° angle to the bone and aim slightly inferior to avoid the growth plate.
   - Insert firmly with a boring or screwing motion; a distinct "pop" should be felt.
   - Remove the stylet, attach the syringe, and try to aspirate marrow.
   - Connect the IV tubing.

   Placement can be verified by:
   - lack of resistance past the "pop"
   - aspiration of bone marrow
   - free flow of fluid into the marrow without subcutaneous infiltration
   - the needle standing up by itself

   Although there are few complications with this procedure, the nurse should be aware of the following:
   - Blood may quickly clot in the needle. Unplug the needle by reinserting the stylet and then flushing with heparinized saline.

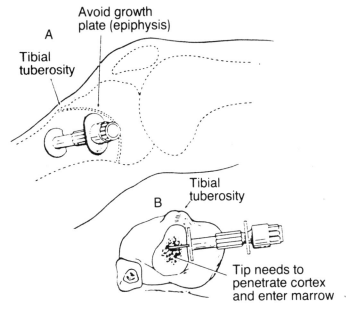

Figure 15-3 Sites for Intraosseous Infusion in the Anterior Tibia. *Source:* Reprinted from *Advanced Pediatric Life Support Manual* with permission of Primary Children's Medical Center, Salt Lake City, Utah, © 1988.

- Subcutaneous infiltration may occur.
- Hypertonic solutions should be diluted to avoid any possible damage to the bone or marrow.
- Growth plate injuries can be avoided by carefully checking anatomic landmarks before inserting the needle.
- The tibial line should be discontinued when peripheral or central vascular access is established and the patient is stable.
- Osteomyelitis is infrequent but may be seen when the IO is used on a long-term basis or in children with sepsis.

The IO route for fluids should be considered before a central line or a cutdown when time is a factor because it takes less time and is easier to do.

2. Central lines: Central lines can deliver fluid rapidly closer to the site of action and allow for measurement of central venous pressure. The use of the subclavian and internal jugular veins is not recommended in the emergency department setting in children less than 8 years of age for the following reasons:[2]

- difficult to insert
- interferes with CPR
- potential for pneumothorax, hemothorax, and dysrhythmia

A femoral vein is a better choice but is not without risk of major complications. The femoral vein has the advantage of not interfering with CPR. Umbilical vessels may be used in infants up to 1 week of age.

Because the risk of complications from central venous cannulation is greater in the pediatric age group, it should only be attempted by those with experience in the procedure.

3. Cutdowns: Cutdowns are useful if peripheral or central venous access cannot be obtained. The preferred site is the saphenous vein. This vein is easily extracted and placement does not interfere with CPR. An infusion pump will be required if the child's perfusion is poor or if pediatric antishock trousers are inflated.

NOTES

1. B. Anderton, et al., *Advanced Pediatric Life Support* (Salt Lake City: Primary Children's Medical Center, 1988), 117.

2. Ibid., 114.

BIBLIOGRAPHY

Anderton, B., et al. *Advanced Pediatric Life Support.* Salt Lake City: Primary Children's Medical Center, 1988.

Chameides, Leon, ed. *Textbook of Pediatric Advanced Life Support.* Dallas: American Heart Association, 1988.

Kanter, R., J. Zimmerman, R. Strauss, and K. Stoeckel, "Pediatric Emergency Intravenous Access." *American Journal of Diseases of Children* 140 (1986): 132–34.

Manley, L., K. Haley, and M. Dick. "Intraosseous Infusion: Rapid Vascular Access for Critically Ill or Injured Infants and Children." *Journal of Emergency Nursing* 14 (1988): 63–69.

Whaley, L., and D. Wong. *Nursing Care of Infants and Children,* 3rd ed. St. Louis: C.V. Mosby Co., 1987.

Chapter 16

Diabetic Emergencies

Jeanette H. Walker

INTRODUCTION

In children, two diabetic emergencies seen in the emergency department are diabetic ketoacidosis and hypoglycemic (insulin) shock. These conditions are discussed in this chapter.

DIABETIC KETOACIDOSIS

Diabetic ketoacidosis (DKA) is a condition caused by an insulin deficiency that results in hyperglycemia, ketoacidosis, and dehydration. DKA exists when the blood glucose concentration exceeds 300 mg/dL, serum pH is 7.30 or less, bicarbonate level is 14 mEq/L or less, and ketonemia is present.

PATHOPHYSIOLOGY OF DKA

Insulin, which is produced in the β cells of the islets of Langerhans in the pancreas, is necessary for the body to metabolize carbohydrates as a source of energy. In DKA, an absolute or relative lack of insulin exists, caused by the body's increased metabolic requirements. This insulin deficiency results in hyperglycemia. As the kidneys attempt to filter out the excess glucose, osmotic diuresis occurs and the body loses large amounts of water and electrolytes. The following events occur:

- Fats and protein are broken down as an alternate source of energy.
- Abnormal metabolism of fats causes ketone bodies to be formed, resulting in ketonemia.
- The number of ketones in the blood exceeds the body's ability to oxidize them, resulting in ketonuria.

141

- Acetone is excreted in the urine due to an excessive accumulation of ketone bodies.
- Increased urine output, dehydration, and further disturbances in fluid and electrolyte balance occur.

The most common illnesses that precipitate DKA in the diabetic child are infections of the skin, respiratory system, and urinary tract. Other factors include the following:

- stress
- trauma
- rapid growth in children without proper adjustments in diet and insulin
- failure to adhere to the insulin, diet, and exercise regimen
- failure of an insulin pump

TRIAGE ASSESSMENT

As in all children, the triage nurse should assess the following:

- airway, breathing, and circulation (ABCs)
- level of consciousness
- hydration status
- vital signs: temperature, pulse, respirations, and blood pressure

The nurse should suspect DKA when the following symptoms are present:

- flushed dry skin
- Kussmaul respirations (deep, labored)
- acetone (fruity) breath odor
- abdominal pain (may or may not be present)
- hypotension
- lethargy or coma

TRIAGE HISTORY

- age of child
- length and history of current illness
- contributing factors such as stress, or failure to adhere to insulin, diet, and exercise regimen

- most recent insulin infusion
- results of urine and blood checks

TELEPHONE TRIAGE GUIDELINES

Any diabetic child who is ill or who has been showing unusually large amounts of sugar or acetone in the urine should be evaluated by a physician as soon as possible. If the child has a decreased level of consciousness, deep respirations, or fruity breath odor, he or she needs immediate treatment.

PRIORITY RATING

Emergent: DKA is a potentially life-threatening condition. Treatment should begin immediately.

TREATMENT AND NURSING CARE

Treatment of a child with diabetic ketoacidosis includes the following:

1. Rehydration
2. Administration of insulin
3. Restoration and maintenance of serum electrolyte and acid base balance
4. Prevention or early detection of cerebral edema and renal failure

Treatment should follow an established protocol such as that shown in Exhibit 16-1. A fluid and insulin administration chart is given in Table 16-1. Table 16-2 lists laboratory tests usually ordered and their significance.

Other nursing actions and interventions include

- providing supplemental oxygen if indicated
- assessing neurological status (especially level of consciousness) every hour or more often if child is unstable
- assessing for other signs and symptoms of illness (including other possible conditions such as appendicitis)
- assessing vital signs every 15 minutes initially, then every hour
- placing cardiac monitor on child
- monitoring intake and output and offering ice chips as tolerated
- monitoring child's response to all interventions

Exhibit 16-1 Emergency Department Diabetic Ketoacidosis Protocol

1. **Admission Assessment:** ABCs, level of consciousness, vital signs (temperature, pulse, respirations, and blood pressure), quality of pulses, capillary refill, hydration status and weight (estimate if unable to stand).

2. **Intravenous (IV) Bolus:** Start an IV, give a bolus of 20 cc/kg of normal saline (NS) over 20–30 minutes. Repeat bolus of 10–15 cc/kg NS if child still showing signs of shock (consult with physician). More aggressive fluid therapy may be necesary if systolic hypotension is present.

3. **Initial Lab Work:** Serum glucose, electrolytes, pH, acetone, phosphorus, blood urea nitrogen (BUN), creatinine, and calcium. Consider urinalysis (UA), complete blood count (CBC), rapid strep screen.

4. **Fluid Orders:** At completion of bolus, start 1/2 NS with 20 mEq potassium acetate and 20 mEq potassium phosphate/L of fluid at 1 and 1/2 maintenance (see Table 16-1 for maintenance calculations). When the serum glucose is less than 250 mg%, change the IV to a dextrose 10% NS with 20 mEq potassium acetate/L and 20 mEq potassium phosphate/L at 1 and 1/2 times maintenance. The fluid rate should provide maintenance and replacement fluids for 10% dehydration over 48 hours. The total given IV plus oral fluids should not exceed 4 L/m²/day.

5. **Insulin Drip:** Start immediately after completion of fluid bolus. Mix 50 U human regular insulin in 500 cc NS (0.1 U/cc concentration). Run 50 cc of solution through tubing (to saturate binding sites on the tubing). Infuse piggyback at a rate of 0.1 U/kg/h (1 cc/kg/h) on infusion pump. Consider this volume in total fluid calculations. When the serum glucose is less than 250 mg% (with a 10% solution infusing) decrease insulin infusion to 0.075 U/kg/h. Continue insulin infusion until serum bicarbonate is greater than 18 mEq/L and serum acetone is less than or equal to 10 mg/dL. Table 16-1 shows a fluid and insulin infusion chart that lists rates per hour on an infusion pump for various units of insulin per hour.

6. **Bicarbonate Therapy:** If the pH is less than 7.00: 80 mEq/m² over 2 hours should be given; if pH is greater than or equal to 7.00, no therapy is necessary.

7. **Laboratory Orders:**
   - Serum glucose every hour
   - Serum electrolytes every 4 hours
   - Serum acetone every 8 hours until acetone less than 10 mg/dL
   - Other studies as indicated by child's condition

8. **Oral Intake:** Sips of clear liquid or ice chips. Advance as tolerated.

This protocol is begun in the ED and continued upon inpatient admission to the hospital as necessary. Physician/nurse collaboration is essential.

Source: Reprinted from *Emergency Department Policy and Procedure Manual,* Primary Children's Medical Center, Salt Lake City, Utah, © 1989.

Table 16-1 DKA Fluid and Insulin Administration Chart

Wt kg	Bolus NS	Maintenance	Insulin	Insulin
	20 cc/kg	1-1/2 Times Minus Insulin Volume (1/2 NS w/ 20 mEq/L Potassium Acetate and 20 mEq/L Potassium Phosphate)	50 Units Regular Insulin 500 cc NS 0.1 U/kg/h	50 Units Regular Insulin 500 cc NS .075 U/kg/h
10	200 cc	52 cc/h	10 cc/h	8 cc/h
11	220 cc	55 cc/h	11 cc/h	8 cc/h
12	240 cc	57 cc/h	12 cc/h	9 cc/h
13	260 cc	59 cc/h	13 cc/h	10 cc/h
14	280 cc	61 cc/h	14 cc/h	11 cc/h
15	300 cc	63 cc/h	15 cc/h	11 cc/h
16	320 cc	65 cc/h	16 cc/h	12 cc/h
17	340 cc	67 cc/h	17 cc/h	13 cc/h
18	360 cc	69 cc/h	18 cc/h	13 cc/h
19	380 cc	72 cc/h	19 cc/h	14 cc/h
20	400 cc	74 cc/h	20 cc/h	15 cc/h
25	500 cc	77 cc/h	25 cc/h	19 cc/h
30	600 cc	79 cc/h	30 cc/h	23 cc/h
35	700 cc	82 cc/h	35 cc/h	26 cc/h
40	800 cc	85 cc/h	40 cc/h	30 cc/h
45	900 cc	88 cc/h	45 cc/h	34 cc/h
50	1000 cc	91 cc/h	50 cc/h	38 cc/h
55	1100 cc	93 cc/h	55 cc/h	41 cc/h
60	1200 cc	96 cc/h	60 cc/h	45 cc/h
65	1300 cc	99 cc/h	65 cc/h	48 cc/h
70	1400 cc	102 cc/h	70 cc/h	52 cc/h
75	1500 cc	105 cc/h	75 cc/h	56 cc/h

PATIENT AND PARENT TEACHING

- insulin: types, action, dosage, preparation, mixing, administration, rotating sites, and storage of medication
- diet: restrictions, modifications to make for increased exercise
- symptoms of hyperglycemia: thirst, deep respirations, fruity odor on breath, vomiting, abdominal and leg cramping, altered level of consciousness
- symptoms of hypoglycemia: headache, irritability, skin cool and clammy, lethargy, altered level of consciousness

Table 16-2 Laboratory Results in Diabetic Ketoacidosis and Their Significance

Lab Test	Expected Value	Causes/Comments
Glucose	> 300 mg/dL	Lack of insulin and body's inability to metabolize glucose as a source of energy
Acetone	Elevated	Breakdown of fats and proteins as an energy source; responsible for the fruity odor on the breath
Sodium	Low, normal, or high	Hyperglycemia causes water to be shifted into the extracellular space resulting in dilutional hyponatremia. Osmotic diuresis also results in loss of sodium. Aldosterone release and dehydration cause the body to retain sodium.
Potassium	Low, normal or high	Acidosis causes excess hydrogen ions to enter cells, resulting in the movement of potassium into the extracellular space. The excess potassium may accumulate in the blood or may be lost via osmotic diuresis or vomiting. As the acidosis is corrected, hydrogen ions leave the cell and potassium re-enters. This may lead to a hypokalemic state.
Bicarbonate	< 15 mEq/dL	Osmotic diuresis which results from the body's attempt to buffer the acidosis
pH	< 7.30	Acidosis
Phosphorus	High or low	Osmotic diuresis results in loss of phosphorus. Like potassium, it moves out of the cell during acidosis but may shift into the cell rapidly once the acidosis is corrected.
BUN	> 20 mEq/dL	Breakdown of amino acids
Creatinine	High	Dehydration
WBC	Normal or high	Infection or an increased catecholamine level
Hemoglobin	High	Dehydration
Hematocrit	High	Dehydration
Urine	Glucose and ketones present	Hyperglycemia and acidosis

NURSING DOCUMENTATION

- level of consciousness
- respiratory status, presence of Kussmaul respirations, fruity odor on breath
- cardiac status (include rhythm strip if abnormalities noted)
- vital signs: temperature, pulse, respirations, blood pressure every hour or more frequently if patient is unstable
- presence of pain
- fluid and insulin therapy; child's response to treatment
- lab values
- intake and output
- infections present, treatment given
- discharge condition
- teaching

HYPOGLYCEMIC (INSULIN) SHOCK

Insulin or hypoglycemic shock is a condition caused by an abnormally low amount of glucose in the blood: 60 mg/100 mL or less.

PATHOPHYSIOLOGY OF INSULIN SHOCK

Insulin shock occurs when the body's requirement for glucose exceeds its supply. Insulin shock is caused by an imbalance in food intake, insulin, and exercise. The most common causes are:

- ingestion of too little food
- increase of exercise without adequate food support
- accidental or intentional increase of insulin without additional food intake

Gastroenteritis, which prevents the absorption of food, is the most serious cause of hypoglycemia.

TRIAGE ASSESSMENT

The triage assessment is the same as for that of DKA. The triage nurse should suspect insulin shock when the following signs and symptoms are present in the diabetic child:

- sweating
- pallor
- irritability
- drowsiness or altered level of consciousness

TRIAGE HISTORY

The triage history is the same as that listed under DIABETIC KETOACIDOSIS.

TELEPHONE TRIAGE GUIDELINES

A diabetic child with symptoms of hypoglycemia (listed under "Triage Assessment") who has not responded to oral glucose or glucagon as ordered by physician needs to be seen immediately. Any child with an altered level of consciousness should be evaluated immediately.

PRIORITY RATING

Emergent: Acute hypoglycemia is an emergent condition; glucose is essential for brain function. Hypoglycemia can result in coma, permanent brain damage, and death.

TREATMENT AND NURSING CARE

The goal of treatment in the child with insulin shock is to increase blood glucose to a level within normal limits for the child. Treatment includes the following:

- Support ABCs.
- Check vital signs every hour; more frequently until stable.
- Monitor blood glucose; initial glucose may be done by Dextrostix. Other laboratory tests as ordered to rule out other causes of coma (toxic ingestion, electrolyte abnormalities, infection).
- Administer simple, fast-acting form of carbohydrate such as orange juice if the child is awake and able to swallow.
- Administer intravenous 25% dextrose, 1–2 mg/kg if the child has a decreased level of consciousness.

PARENT/PATIENT TEACHING

- Hypoglycemia is preventable.
- Modify diet according to exercise and insulin.
- Eat meals on time.
- Monitor insulin regimen carefully.
- Keep simple sugars and glucagon available at all times.

NURSING DOCUMENTATION

- ABCs
- level of consciousness
- vital signs
- laboratory tests
- treatment and response
- teaching and follow-up instructions

NURSING DIAGNOSES FOR THE CHILD WITH A DIABETIC EMERGENCY

- alteration in nutrition (more than body requirements or less than body requirements)
- fluid volume deficit related to decreased intake or vomiting
- alteration in cerebral tissue perfusion
- alteration in comfort (e.g., abdominal pain)
- knowledge deficit regarding insulin therapy, glucose and acetone monitoring, diet, and exercise
- noncompliance related to nonacceptance of disease

BIBLIOGRAPHY

Bourg, P., C. Sherer, and P. Rosen. *Standardized Nursing Care Plans for Emergency Departments.* St. Louis: C.V. Mosby Co., 1986.

Butts, D. "Fluid and Electrolyte Disorders Associated with Diabetic Ketoacidosis and Hyperglycemic Hyperosmolar Nonketonic Coma." *Nursing Clinics of North America* 22 (1987): 827–36.

Greenberg, C. "The Child with Diabetes." In *Nursing Careplanning Guides for Children,* 104–12. Baltimore: Williams & Wilkins, 1988.

Lindsay, R., and R. Bolte. "The Use of Insulin Bolus in Low-Dose Insulin Infusion for Pediatric Diabetic Ketoacidosis." *Pediatric Emergency Care* 5 (1989): 77–79.

Lumley, W. "Controlling Hyperglycemia and Hypoglycemia." *Nursing* 88/10 (1988): 620–23.

Moorman, N. "Acute Complications of Hyperglycemia and Hypoglycemia." *Nursing Clinics of North America* 18 (1983): 707–19.

Primary Children's Medical Center. *Policy and Procedure Manual, Protocol for Diabetic Keto-acidosis*. Salt Lake City, Utah: Primary Children's Medical Center, 1990.

Sabo, C., and S. Michael. "Diabetic Ketoacidosies: Pathophysiology, Nursing Diagnosis and Nursing Intervention." *Focus* 16 (1989): 21–28.

Sperling, M. "Diabetic Ketoacidosis." *Pediatric Clinics of North America* 31 (1984): 591–608.

Whaley, L., and D. Wong. "The Child with a Disturbance of Regulatory Mechanisms." In *Essentials of Pediatric Nursing*, 2d ed., 778–80. St. Louis: C.V. Mosby Co., 1985.

Part VI

Neurological Problems

Chapter 17

Seizures

Donna Ojanen Thomas

INTRODUCTION

Seizures are one of the most common neurological problems in children seen in an emergency department. Between 4 and 6% of all children will have at least one seizure in the first 16 years of life.[1]

Seizures or convulsions are defined as a paroxysmal disturbances in nerve cells resulting in abnormalities in motor, sensory, autonomic, or psychic function. Seizures that last more than 30 minutes are termed status epilepticus, or status seizures. Seizures are further classified according to parts of the body involved, symptoms, and whether impairment of consciousness exists.

Because a febrile episode is the most common cause of seizures seen in the ED, febrile seizures are discussed in this chapter.

PATHOPHYSIOLOGY

During a generalized seizure, large numbers of neurons discharge simultaneously, increasing the metabolic activity of the brain. Cerebral blood flow increases to provide adequate oxygen and glucose. If the seizure is prolonged, the requirements of the brain for oxygen and glucose may exceed the ability to deliver. Children already have an increased metabolic rate and oxygen demand, which compounds the problem. Hypoxia can occur because of the increased oxygen demands, accumulation of secretions in the pharynx and irregular respirations. Hypoxia leads to cerebral edema, which decreases blood flow to the brain. If the seizure is longer than 30 minutes, brain damage can occur.

Causes of seizures in children are listed in Exhibit 17-1.

Exhibit 17-1 Causes of Seizures in Children

INFECTIONS
Meningitis
Encephalitis
Shigellosis

TOXIC/METABOLIC DISTURBANCES
Electrolyte imbalances: hypogylcemia, hypernatremia
Liver disorders
Inherited metabolic disorders
Toxins: ingested drugs; tricyclic antidepressants, lidocaine

INTRACRANIAL CAUSES
Trauma resulting in intracranial bleeding
Hypertension
Anoxia
Brain tumors

OTHER
Noncompliance with routine anticonvulsant therapy
Breath-holding spells
No known cause

FEBRILE SEIZURES

Febrile seizures are seizures associated with fevers and without evidence of a defined cause. They occur in 3 to 5% of all children and show a familial tendency. The majority of febrile seizures occur in children between the ages of 1 and 3 years, but can occur any time between the ages of 3 months and 5 years. They are usually associated with a temperature of 38.3 to 40.0° C.

Febrile seizures can be classified into two categories.

1. Simple: generalized seizures lasting less than 15 minutes that are not recurrent in a 24-hour period
2. Complex: focal seizures lasting longer than 15 minutes and usually reoccurring within a 24-hour period

PATHOPHYSIOLOGY OF FEBRILE SEIZURES

The cause of febrile seizures is not clearly understood; however, since they occur in a restricted age group, they are thought to be related to the lack of myelinization in the immature brain, and the differences in structure and in water and electrolyte balance in the brains of children at various ages.[2,3] Evidence of a familial tendency exists. The incidence of long-term complications depends on the following:

- age of the child
- family history
- type of seizure
- previous abnormal neurological states

Children less than 6 months of age are more at risk for developing epilepsy. Recurrence of the seizure with the same illness is rare, but recurrence with future illness is common.[4]

TRIAGE ASSESSMENT

- airway, breathing, circulation
- level of consciousness
- presence of fever
- other signs and symptoms of illness
- signs and symptoms of trauma

TRIAGE HISTORY

1. Symptoms associated with seizure activity
   - events preceding the seizure: change in facial expression, crying
   - body movement: focal (affecting only one side of the body) or generalized (affecting the entire body)
   - color: presence of cyanosis
   - eyes: pupillary changes
   - respiratory changes: apnea, gasping
   - presence of incontinence of urine or stool
2. Current medications the child is taking
3. Associated current illness, fever, or recent immunizations
4. Family history of seizures
5. Possibility of ingestion of toxic substance

The history is important to differentiate true seizure activity from another condition such as hyperventilation syndrome or syncope.

TELEPHONE TRIAGE GUIDELINES

Every child who has experienced a first-time seizure should be seen by a physician as soon as possible to determine the cause. If the child has a history of a seizure disorder, the parents need to contact their physician to determine if the child needs to be seen to have drug levels drawn or to have medication adjusted. A parent who states that the child is having seizure activity should be directed to[5]

- position child on side to assure adequate airway
- arrange transportation to ED; call the emergency medical services (EMS)

Parents should be instructed to have someone drive them: even if the seizure has stopped it may recur on the way to the hospital and they may need additional help.

PRIORITY RATING

Emergent: A child who is having seizure activity or has a decreased level of consciousness after a first-time seizure; any child with a history of having a seizure after a head injury; any child who looks ill.

Urgent: A child who has experienced a first time seizure, or a child with a known seizure disorder who is currently awake and alert. If the child is febrile, acetaminophen should be given as soon as possible (15 mg/kg).

TREATMENT AND NURSING CARE

Nursing care of the child who is experiencing a seizure includes the following:

1. Airway
   - Maintain an open airway.
   - Turn child on side to prevent aspiration.
   - Maintain cervical spine immobilization if the possibility of head injury exists.
   - Apply suction as needed.
   - Do not attempt to put anything in the child's mouth.
2. Breathing
   - Provide oxygen by mask.
   - Be prepared to provide respiratory support; have a bag and mask available.
   - Be prepared to assist with intubation.
3. Circulation
   - Start an IV line as ordered to give medications if the seizure is prolonged.

- Place a cardiac monitor and pulse oximeter on the child, especially if anticonvulsants are to be given.

4. Vital signs: temperature, pulse, respirations, and blood pressure
5. Protection from injury
   - Don't leave the child unattended.
   - Position child on side during seizure to prevent aspiration.
6. Medications: Table 17-1 lists drugs used to stop seizures and nursing implications.

Table 17-1 Drugs Used To Stop Seizure Activity in Children

Drug	Initial Dose/Route	Nursing Considerations
Phenobarbital	10–20 mg/kg IV (up to 300 mg)	Observe for hypotension and respiratory depression. Dilute with an equal amount of IV fluid. Rate not to exceed 1 mg/kg/min.
Diazepam (Valium)	0.1–0.2 mg/kg	Observe for respiratory depression. Give slow IV push. Have bag and mask ready to provide respiratory support if needed. Very caustic, avoid infiltration. Make sure IV is patent before administering.
Lorazepam (Ativan)	0.05–0.1 mg/kg IV	Same precautions as Valium. May be preferred over Valium because it is less caustic to the tissue and has a greater duration of action than Valium.
Phenytoin (Dilantin)	15 mg/kg IV, up to 1 g	May cause venous irritation, hypotension. Give at a rate not to exceed 1 mg/kg/min. Hot packs to infusion site may reduce irritation after infusion. Will precipitate when infused with a glucose solution.
Paraldehyde	0.3 mg/kg in oil, rectally	Do not give IV. May cause respiratory depression.

GENERAL PRECAUTIONS FOR ADMINISTERING ALL ANTICONVULSANT DRUGS

1. Don't mix medications; dilute with normal saline.
2. Don't give as a continuous infusion.
3. Be ready for respiratory depression; have necessary equipment to support the airway at the bedside.
4. Place child on cardiac monitor and oxygen saturation monitor.
5. Monitor vital signs before and after administration of medication.

Source: P. Ferry, W. Banner, and R. Wolf, *Seizure Disorders in Children* (Philadelphia: J.B. Lippincott Co., 1986), 176–90.

Other treatment will be done based on the child's signs and symptoms. Nursing care after the seizure activity has stopped is mainly supportive.

1. Diagnostic studies may include the following:
   - complete blood count (CBC)
   - electrolytes
   - glucose
   - toxicology screen
   - anticonvulsant levels (if the child routinely takes anticonvulsants)
   - computerized tomography (CT) scan
2. Anticipate recurrence of seizures.
3. Support the family and provide information on treatment.
4. Assist the physician with any diagnostic procedures or treatments.

PARENT TEACHING

- cause of seizure
- treatment prescribed: medications, fever control
- treatment if seizure occurs at home
- safety measures: not leaving child unattended in bathtub, preventing injury during seizure activity
- follow-up care

NURSING DOCUMENTATION

- history, including type of seizure, any medications the child is currently taking
- time current seizure activity started, type of seizure, and response to medications given
- ED treatment, including airway management, drug therapy, and laboratory tests, and child's response to treatment
- vital signs: at least q 15 minutes initially
- follow-up plans

NURSING DIAGNOSES

- ineffective airway clearance relating to seizure activity and increased secretions
- ineffective breathing patterns related to seizure
- alteration in cerebral tissue perfusion related to seizure activity
- alteration in body temperature (hyperthermia)
- fear relating to child's age and unfamiliarity with ED personnel
- knowledge deficit of parents related to child's condition and ED treatment
- noncompliance with prescribed seizure medication

NOTES

1. R. Packer and P. Berman, "Neurologic Emergencies," in *Textbook of Pediatric Emergency Medicine,* eds. G. Fleisher and S. Ludwig (Baltimore: Williams & Wilkins Co., 1988), 399–412.

2. Eileen M. Ouellette, "The Child Who Convulses with Fever," *Pediatric Clinics of North America* 21 (1974): 467–81.

3. J.C. Lagos, "Febrile Seizures: To Treat or Not To Treat," *Postgraduate Medicine* (February 1970): 189–93.

4. P.G. Vining and John M. Freeman, "Seizures Which Are Not Epilepsy," *Pediatric Annals* 14 (1985): 711–22

5. Jeffrey L. Brown, *Pediatric Telephone Medicine: Principles, Triage, and Advice.* Philadelphia: J.B. Lippincott Co., 1989): 111.

BIBLIOGRAPHY

Evans, O.B. *Manual of Child Neurology.* New York: Churchill Livingstone, 1987.

Ferry, P., W. Banner, and R. Wolf. *Seizure Disorders in Children.* Philadelphia: J.B. Lippincott Co., 1986.

Kempe, C., H. Silver, and D. Obrien. *Current Pediatric Diagnosis and Treatment.* 9th ed. Norwalk, Conn.: Appleton & Lange, 1987.

Strange, G.R. "Febrile Seizures: Evaluation and Management." In *The Emergently Ill Child,* edited by R.M. Barkin, 201–06. Gaithersburg, Md.: Aspen Publishers, Inc., 1987.

Vining, P.G., and J.M. Freeman. "Classification and Evaluation of Seizures." *Pediatric Annals* 14 (1985): 738–39.

Vining, P.G., and J.M. Freeman. "Discussion and Explanation of Seizures to the Parents and Child." *Pediatric Annals* 14 (1985): 738–39.

Zimmerman, S.S., and J.H. Gildea. *Critical Care Pediatrics: A Problem Oriented Approach.* Philadelphia: W.B. Saunders Co., 1985.

Chapter 18

Meningitis

Ramona F. Randolph

INTRODUCTION

Meningitis is an inflammation of the meninges, the covering of the brain and spinal cord. Meningitis occurs more frequently during childhood than at any other time in the life cycle and is potentially a life-threatening condition. Bacterial meningitis may occur at any age, but one-fourth of all cases occur in the first year of life and two-thirds of all cases occur before age 5. Three-fourths of all cases occur prior to adulthood.[1]

PATHOPHYSIOLOGY

Meningitis can be caused by either a bacterial or a viral organism. These organisms reach the meninges via any of several routes.

- through the bloodstream from a focus of infection in the body
- from structures that adjoin the central nervous system
- through fractures via the paranasal sinuses resulting from head trauma
- by direct communication between the skin and meninges due to congenital conditions, such as meningomyelocele
- after a neurosurgical procedure

Almost any bacteria can cause meningitis, but the following five organisms cause the majority of cases:

1. *H. influenzae*
2. *S. pneumoniae*
3. *N. meningitidis*

4. *E. coli*

5. Group B *Streptococcus*

The most common organism varies with the age of the child. *E. coli* and group B streptococcus are most common in the first month of life. After the first two months of life, *H. influenzae* is the most common cause.

Viral meningitis is generally milder than bacterial meningitis and is usually self-limiting, without specific therapy. The most common causes of viral meningitis are:

- coxsackie B
- echovirus
- rubella virus

TRIAGE ASSESSMENT

The triage assessment focuses on recognition of the ill infant who may not "look" overtly ill. The triage assessment includes the following:

- airway, breathing, circulation
- level of consciousness, including extreme irritability, lethargy, or seizures
- tense or bulging anterior fontanelle in children less than 2 years of age
- presence of nuchal rigidity, headache
- presence of rashes, especially a petechial rash (a round, purplish rash caused by intradermal hemorrhage, which can be indicative of meningococcal infection)
- vital signs (fever in a child less than 3 months of age is an emergent condition)

The signs and symptoms of meningitis vary depending on the age of the child, the infecting organism, and the duration of the illness. The clinical signs and symptoms can include the following:

- irritability
- lethargy or altered level of consciousness
- vomiting
- anorexia
- fever
- nuchal rigidity
- seizures

- bulging anterior fontanelle (0 to 2 years of age)
- positive Kernig's sign (pain with flexion and extension of the legs at the hips and knees)
- positive Brudzinski's sign (flexion of the child's hips and knees in response to flexion of the neck)

TRIAGE HISTORY

- age of the child
- pre-existing condition and medications child may be taking
- length of present illness
- activity level
- prior exposure to illness
- presence of rashes

TELEPHONE TRIAGE GUIDELINES

Any child, especially infants less than 3 months of age, with a history of fever, lethargy, rash, and/or a complaint of a stiff or sore neck should be evaluated by a physician as soon as possible.

The nurse needs to give advice with caution to parents who call with vague complaints of fever, rash, or irritability. Often the signs and symptoms of meningitis are subtle. For this reason, the nurse should encourage the parents to call their own physician, and let them know they can be seen in the ED at any time.

PRIORITY RATING

Emergent: A child who exhibits signs and symptoms of meningitis should be considered a medical emergency and treatment should be started immediately.

Urgent: A child less than 3 months of age with a fever who is awake and alert with good perfusion should be seen as soon as possible.

TREATMENT AND NURSING CARE

Treatment should be directed toward stabilization: maintenance of airway, breathing, circulation, and control of seizures. Antibiotic therapy is started in the ED as the child is being stabilized.

Nursing care of the child should include the following:

1. Assess respiratory, circulatory, and neurological status frequently.
2. Administer oxygen by mask or nasal cannula. Be ready to assist with intubation, if necessary.
3. Monitor vital signs: temperature, pulse, respirations, and blood pressure. Note capillary refill time: delayed capillary refill time with tachycardia and decreasing level of consciousness may indicate shock. A decrease in blood pressure is a *late* sign of shock.
4. Administer antipyretic medication: 15 mg/kg of acetaminophen is preferred; aspirin products should be avoided.
5. Establish an IV line for fluid resuscitation and antibiotic therapy. Lactated Ringer's or normal saline is the preferred isotonic solution. A child in shock may need to be bolused with 20 cc/kg. More may be needed depending on the response of the child.
6. Assist with diagnostic tests (discussed below).
7. Administer antibiotics appropriate for the causative agent.
8. Administer anticonvulsants to bring seizures under control if necessary and as ordered (see Chapter 17).
9. Prepare child and family for admission to the hospital—usually 10–14 days for IV antibiotic therapy.

Antibiotic therapy depends on the age of the child and the organism causing the meningitis. The following antibiotics can be used:

- ampicillin and ceftriaxone (or another third-generation cephalosporin) for children less than 1 month
- ampicillin and chloramphenicol for children older than 1 month

The occurrence and sensitivity of various pathogens as well as antibiotic efficacy vary over time and from one area to another. Nurses need to be familiar with appropriate antibiotics used in their practicing area and those antibiotics' doses and methods of administration. For further information, nurses should refer to a standard medical textbook.

Diagnostic tests should be started immediately after the child is stabilized. The lumbar puncture or spinal tap is necessary to collect cerebrospinal fluid (CSF) for analysis. CSF should be clear as water and becomes opaque with multiple white cells, indicating infection. Tests that are done on the CSF include a differential cell count, glucose, protein, and Gram stain and culture. The Gram stain is done to determine the organism to be treated. The physician needs to obtain informed consent from the parents for the spinal tap. Other tests that may be done include the following:

- CBC with differential
- blood cultures
- electrolytes
- serum glucose
- urinalysis

PARENT TEACHING

Parents will need reassurance and information about meningitis and how it is treated. Parent teaching should start with an explanation of the lumbar puncture, since parents seem to have many fears about this procedure. When the diagnosis is confirmed, explain to the parents about meningitis and the treatment that will be needed. Written information should be provided. The ED nurse can be helpful in preparing the family for the hospital stay.

Parents are often very concerned about their other children being exposed to this disease. Prophylaxis is recommended for secondary contacts under the age of 6. The drug recommended is rifampin 20 mg/kg/day, given in four doses (every 6 hours) per day for 5 days.

NURSING DOCUMENTATION

- vital signs: temperature, pulse, respiration, blood pressure, and weight in kilograms
- respiratory, circulatory, and neurological assessment
- type, amount, site of IV fluids infused in the ED
- medications administered
- child's response to interventions
- procedures performed, child's response
- disposition of child to nursing unit

NURSING DIAGNOSES

- hyperthermia related to the infectious process
- fluid volume deficit related to increased metabolic needs, increased losses, and decreased intake

- alteration in cerebral or cardiopulmonary tissue perfusion related to possible shock
- potential for infection of hospital staff, family members, and other ED patients
- knowledge deficit related to disease process and hospital care

---

NOTE

1. Gary R. Fleisher, "Infectious Disease Emergencies," in *Textbook of Pediatric Emergency Medicine,* eds. Gary R. Fleisher and Stephen Ludwig (Baltimore: Williams & Wilkins Co., 1988): 421.

BIBLIOGRAPHY

Feigin, R., and J. Cherry. *Textbook of Pediatric Infectious Diseases,* 2d ed. Philadelphia: W.B. Saunders Co., 1987.

Fleisher, G., and S. Ludwig. *Textbook of Pediatric Emergency Medicine,* 2d ed. Baltimore: Williams & Wilkins Co., 1988.

Kelley, S. *Pediatric Emergency Nursing.* Norwalk, Conn.: Appleton & Lange, 1988.

Overturf, G. "Meningitis." *Topics in Emergency Medicine* 14 (1982): 16–25.

Chapter 19

Encephalitis

Donna Ojanen Thomas

INTRODUCTION

Encephalitis is an inflammation of the brain that produces various forms of central nervous system (CNS) dysfunction. It is often hard to distinguish initially from other CNS infections or conditions, and is a serious illness that can leave children with permanent neurological impairment.

PATHOPHYSIOLOGY

The CNS dysfunction results from direct invasion of the brain, most frequently by a virus or as a complication of a viral infection. The onset of encephalitis may be abrupt or insidious and is usually associated with fever, headache, and signs of meningeal irritation. Signs and symptoms depend on the degree and location of cerebral involvement.

The exact cause of the majority of the cases of encephalitis is unknown because of the difficulty of identifying the virus in the CNS.

Cases resulting from direct invasion of the CNS are most often caused by the arboviruses (arthropod-borne viruses). The vector for these viruses is the mosquito. Infections caused by these viruses most often occur in the summer and fall and are endemic in various areas of the United States. Sporadic cases may occur during any season.

Postinfectious causes of encephalitis are usually related to complications after infection with any of the following:

- herpes simplex
- enteroviruses
- varicella

- mumps
- measles

Herpes simplex, responsible for 10% of all cases of encephalitis, is probably the most severe form of encephalitis and results in death in 50–70% of all cases.[1]

TRIAGE ASSESSMENT

The most prominent finding during the initial triage assessment may be an altered level of consciousness. Signs and symptoms of encephalitis may mimic those seen in children with meningitis and other conditions that affect the CNS, including the following:

- malaise
- fever
- headache
- dizziness
- stiff neck
- nausca and vomiting
- ataxia (commonly seen in varicella zoster infections)
- tremors
- hyperactivity
- speech difficulties
- seizures

TRIAGE HISTORY

- recent viral infections or exposures
- exposures to vectors, such as ticks and mosquitoes
- exposure to animals that may be reservoirs for arboviruses
- exposure to heavy metals or pesticides
- trauma
- recent injections

The triage history will help in the differential diagnosis. Considerations should include the following:

- trauma; possible head injury
- poisoning—lead, ethanol, carbon monoxide, antiemetics, salicylates

- bacterial meningitis
- Reye's syndrome
- confusional migraines
- diabetic coma or ketoacidosis

TELEPHONE TRIAGE GUIDELINES

Telephone triage guidelines should be the same as for the child with a fever or suspected meningitis. The best guideline to follow is that any child with a history of altered level of consciousness, or CNS signs and symptoms such as ataxia, should be evaluated as soon as possible.

PRIORITY RATING

The priority rating is the same as for the child with suspected meningitis (Chapter 18). Any child with an altered level of consciousness is considered emergent.

TREATMENT AND NURSING CARE

Treatment and nursing care are the same initially as for the patient with meningitis and include the following:

1. Support airway, breathing, circulation (the ABCs); provide supplemental oxygen.
2. Monitor neurological status. Watch for signs and symptoms of increased intracranial pressure and seizures.
3. Monitor fluid intake. IV therapy will be ordered and a Foley catheter placed to monitor output. Fluids will be restricted to two-thirds maintenance to prevent overhydration unless clinical signs and symptoms of shock are apparent.
4. Administer drugs as appropriate.
   - antipyretics—acetaminophen
   - anticonvulsants as necessary (see Chapter 17)
   - antibiotics: may be ordered until a bacterial infection is ruled out
   - specific medications: acyclovir may be considered in suspected cases of herpes encephalitis, but is usually not started in the emergency department
5. Assist with laboratory studies.
   - lumbar puncture
   - cultures: viral and bacterial of blood, stool, urine, and pharynx

- CBC with differential: helps to differentiate between viral and bacterial infections
- electrolytes
- glucose
- toxic screen of blood and urine: should be considered depending on history and other findings
- computerized tomography scan: may be ordered to rule out head injury, brain abscess

PARENT TEACHING

Parent teaching is similar to that for meningitis since many of the same tests are done, and includes the following:

- Explain all procedures to child and family.
- Prepare for possible admission to the intensive care unit.
- Encourage parents to remain with child.
- Involve hospital social services if necessary.
- Explain disease process and possible outcomes (in collaboration with ED physician).

NURSING DOCUMENTATION

- initial assessment
- history
- presenting signs and symptoms
- diagnostic studies done
- interventions and response

NURSING DIAGNOSES

Nursing diagnoses are the same as for the child with meningitis (see Chapter 18).

NOTE

1. Richard S.K. Young, "Meningoencephalitis," in *Primary Pediatric Care*, ed. Robert A. Hockelman (St. Louis: C.V. Mosby Co., 1987): 1364.

BIBLIOGRAPHY

Behrman, R., and V. Vaughan, eds. *Nelson Textbook of Pediatrics,* 13th ed. Philadelphia: W.B. Saunders Co., 1987.

Fleisher, G., and S. Ludwig. *Textbook of Pediatric Emergency Medicine.* Baltimore: Williams & Wilkins Co., 1988.

Hockelman, R, ed. *Primary Pediatric Care.* St. Louis: C.V. Mosby Co., 1987.

Moffet, H. *Pediatric Infectious Diseases: A Problem-Oriented Approach.* Philadelphia: J.B. Lippincott Co., 1989.

Steele, R. *A Clinical Manual of Pediatric Infectious Disease.* Norwalk, Conn.: Appleton-Century-Crofts, 1986.

Whaley, L., and D. Wong. *Nursing Care of Infants and Children,* 3d ed. St. Louis: C.V. Mosby Co., 1987.

Zimmerman, S.S., and G. Gildea. *Critical Care Pediatrics: A Problem Oriented Approach.* Philadelphia: W.B. Saunders Co., 1985.

Chapter 20

Reye's Syndrome

Donna Ojanen Thomas

INTRODUCTION

Reye's syndrome has been defined as an acute, noninflammatory encephalopathy associated primarily with the brain and liver. It occurs in infants and children of all age groups, but the highest incidence has been reported in the 5- to 14-year-old age groups. The mortality rate has decreased from 80% to less than 30% due to early recognition and treatment.

PATHOPHYSIOLOGY

Multiple metabolic abnormalities are present, including:

- fat accumulation in the liver and functional derangements leading to liver failure
- fatty infiltration of the heart, skeletal muscle, and kidney tubule cells
- mitochondrial changes in the liver and brain
- brain swelling (usually the cause of death)
- hyperammonia due to the reduction of enzymes that convert ammonia to urea
- hypoglycemia

The causes of Reye's syndrome are still not clear, but appear to be related to mitochondrial damage. Four current theories are as follows:[1]

1. intrinsic toxin affecting mitochondrial metabolism following a viral illness, most commonly varicella (chickenpox) or influenza
2. extrinsic toxin—environmental chemicals or drugs, such as salicylates

3. genetic predisposition
4. primary metabolic disorder in lipid and ammonia metabolism that is unmasked during a viral illness

Because of a correlation between the use of salicylates and Reye's syndrome, the American Academy of Pediatrics (AAP) recommends that products containing salicylates not be used in children who have chickenpox or flulike symptoms. Since this recommendation, the incidence of Reye's syndrome has decreased significantly.

TRIAGE ASSESSMENT

Prompt recognition is the most important factor in the outcome of the disease. The signs and symptoms are different in infants than in older children. Infants (less than 2 years of age) are particularly susceptible to profound hypoglycemia. In addition, they may exhibit signs and symptoms similar to meningitis including:[2]

- fussiness
- inappropriate gazing
- twitching or seizure activity
- floppiness
- lethargy
- high-pitched cry
- respiratory distress

The highest incidence of Reye's syndrome occurs in the age group of 5 to 15 years. Children in this age group usually present with the following signs and symptoms:

- persistent vomiting not relieved by antiemetics (uncommon in infants)
- behavior changes—confusion to lethargy, combativeness
- hyperventilation
- seizures—usually a late sign in this age group

The adolescent patient age 12 to 18 exhibits similar behavior, but this behavior is often attributed to alcohol or drug abuse. This should be considered in the differential diagnosis along with Reye's syndrome.

TRIAGE HISTORY

Children with Reye's syndrome present with a history of a recent viral infection (commonly varicella or influenza), a brief recovery period, and then a relapse. The triage history should include the following:

- history of recent illnesses
- history of current medications, especially any that contain salicylates, such as Pepto Bismol. Children on chronic salicylates (e.g., for rheumatoid arthritis) are at risk for Reye's syndrome.
- possibility of other toxic ingestions
- history of trauma

TELEPHONE TRIAGE GUIDELINES

Any child with an altered level of consciousness and/or persistent vomiting should be seen immediately. Infants may need to be seen just on the basis of "not acting normally."

Parents should always be instructed to avoid salicylates any time their child has a viral-type infection.

PRIORITY RATING

Emergent: Any child who presents with an altered level of consciousness and/or persistent vomiting, or an infant with marked behavioral changes should be given immediate attention.

TREATMENT AND NURSING CARE

1. *Recognition.* The nurse will assist the doctor in confirming the diagnosis. The following characteristics will aid in the diagnosis of Reye's syndrome:[3]
   a. child's presentation
      - history
      - altered level of consciousness
      - hyperactive reflexes
   b. diagnostic studies
      - elevated liver enzymes: serum glutamic-oxaloacetic transaminase (SGOT), serum glutamic-pyruvic transaminase (SGPT)

- elevated serum ammonia
- prolonged prothrombin (PT) time
- decreased blood glucose (most common in children less than one year of age)
- metabolic acidosis, respiratory alkalosis
- increased free fatty acids
- abnormal electroencephalogram (EEG)
- normal bilirubin
- normal cerebral spinal fluid (CSF)

2. *Staging.* Once the diagnosis is made, the child is usually staged according to Lovejoy's criteria, presented in Table 20-1:[4]

3. *Management in the ED.* The child with suspected Reye's syndrome needs to be admitted to a pediatric intensive care unit (PICU). Provisions should be made to transfer the child to another facility if necessary, after the child is stabilized. Treatment in the ED includes the following:

a. Check vital signs.

- Check temperature, pulse, respiratory rate, blood pressure—monitor frequently.
- Keep temperature near normal to decrease oxygen demand and cerebral metabolism.
- Obtain weight or estimate.
- Place cardiac monitor on child.

Table 20-1 Clinical Stages of Reye's Syndrome

Stage	Signs and Symptoms
I	Vomiting, lethargy, and sleepiness
II	Disorientation, delirium, combativeness
III	Obtunded, coma, hyperventilation, inappropriate response to noxious stimuli, decorticate posturing, preservation of pupillary, light, and oculovestibular reflexes (doll's eyes)
IV	Deeper coma, decerebrate rigidity, loss of occulovestibular reflexes, dilated and fixed pupils, dysconjugate eye movements in response to caloric stimulation
V	Seizures, absent deep-tendon reflexes, respiratory arrest, flaccid paralysis

b. Monitor neurological status.
- Watch for signs and symptoms of increased intracranial pressure (ICP): decreased level of consciousness, changes in respiratory rate and depth, bradycardia.
- Elevate head of bed.
- Maintain quiet environment.

c. Administer and monitor fluids.
- Start IV infusion and deliver 10% dextrose solution at two-thirds maintenance unless clinical signs and symptoms of shock are apparent.
- Insert Foley catheter to monitor output.
- Monitor intake and output carefully.

d. Make transfer arrangements if necessary; children may progress rapidly to deeper stages.

e. Support child and family.
- Explain all procedures and the disease process.
- Prepare for PICU admission.
- Evaluate family's need for additional support.

Children in stages III, IV, and V will require more aggressive treatment that may include the following:

1. intubation and mechanical ventilation
2. nasogastric tube to decompress the stomach and prevent aspiration
3. central line placement
4. medications as ordered by the physician:
   - mannitol, 1 g/kg to decrease ICP (if shock isn't present)
   - neomycin, 50 mg/kg/day to reduce serum ammonia
   - dexamethasone, loading dose of 0.2 mg/kg IV to reduce cerebral edema (controversial)
5. further intervention for acute increased ICP
   - hyperventilation as ordered by physician
   - equipment ready for placement of intraventricular catheter or craniotomy

PARENT TEACHING

Nurses can teach parents both in the community and in the ED about signs and symptoms of Reye's syndrome, including:

- persistent vomiting
- hyperventilation or changes in breathing patterns

- seizures
- changes in level of consciousness

Parents should also be warned against the use of salicylates, especially when the child has a viral infection. Parents can contact the National Reye's Syndrome Foundation at the following address:

National Reye's Syndrome Foundation
426 North Lewis
Bryan, Ohio 43506

NURSING DOCUMENTATION

- history and initial assessment
- laboratory studies done
- clinical staging of Reye's syndrome
- interventions: fluids, medications
- response to interventions
- disposition of patient with a complete copy of the child's chart sent to receiving hospital if child is to be transferred

NURSING DIAGNOSES

- hyperthermia related to infectious process
- potential for fluid volume deficit related to decreased intake and increased vomiting
- potential for ineffective breathing patterns related to disease process
- fear of child related to ED and procedures
- knowledge deficit of parents related to cause of illness and disease process

NOTES

1. John T. Boyle and John B. Watkins, "Gastrointestinal Emergencies," in *Textbook of Pediatric Emergency Medicine*, eds. Gary Fleisher and Stephen Ludwig (Baltimore: Williams & Wilkins Co., 1988): 697.

2. Mary Martelli, "Reye's Syndrome: An Update," *Journal of Emergency Nursing* 10 (1984): 287–88.

3. Peggy Dalgas, "Reye's Syndrome Update," *Maternal Child Nursing* 8 (1983): 346–47.

4. Frederick Lovejoy, et al., "Clinical Staging in Reye's Syndrome," *American Journal of Diseases of Children* 128 (1974): 36–41.

BIBLIOGRAPHY

Boyle, J., and J. Watkins. "Gastrointestinal Emergencies." In *Textbook of Pediatric Emergency Medicine,* edited by G. Fleisher and S. Ludwig, 688–708. Baltimore: Williams & Wilkins Co., 1988.

MacGregor, D., and S. Zimmerman. "Reye's Syndrome." In *Critical Care Pediatrics: A Problem Oriented Approach,* edited by S. Zimmerman and J. Gildea, 282–91. Philadelphia: W.B. Saunders Co., 1985.

Martelli, M. "Teaching Parents about Reye's Syndrome." *American Journal of Nursing* (February 1982): 260–63.

Ribovich, R. "Reye's Syndrome." In *Primary Pediatric Care,* edited by R. Hockelman, 1449–53. St. Louis: C.V. Mosby Co., 1987.

Robinson, R. "Differential Diagnosis of Reye's Syndrome." *Developmental Medicine and Child Neurology* 29 (1987): 110–16.

Whaley, L., and D. Wong. *Essentials of Pediatric Nursing,* 3d ed. St. Louis: C.V. Mosby Co., 1989, 918–20.

Part VII

Pediatric Trauma

Chapter 21

Multiple Trauma: An Overview

Donna Ojanen Thomas

INTRODUCTION

Trauma is the leading cause of death and disability in children older than 1 year. Because the care given in the first hour following the injury often determines the final outcome, the initial assessment of the child must be performed in the proper sequence and the unique characteristics of the child must be understood. Care of the pediatric trauma victim must be delivered with a team approach. The team should be governed by protocols specific to the pediatric patient. Nurses caring for the pediatric patient must possess special skills. Recognition of respiratory distress and shock in the child and knowledge of appropriate interventions are two of the most important skills for the nurse to develop. These skills are mismanaged the most often in the initial treatment and stabilization.

Recommended knowledge and skill requirements of nurses caring for pediatric trauma patients are listed in Exhibit 21-1. See also Exhibits 21-2 and 21-3.

PATHOPHYSIOLOGY

The main causes of pediatric trauma are as follows:

1. motor vehicle accidents (mostly auto–pedestrian accidents)
2. drownings
3. fires, burns
4. firearms
5. poisoning
6. falls

Exhibit 21-1 Recommended Knowledge and Skill Requirements for Nurses Caring for Pediatric Trauma Victims

---

PEDIATRIC ASSESSMENT SKILLS
Knowledge of anatomic and physiological variables in children
Signs and symptoms of shock, respiratory distress, and other life-threatening emergencies
Ongoing education on pediatric emergencies

ADVANCED PEDIATRIC LIFE SUPPORT
Pediatric airway management
Management of shock—IV access
Management of dysrhythmias
Management of CNS injuries
Routine practice pediatric megacodes
Knowledge of pediatric advanced life support medications: dosages, administration, and effects

PROTOCOLS FOR PEDIATRIC TRAUMA
Assigned roles for team members (example in Exhibit 21-2)
Transfer agreement with pediatric facility where appropriate
Protocols dealing with specific injuries
Knowledge of how to initiate trauma team

EQUIPMENT
  Equipment specific to pediatric patients (drugs, airway equipment, life support equipment).
Recommended equipment necessary to manage pediatric trauma is listed in Exhibit 21-3.

Ninety percent of pediatric injuries are the result of blunt trauma rather than penetrating injury. Because of less body fat, increased elasticity of connective tissue, and close proximity of organs, the child often has injuries to multiple organs.

PRIORITY RATING

All children experiencing a traumatic injury are given an emergent rating until they have been thoroughly examined and the mechanism of injury is known. The mechanism of injury is an important consideration in judging severity despite the appearance of the child.

NURSING ASSESSMENT AND CARE

The nursing assessment is done in conjunction with life-saving interventions. As in adults, the assessment begins with the primary assessment.

Exhibit 21-2 Pediatric Trauma: Nursing Roles

NURSE RIGHT

Room Setup Duties
- Set up respiratory therapy supplies: intubation equipment, suction, nasogastric (NG) tubes.
- Set up cardiac monitor/oximeter: leads and probes.
- Set up Foley catheter tray/bag.

Patient Care Duties
- Assist with IV and fluids on the right side of the patient.
- Assist with any procedures on the right side of the patient: cutdowns, chest tubes, central line placement.
- Control bleeding.
- Insert Foley catheter and NG tube.
- Handle right-sided monitors: cardiac, Doppler, oximeter.
- Assist with MAST inflation/deflation.
- Check vital signs.
- See that chart is completed.
- Accompany patient to CT scan/ICU or OR.

Nurse Right calls out all procedures to the nurse who is charting. Example: "Foley cath, #8, inserted at 1500."

NURSE LEFT

Room Setup Duties
- Set up hypothermia unit, heat lamps, humidified oxygen.
- Set up IV solutions, blood warmer.
- Assist with preparing medications.

Patient Care Duties
- Expose child; remove all clothing.
- Communicate with child even if he or she appears unconscious.
- Keep child warm; apply heat lamps, hypothermia unit, as needed.
- Give medications (if staffing permitted, this person would just give them and not draw them up).
- Assist with left-sided IVs, administer blood.
- Assist with left-sided surgical procedures: chest tubes, etc.

MEDICATION NURSE

Room Setup Duties
- Get out intubation drugs, draw up saline flushes, prepare arrest cart.
- Set up arterial lines, medication drips as necessary.

Patient Care Duties
- Assist with blood drawing.
- Prepare all medications and drips.
- Set up arterial lines.
- Document all care given.

Exhibit 21-3 Pediatric Trauma Supplies and Equipment

AIRWAY/BREATHING
Oxygen masks: sizes neonatal, child, adult
Oxygen nasal cannulas
Ambu bags: sizes pediatric and adult
Portable oxygen
Oral airways: sizes 00–10 cm
Ventilation masks: sizes 1–5 (neonatal to adult)
Intubation blades: sizes 0.1, 1.5, 2, 3
Intubation handles
Large and small stylets
McGill forceps
Uncuffed endotracheal (ET) tubes: sizes 2.5, 3.0, 3.5, 4.0, 4.5, 5.0
Cuffed ET tubes: sizes 5.0, 5.5, 6.0, 6.5, 7.0, 7.5, 8.0, 8.5
Tracheostomy tray
Tracheostomy tubes: sizes 00, 1, 2, 3, 4
Tracheostomy ties
Cricothyroidotomy setup
Arterial blood gas kits
Pulse oximeter (optional but very useful) to assess oxygen saturation

CERVICAL SPINE
Backboard or scoop stretcher
Cervical collars: stiff necks or Philadelphia, sizes pediatric to adult
IV fluid bags: can be used to help stabilize the neck and are preferred over sandbags
Gardner–Wells (Crutchfield) tongs

CIRCULATION/CARDIOVASCULAR RESUSCITATION
IV catheters: sizes 14–24 gauge
Pediatric and adult IV tubing with volume control attachment
IV extension tubing

IV pressure bags and pump
Catheters for arterial lines: sizes 2.5, 3.0, 4.0, 5.0
Central venous pressure (CVP) catheters, 14–22 gauge
Blood warmer/infuser
Tibial infusion needles or bone marrow needles
Syringe pump for administering drip medications
Umbilical artery catheters
Doppler device
Blood pressure cuffs: 5, 7, 9, 12, 14 cm
Cardiovascular monitor with strip recorder and ability to monitor central lines
Defibrillator with pediatric paddles
MAST pants: toddler, child, and adult
Heimlich valve for chest drainage
Chest drainage setup
Thoracotomy tray with rib spreader
Thoracentesis tray
Chest tubes

DRUGS* (See Chapters 7 and 22)
Resuscitation drugs in pediatric doses
Vasoactive drugs
Intubation drugs
Anticonvulsant drugs
Diuretics
Antibiotics
Tetanus

OTHER
Femur traction splints, pediatric size
Hypothermia thermometer
Warming lights
Hypothermia blankets
Pediatric nasogastric tubes

*Recommended dosages and drugs may vary in different areas but should be standard in emergency departments. A chart with pediatric drugs and doses per weight should be posted in the trauma or resuscitation room.

Primary Assessment

The primary assessment consists of an evaluation of the airway, breathing, cervical spine, circulation (the ABCs), a brief neurological exam, and appropriate life-saving interventions. Many life-saving interventions are independent nursing functions. Table 21-1 lists assessment parameters and interventions for the primary assessment. Table 21-2 lists some life-threatening chest injuries that require immediate recognition and intervention during the primary assessment.

Secondary Assessment

The secondary assessment consists of a brief history of the injury and a complete head-to-toe evaluation of the child. Table 21-3 lists the components of this exam and possible interventions. Table 21-4 lists signs and symptoms of, and interventions for, abdominal and genitourinary trauma.

PARENT TEACHING

It is inappropriate to discuss preventive measures with parents whose child is severely injured as it will increase their feelings of guilt. Since prevention is the key in reducing deaths in the pediatric age group due to trauma, accident prevention should be discussed with all families when appropriate, include the following:

- Always use child safety seats while driving.
- Teach children safety habits concerning bicycles (e.g., wearing helmets).
- Teach water safety and never leave children unattended while near water.
- Do not keep firearms in the home.

Other age-related aspects of prevention are discussed in Chapter 3.

NURSING DOCUMENTATION

A trauma flow sheet is useful. The following should be documented:

- history and mechanism of injury
- prehospital care given
- primary and secondary survey, interventions and child's response
- disposition of child

Table 21-1 The ABCs of the Pediatric Primary Assessment

Assessment Parameter	Interventions
Airway with cervical spine control	Positioning—jaw thrust; suctioning to clear the airway; stiffneck collar, backboard

Breathing
Assess:
  Air exchange
  Chest movements
  Breath sounds
	Provide supplemental oxygen by mask, bag mask; prepare for intubation; assemble intubation drugs.

Circulation
Assess for presence of shock:
  Pulse
  Perfusion (capillary refill)
  Blood pressure
  ECG
	IV access (see Chapter 15)
	Fluids—lactated Ringer's, blood; obtain blood for laboratory studies.

Assess heart sounds	Apply cardiac monitor, blood pressure monitor; pulse oximeter; prepare for chest tube insertion (see Table 21-2 for further interventions of life-threatening chest injuries).
Dextrose	Consider need for 25% dextrose.

Disability
Assess:
  Neurological status
  Signs and symptoms of increased
   intracranial pressure (ICP)
  Presence of seizures
	Glasgow coma score (see Chapter 22)
	Raise head of bed, hyperventilate per physician order for increased ICP.
	Have anticonvulsant drugs ready.

Distention
  Abdominal
 	
  Urinary
	Insert nasogastric tube (except with multiple facial fractures, basilar skull fracture).
	Insert urinary catheter, watch for blood at urethral meatus.

Exposure Temperature control	Remove clothing; cut if necessary. Prevent hypothermia: • warm blood/fluid • radiant warmers • warmed O_2

Note: Other life-saving interventions can be performed during the primary survey depending on findings. These interventions are discussed in Tables 21-2, 21-3, and 21-4.

Table 21-2 Chest Injuries in Children: Recognition and Treatment

Injury/Definition	Signs and Symptoms	Collaborative and Nursing Interventions/Comments
1. *Pulmonary contusion.* Most common type of potentially lethal chest injury, usually due to blunt trauma	May have bruising to the chest. Initially, may be asymptomatic. Later signs and symptoms include: • tachycardia • rales • hemoptysis • falling PO$_2$	Early recognition Frequent observation of respiratory status Provide oxygen* Raise head of bed Limit fluids unless shock is present
2. *Pneumothorax.* Air in the pleural space from lung or tracheobronchial injury	Hypoxia; hyperresonance to percussion; decreased breath sounds; asymmetry of chest wall movement; breath sounds may be absent if the child has bilateral pneumothoraxes	Oxygen. Prepare for chest tube, thoracostomy to affected side.
a. *Open pneumothorax.* Open chest wound—may be sucking or non-sucking	Open chest wound with signs and symptoms as above	Occlusive dressing (petroleum jelly gauze). Prepare for chest tube insertion. If child experiences sudden respiratory distress after placement of the occlusive dressing, suspect tension pneumothorax; remove dressing briefly to let air escape until chest tube can be placed.
b. *Tension pneumothorax* (second most common lethal chest injury). Air leak accumulates without means of escape and compresses both lungs	Distended neck veins; tracheal deviation to contralateral side; decreased breath sounds; cyanosis; signs and symptoms of shock due to decreased cardiac output	Immediate recognition, especially prior to air transport. Prepare for thoracentesis to convert tension pneumothorax to simple pneumothorax. Must be done immediately to improve cardiac output prior to chest tube insertion. Prepare for tube thoracostomy.

continues

Table 21-2 continued

Injury/Definition	Signs and Symptoms	Collaborative and Nursing Interventions/Comments
c. *Traumatic hemothorax.* Blood in the chest cavity resulting from blunt or penetrating trauma	Hypoxia; signs and symptoms of shock	Prepare for chest tube insertion. Volume replacement. May require open thoracotomy.
3. *Traumatic asphyxia* due to sudden, massive decompression of the chest, transmitting pressure to the heart, lungs, vena cava, neck and head	Petechiae of head and neck; subconjunctival hemorrhages; depressed level of consciousness; hemoptysis, pulmonary contusion, and great vessel injury may be present; epistaxis and hematemesis may be present	Assess for associated injuries. Prepare for chest tube insertion. Limit fluids unless signs and symptoms of shock are present. Elevate head of bed.
4. *Cardiac tamponade.* Accumulation of blood in the pericardial sac due to penetrating or crush injuries	Shock: • Narrow pulse pressure • Distended neck veins • Muffled heart sounds	Fluids—treat for shock. Prepare for pericardiocentesis.

*All children with known or suspected chest trauma should receive supplemental oxygen and constant cardiac and oxygen saturation monitoring by oximeter. The nurse should be prepared to assist with intubation and mechanical ventilation.

Source: American Academy of Pediatrics and American College of Emergency Physicians, *Advanced Pediatric Life Support* (Elk Grove Village, Ill.: American Academy of Pediatrics; and Dallas: American College of Emergency Physicians, 1989), 86–90.

Table 21-3 The Pediatric Secondary Assessment

Assessment Parameter	Interventions
Head and Face Bony deformities Full anterior fontanelle Surface trauma Impaled objects Visual acuity (if appropriate) Edema Malocclusion Facial nerve weakness Otorrhea/rhinorrhea Nasal flaring Changes in level of consciousness Seizures	Continually reassess airway and maintain cervical spine immobilization. X-rays. Correlate findings with other signs and symptoms. Comfort child. Allow parents to be present as appropriate.
Neck Tracheal deviation Distended or flat neck veins Edema Hoarseness Subcutaneous emphysema Cervical spine tenderness	Maintain immobility. May need intervention for respiratory emergency such as pneumothorax, cardiac tamponade, etc. Correlate findings with other signs/symptoms. Comfort child.
Chest Surface trauma Pain on palpation Respiratory rate Stridor/retractions Dyspnea Chest movement—equal or unequal Breath sounds Crepitus Muffled heart sounds	Reassess airway; may need to prepare for chest tube insertion. Chest x-ray. ECG monitor. IV, lab work. Monitor blood loss. Orogastric or NG tube (distended abdomen can put pressure on diaphragm and compromise breathing). Check NG aspirate. Consider transport to a tertiary care facility.
Abdomen Surface trauma Distention Rigidity Guarding Pain Absent bowel sounds Increased girth Rebound tenderness Entry or exit wound	CT scan or peritoneal lavage. Urinary catheterization. X-ray. IV. Surgical evaluation. Monitor vital signs. Consider blood loss leading to impending shock.

continues

Table 21-3 continued

Assessment Parameter	Interventions

Pelvis/Genitalia
  Suprapubic mass
  Soft tissue edema
  Hematoma
  Unstable pelvis
  Pain
  Blood at meatus
  Anal/vaginal trauma
	Immobilize. Urinary catheterization. Urology consult. Monitor vital signs. Comfort child.
	
	Consider sexual abuse with anal or vaginal trauma. (See Table 21-4 for further interventions of abdominal and genitourinary trauma.)

Extremities
  Surface trauma
  Edema
	Splint. X-ray. Orthopedic consult (see Chapter 23).

Five "P"s:
  Pain
  Pallor
  Paralysis
  Pulselessness
  Paresthesia
 	
  Deformities
  Crepitus
  Capillary refill time
	Consider blood loss. Consider pain medications when possible. Monitor vital signs. Comfort child.

Posterior
  Surface trauma
  Bruising
  Swelling
  Pain
	Maintain cervical spine. Log roll to assess back.

Miscellaneous
  Tetanus status
  Parental support
	Immunize as needed. Refer to social services, clergy, etc., as appropriate. Keep parents updated on child's condition.

Table 21-4 Abdominal and Genitourinary Injuries in Children: Recognition and Treatment

Injury	Signs and Symptoms	Collaborative and Nursing Interventions/Comments
Abdominal:		
1. Liver and spleen: commonly injured in children by blunt trauma	Onset of signs and symptoms may be rapid depending on injury—shock may be present. Symptoms may be gradual due to chemical or bacterial peritonitis. General signs and symptoms of intra-abdominal injury include:	Oxygen. Treat for shock if present. Frequently assess vital signs. Insert nasogastric tube to decompress the stomach. Surgical consult. Prepare child for abdominal CT scan or peritoneal lavage. Prepare for admission or for surgery. Diagnostic tests.
2. Pancreas: may be injured in a high-speed deceleration accident or by direct blows to upper abdomen	• *Kehr's sign.* Pain in the left shoulder caused by irritation of the diaphragm and phrenic nerve by free blood in the abdomen. Pain is referred to the left shoulder by the phrenic nerve.	
3. Duodenum: duodenal hematomas can occur in children who fall against handle bars of bicycle; may be present in cases of child abuse	• *Seat belt sign.* Compression of a lap belt causes ecchymosis over the lower abdomen. • *Cullen's sign.* Periumbilical ecchymosis caused by intra-abdominal bleeding from a ruptured spleen (rare).	
4. Intestinal: uncommon; may be perforated by deceleration trauma	Abdominal pain/rigidity; absent or decreased bowel sounds; gastric distention	
Genitourinary Injuries*		
1. Renal: minor contusions most common; lacerations and major vascular injuries less common	Hematuria; flank or abdominal pain; flank abrasion, contusion or ecchymosis	Frequent observation of vital signs. Prepare for intravenous pyelogram (IVP). For serious injury, surgical intervention and management in the intensive care unit may be necessary.

continues

Table 21-4 continued

Injury	Signs and Symptoms	Collaborative and Nursing Interventions/Comments
2. Bladder: usually secondary to severe blunt trauma causing rupture	Hematuria; abdominal pain; inability to void; pelvic fracture; renal injury	Recognition. Prepare for cystography. May need surgical repair. Don't pass urethral catheter until ureteral injuries are ruled out.
3. Ureteral: traumatic disruption of the ureter from the renal pelvis (rare in children)	Flank pain; flank mass; penetrating injury; inability to void	Prompt recognition. Prepare child for surgical intervention.
4. Urethral: most commonly results from pelvic fractures, straddle injuries, or urethral manipulation	Blood at urethral meatus; inability to void; lower abdominal or pelvic pain; scrotal hematoma or pelvic swelling; high-riding prostate; hematuria	Do not insert urethral catheter. Prepare for retrograde urethrography. May need surgical intervention.
5. Genital injuries: may be injured in sporting activities, burns, accidental mutilation, and sexual abuse; most injuries are minor	Swelling; ecchymosis; hematoma; perineal tears; lacerations	Recognition. Consider sexual abuse if injury inconsistent with history given. Minor injuries usually treated with analgesics and ice packs. Surgical exploration and repair may be necessary.

*Genitourinary trauma should always be suspected in any child with abdominal or flank tenderness, pelvic fracture, lower rib fracture, or perineal swelling.

Source: American Academy of Pediatrics and American College of Emergency Physicians, *Advanced Pediatric Life Support* (Elk Grove Village, Ill.: American Academy of Pediatrics; and Dallas: American College of Emergency Physicians, 1989), 91–93; Lisa Peckham and Louann Kitchen, "Abdominal and Genitourinary Trauma," in *Pediatric Trauma Nursing*, ed. Connie Joy (Gaithersburg, Md.: Aspen Publishers, Inc., 1989), 102–17.

NURSING DIAGNOSES FOR THE PEDIATRIC TRAUMA VICTIM

- ineffective airway clearance related to vomitus and blood in airway
- potential for aspiration related to blood or vomitus in airway
- ineffective breathing pattern related to possible chest injury
- decreased cardiac output related to hypovolemia
- potential for fluid volume deficit related to blood loss
- alteration in cerebral and cardiopulmonary tissue perfusion related to shock state
- alteration in body temperature (e.g., hypothermia)
- potential for infection related to injuries
- fear of child related to ED and procedures
- alteration in comfort, pain related to injuries and procedures
- potential for alteration in growth and development related to severity and type of injuries
- anticipatory grieving of parents related to seriousness of child's condition
- ineffective family coping related to child's condition and effect on family

BIBLIOGRAPHY

American Academy of Pediatrics and American College of Emergency Physicians. *Advanced Pediatric Life Support.* Elk Grove Village, Ill.: American Academy of Pediatrics; and Dallas: American College of Emergency Physicians, 1989.

Curley, M., and S. Vaughan. "Assessment and Resuscitation of the Pediatric Patient." *Critical Care Nurse* 7 (1984): 26–42.

Eichelberger, M., and G. Pratsch. *Pediatric Trauma Care.* Gaithersburg, Md.: Aspen Publishers, Inc., 1987.

Eichelberger, M., and G. Randolph. "Pediatric Trauma: An Algorithm for Diagnosis and Therapy." *Journal of Trauma* 23 (1983): 91–97.

Fleisher, G., and S. Ludwig. *Textbook of Pediatric Emergency Medicine.* Baltimore: Williams & Wilkins Co., 1988.

Hodge, D. "Pediatric Emergency Office Equipment." *Pediatric Emergency Care* 4 (1988): 212–14.

Joy, C. *Pediatric Trauma Nursing.* Gaithersburg, Md.: Aspen Publishers, Inc., 1989.

Kelley, S, ed. *Pediatric Emergency Nursing.* Norwalk, Conn.: Appleton & Lange, 1988.

Luten, R., ed. *Problems in Pediatric Emergency Medicine.* New York: Churchill Livingstone, 1988.

Manley, L. "Pediatric Trauma: Initial Assessment and Management. *Journal of Emergency Nursing* 13 (1987): 77–90.

Selbst, S., and S. Torrey. *Pediatric Emergency Medicine for the House Officer.* Baltimore: Williams & Wilkins Co., 1988.

Chapter 22

Head and Neck Trauma

Laurel S. Campbell

INTRODUCTION

One of the most frequent chief complaints among pediatric patients in the emergency department is head injury. Children are prone to having head injuries due to their activity level, participation in contact sports, and lack of motor coordination, especially in their early years. Children under the age of 2 have open sutures, relative elasticity of the skull, weak neck musculature, and relatively large heads, all of which predispose them to head injury.

The most common head injuries in children are (1) skull fractures and (2) closed head injuries involving concussion, contusion, intracranial hemorrhage, and cerebral edema.

PATHOPHYSIOLOGY

1. Skull fractures. Skull fractures can be generally classified as open or closed and are usually caused by a collision of the head with a solid object such as a table or the floor. Some common types of skull fractures include the following:

- linear: a straight line fracture.
- depressed: an indented fracture usually caused by a flying object against the head (horseshoes, golf clubs, baseballs) in which inwardly penetrating skull fragments can press on or damage underlying structures.
- basilar: a fracture in any of the bones that form the base of the skull. This type of fracture is often difficult to diagnose on x-ray and may require a CT scan for diagnosis. The diagnosis is often made by history and assessment of presence of the "classic signs" of a basilar skull fracture:[1]
  - "Battle's sign": bruising over the mastoid area

197

- "raccoon eyes": periorbital ecchymosis
- hemotympanum
- cerebrospinal fluid (CSF) drainage from the nose, ears

2. Closed head injuries

- Concussion: a closed head injury often associated with a transient loss of consciousness, nausea, vomiting, headache; usually not associated with any long-term neurological deficits.
- Contusion: a "bruising" of the cortical surface of the brain, usually associated with impaired nerve function, transient loss of consciousness, vomiting, headache, memory loss (transient).
- Cerebral edema: any injury producing cerebral hypoxia. Trauma or ischemia may cause cerebral edema, or swelling of the cerebral cells. This swelling of the brain tissue results in an increase in intracranial volume and therefore an increase in intracranial pressure.

3. Intracranial hemorrhages. Intracranial hemorrhages are often associated with a high morbidity and mortality rate in children since symptoms may not develop immediately and are not easily identified if the child is too young to complain. Table 22-1 compares the signs and symptoms and other factors that differentiate these hemorrhages.

4. Increased intracranial pressure. Intracranial pressure (ICP) is determined by the volume of the main components in the cranial vault: blood, brain, and CSF. An increase in the size or amount of any one component due to trauma can result in an increase in intracranial pressure. An increase in ICP may reduce cerebral blood flow and cause ischemia. Increased ICP can also cause vital sign deterioration due to brainstem compression and decreased cerebral perfusion.[2] A normal ICP should be in the range of 80–180 mm H_2O or 0–15 mm Hg.[3]

5. Cervical spine injuries. Pediatric spinal cord injury accounts for 1–5% of all cases of spinal cord injury in the United States. Injuries in the first decade of life usually result from motor vehicle accidents, and those in the second decade of life are usually due to sports and recreational activities. Cervical spine injuries are associated with a high morbidity and mortality rate due to the permanent paralysis accompanying cord trauma or transection.[4] All pediatric trauma patients with a head injury should be suspected of having a cervical spine injury until examined by a physician.

TRIAGE ASSESSMENT

A thorough neurological assessment should be done on all children with suspected head injury. General assessment parameters that should be initiated with all head injuries are listed below:

Table 22-1 Intracranial Hemorrhages

	Epidural Hematoma	Subdural Hematoma	Subarachnoid Hemorrhage
Location of bleed	Between skull and dura matter	Between dura mater and arachnoid mater	Between arachnoid mater and pia mater
Bleed source	Usually arterial	Usually venous	Usually arterial
Incidence	Lower	Higher	Higher
Intracranial pressure	Increased	Increased	Increased
Laterality	Usually unilateral	Bilateral in 75%	Either
Causes	Blunt trauma	Trauma, violent shaking (child abuse)	Trauma, ruptured cerebral artery, arteriovenous malformation bleeds
Classic symptoms	Initial loss of consciousness followed by transient consciousness followed by unconsciousness in 35–50% of pediatric patients; ipsilateral pupil dilation, contralateral paresis, paralysis; vital sign deterioration	Headache, severe deterioration in level of consciousness	Headache, meningeal signs (see Chapter 18)

Source: Adapted from N.P. Rossman, "Pediatric Emergencies: Managing Acute Head Trauma" in *Contemporary Pediatrics*, November 1986, p. 43, with permission of Contemporary Pediatrics, © 1986.

- airway, breathing, and circulation (the ABCs)
- cervical spine immobilization measures
- vital signs (pulse, blood pressure, rate and quality of respirations)
- verbal response, motor response, eye opening in response to stimuli (Glasgow coma score)
- pupil size and reaction to light
- level of consciousness/orientation
- cranial nerve deficits
- gait difficulties
- neck stiffness or pain
- hyperventilation
- scalp: areas of edema, depression
- anterior fontanelle (if open)
- evaluation for other injuries (chest, abdomen, extremities)

Table 22-2 Adaptation of the Glasgow Coma Score for Pediatric Patients

Traditional Score*		Pediatric Adaptation†	
Eye Opening:		Eye Opening:	
Spontaneous	4	Spontaneous	4
To speech	3	To sounds	3
To pain	2	To painful stimuli	2
None	1	None	1
Motor Responses:		Motor Responses:	
Obeys commands	6	Spontaneous movement	6
Localizes pain	5	Localizes to pain	5
Withdrawal	4	Withdraws	4
Abnormal flexion	3	Reflex flexion	3
Extensor rigidity	2	Reflex extension (decerebrate)	2
None	1	None (flaccid)	1
Verbal Responses:		Verbal Responses:	
Oriented	5	Appropriate words or social smile; fixes and follows	5
Confused	4	Cries, but consolable	4
Inappropriate	3	Persistently irritable	3
Incomprehensible	2	Restless, agitated	2
None	1	None	1

Source: *Reprinted from *Lancet,* Vol. 2, p. 81, with permission of The Lancet, Ltd., © 1974; and †reprinted with permission of Thomas G. Luerssen, Associate Professor of Surgery, Pediatric Neurosurgery Division, James Whitcomb Riley Hospital for Children, Indianapolis, Indiana.

Additional tests can include oculomotor-vestibular reflexes (doll's eyes, cold calorics), gag reflex, Babinski reflex, retinal exam, and pain response.

Table 22-1 lists specific assessment findings associated with the different entities of head injuries. The Glasgow coma score has been used for years to give an objective scoring to neurological status, but it is often difficult to assess pediatric patients using the adult responses listed in the score. Table 22-2 lists an adaptation of the Glasgow coma score for assessment of verbal response, motor response, and eye opening in children.

TRIAGE HISTORY

- age of child
- developmental level
- mechanism of injury
- loss of consciousness
- history of nausea, vomiting, headache, weakness, lethargy, irritability postinjury
- allergies to medicines
- past medical history of neuromuscular disorders (seizures, cerebral palsy, etc.)

TELEPHONE TRIAGE GUIDELINES

Before the emergency nurse can use clinical judgment in providing telephone advice to parents of children with possible head or neck injury, several factors must be determined. These include the following:

- age of the child (if less than 6 months of age, nonaccidental trauma must be considered)
- mechanism of injury: high speed, long fall
- length of time since injury occurred
- loss of consciousness or decrease in level of consciousness
- child's current behavior compared with normal
- presence of vomiting, blurred vision, lethargy, dizziness, neck pain, difficulty in walking or talking, seizure activity
- presence of open or bleeding skin on the head

The ED nurse should recommend evaluation by a physician if the child has exhibited any of the signs and symptoms of head injury (see "Triage Assessment") or if the parents are at all concerned about their child's status. If the injury is minor and the child is functioning at a normal level, the nurse could recommend at-home observation with instruction to seek medical care if the child's condition changes. These instructions should include a recommendation to wake the child up during the night to check neurological status and to avoid giving pain medications pending evaluation by a physician.

PRIORITY RATING

Emergent: Hemodynamically unstable child with apnea or bradypnea, unequal and/or unresponsive pupils, decerebrate or decorticate posturing, seizures, full tense anterior fontanelle in infants, decreased level of consciousness, vomiting, airway instability.

Urgent: Hemodynamically stable child with history of transient loss of consciousness, lethargy, confusion, vomiting, dizziness.

Nonurgent: Hemodynamically stable child with history of head contact with a solid object with local swelling, no loss of consciousness, transient vomiting; child alert, active, playful.

TREATMENT AND NURSING CARE

General care of the child with a head injury should begin with close and consistent observation of the child's neurological status for signs of improvement or deterioration. Other general care guidelines for head injury include the following:

1. airway management
   - jaw thrust, bag, and mask ventilations, initially if child is comatose or child's ability to maintain an open airway is insufficient.
   - endotracheal intubation: may be necessary if oropharyngeal secretions/ bleeding could possibly obstruct the airway or if bag and mask ventilations must be continued past the initial stabilization period.
   - hyperventilation: lowering the carbon dioxide level by deliberate hyperventilation causes cerebral vasoconstriction, which lowers intracranial blood volume.[5] Often children with severe head injuries present with hyperventilation as a physiological means of decreasing their carbon dioxide level and therefore their ICP. Deliberate hyperventilation should be accomplished using bag and mask ventilations or bag and endotracheal tube ventilations.
2. nasogastric (NG)/orogastric (OG) tube. An NG or OG tube should be placed in the stomach for decompression and to minimize the risk of vomiting and

aspiration. If there is any possibility of basilar skull fracture, the OG tube is preferred over the NG to prevent tube placement through the fracture.

3. cervical spine immobilization. One of the "rules" in trauma management states that any child suspected of having a traumatic head injury should also be suspected of having a cervical spine injury until proven otherwise.

- Cervical spine immobilization should be accomplished using an appropriately sized "stiff" collar.
- Sandbags are usually ineffective in immobilizing a child's head and neck and should be used only if no other means of immobilization are available.

4. fluid therapy. In the ill or injured child IV access is essential if a route is needed for administration of diuretics, neuromuscular blockers, anticonvulsants, and critical fluids. However, an increase in circulating blood volume results in an increased cerebral blood volume and an increase in ICP.

- Fluid intake should be restricted to one-half to two-thirds maintenance volume if there are no signs of major blood loss.[6]
- Maintenance fluids include isotonic solutions such as lactated Ringer's, normal saline, or blood.[7]

5. drug therapy. Drugs commonly used in the management of increased ICP and head injury are listed in Table 22-3.

6. seizure precautions. Anticonvulsants used in the prophylactic or actual treatment of seizures related to head injuries are listed in Table 22-3.

7. lab/radiology tests. Should only be initiated after initial stabilization measures are established.

- CBC, electrolytes, metabolic studies
- skull x-rays
- CT

8. ICP monitoring. Many devices can be used to measure ICP, including insertion of an intraventricular catheter, a fiberoptic ICP monitor, or a subarachnoid bolt screw. Insertion of these devices is an invasive procedure and subjects the patient to possible cross-contamination from other ED patients; therefore, insertion of these devices should be done in a controlled setting such as the operating room or pediatric intensive care unit.

9. surgical intervention. Most intracranial hemorrhages require surgical ligation and evacuation of the hematoma. Preoperative measures should include parent teaching, keeping the patient NPO (nothing by mouth), establishing vascular access, and airway management and support.

10. antibiotic, tetanus prophylaxis. Usually initiated if there is a basilar skull fracture or an open wound over a depressed skull fracture (see Chapter 3 for tetanus prophylaxis guidelines).

Table 22-3 Medications Used in Treatment of Head Injuries

Medication	Indications	Dose*/Route	Nursing Implications
Furosemide	Diuretic, used for acute episodes of increased ICP	1 mg/kg IV	May cause hypokalemia, dehydration. Monitor intake and output.
Mannitol	Osmotic diuretic, used for acute episodes of increased ICP with rapid clinical deterioration	0.25–1.0 g/kg IV	Administer over 3–5 min. If no response, may repeat every 5 min. May cause circulatory overload, electrolyte imbalance. Monitor intake and output.
Dexamethasone	Steroid, used for acute episodes of increased ICP	Initial dose 0.5–1.5 mg/kg IV, IM	Followed by maintenance doses.
Diazepam	Muscle relaxant, used for initial intervention in seizure control	0.2–0.5 mg/kg/dose IV (status epilepticus dose range)	Causes respiratory depression.
Lorazepam	Central nervous system depressant, used for initial intervention in seizure control	0.03–0.05 mg/kg/dose IV	Causes respiratory depression.
Phenytoin	Anticonvulsant	15–20 mg/kg IV	Administration rate should not exceed 50 mg/min. May cause bradycardia, hypotension. Compatible only with normal saline base solution.

*Doses from Peter C. Rowe, *The Harriet Lane Handbook* (Chicago: Yearbook Medical Publishers, 1987), 150–151, 161, 172–173, 188.

PARENT TEACHING

The parent may be very anxious about taking the child home for observation. The following guidelines are useful to help parents determine whether or not to return to the ED:

1. Observe for changes in the child's level of consciousness.
2. Observe for symptoms of severe headache, restlessness, agitation.
3. Keep the child on clear liquids for a few hours after injury, then advance to regular diet. Vomiting is common after even the mildest head injury. If vomiting is forceful or persistent, call the pediatrician or return to the emergency department.
4. Return to the ED if any of the following occur:
   - seizures
   - changes in the level of consciousness
   - persistent vomiting
   - unequal pupils
   - weakness or loss of use of extremity
   - slurred speech
   - blurred vision
   - severe headache

Safety measures such as the use of helmets while riding bicycles and the use of seat belts in automobiles should also be discussed.

NURSING DOCUMENTATION

- initial assessment data
- historical data, including mechanism of injury
- vital signs
- ongoing neurological evaluation data (Glasgow coma score, pupil size and reaction)
- medical and nursing interventions and patient response
- condition on discharge/admission
- discharge instructions
- follow-up care

NURSING DIAGNOSES

- alteration in comfort, pain related to intracranial pressure and/or neck trauma
- alteration in cerebral tissue perfusion related to increased intracranial pressure and/or hemorrhage
- ineffective airway clearance related to secretions and/or possible paralysis
- impaired gas exchange related to hyperventilation, hypoventilation and/or apnea
- child's fear related to hospitalization, procedures
- knowledge deficit related to at-home observation for signs and symptoms of head injury

---

NOTES

1. M. Yaster and J.A. Haller, "Multiple Trauma in the Pediatric Patient," in *Textbook of Pediatric Intensive Care,* ed. Mark Rogers (Baltimore: Williams & Wilkins Co., 1987): 1299.

2. D. Bruce, L. Schut, and L. Sutton, "Neurosurgical Emergencies," in *Textbook of Pediatric Emergency Medicine,* eds. Gary Fleisher and Stephen Ludwig (Baltimore: Williams & Wilkins Co., 1988): 1114.

3. J. Harr and M.F. Hazinski, "Neurologic Disorders," in *Nursing Care of the Critically Ill Child,* ed. M.F. Hazinski (St. Louis: C.V. Mosby Co., 1984): 378.

4. M. Yaster and J.A. Haller, "Multiple Trauma in the Pediatric Patient," 1305.

5. Harr and Hazinski, "Neurologic Disorders," 372.

6. S. DeJong, "Traumatic Head Injury," in *Pediatric Trauma Nursing,* ed. Connie Joy (Gaithersburg, Md.: Aspen Publishers, Inc., 1989): 49.

7. M. Dean and D. Hanley, "Evaluation of the Comatose Child," in *Textbook of Pediatric Intensive Care,* ed. Mark Rogers (Baltimore: Williams & Wilkins Co., 1987): 599.

BIBLIOGRAPHY

Fleisher, G., and S. Ludwig, eds. *Textbook of Pediatric Emergency Medicine.* Baltimore: Williams & Wilkins Co., 1988.

Hazinski, M.F., ed. *Nursing Care of the Critically Ill Child.* St. Louis: C.V. Mosby Co., 1984.

Joy, C., ed. *Pediatric Trauma Nursing.* Gaithersburg, Md.: Aspen Publishers, Inc., 1989.

Kelley, S., ed. *Pediatric Emergency Nursing.* Norwalk, Conn.: Appleton & Lange, 1988.

Meier, E. "Evaluating Head Trauma in Infants and Children." *Maternal Child Nurse* 8/1 (1983): 54–57.

Rogers, M., ed. *Textbook of Pediatric Intensive Care.* Baltimore: Williams & Wilkins Co., 1987.

Chapter 23

Orthopedic Trauma

Laurel S. Campbell and John D. Campbell

INTRODUCTION

Orthopedic trauma is common in the pediatric patient due to several factors, including bone immaturity and a tendency among children to engage in high-contact play activities. Injuries may be caused by applied forces, such as direct impact associated with motor vehicle accidents, or intentional forces such as those associated with child abuse. Pathological conditions such as osteochondrosis, metabolic disorders, and tumors may also predispose the child to orthopedic injury. Consequences of orthopedic trauma include neurovascular compromise and impaired activity level for extended periods of time; in addition, fractures can affect future growth and function of bone.

PATHOPHYSIOLOGY

The following terms are commonly used to define and describe orthopedic injuries:

- sprain: an injury involving the *ligaments,* commonly seen when the joint exceeds its normal limits
- strain: an injury involving the *muscle,* usually associated with a weakening or overstretching of the muscle where it attaches to the tendon
- contusion: a "bruise" or extravasation of blood into tissues, usually the result of a blunt force
- fracture: a disruption or break in the bone
- dislocation: acute or chronic disruption of a joint whereby the two joint surfaces are no longer in contact
- subluxation: an incomplete dislocation in which the joint relationship is altered but the articular surfaces are partially intact

- amputation: the cutting off (either partial or complete) of a body part by a traumatic force

There are several types of fractures, most of which can be classified as either closed or open. A closed fracture can be described as a fracture in the bone without a break in the skin surface above the fracture. An open fracture involves a break in the skin above the fracture, due to the disruption of the skin by the fragmented bone or by the force that actually caused the fracture. Other classifications of fractures may include the following:

- greenstick. Commonly seen in children; involves a partial fracture that does not extend completely through the bone.
- transverse. A horizontal fracture that usually results from a direct force.
- oblique. A diagonal fracture, usually resulting from a twisting force.
- spiral. A fracture line that spirals around the bone, commonly seen with application of direct force to a bone while one end is firmly held or planted.
- comminuted. A fracture with three or more fragments.
- epiphyseal. Fractures involving the bone growth plate. These fractures are divided into five categories (Salter I–V) with Salter V fractures having the worse prognosis for return to normal growth.

TRIAGE ASSESSMENT

Many orthopedic injuries present with similar assessment findings. Long bone fractures may be accompanied by neurovascular damage and severe blood loss, so that a brief but thorough assessment of the injured extremity should include neurovascular checks distal to the site of injury. Triage assessment should include the following:

1. airway, breathing, circulation (ABCs), level of consciousness
2. vital signs, including signs of shock
3. injured site assessment: edema, erythema, ecchymosis, obvious angulation, the five "Ps": pain, pallor, paralysis, paresthesia, pulselessness

TRIAGE HISTORY

- age of child
- mechanism of injury (fall, blow from foreign object, motor vehicle accident)

- time of last food and water intake
- first aid measures taken at home
- present history: activity level, current medications, allergies
- past history: previous orthopedic injuries, especially to the same site/extremity

As an added precaution, the nurse should be aware of discrepancies between the history of how the injury occurred and the actual extent or type of injury. These discrepancies may indicate a situation involving child abuse or neglect.

TELEPHONE TRIAGE GUIDELINES

Emergency nurses often see cases of orthopedic trauma in which the child has been walking on or using a fractured extremity for hours to days after being injured. Since an untreated fracture can result in future impairment of bone growth and function, most orthopedic injuries should be seen for evaluation by a physician within a reasonable period of time after the injury occurs. In view of this, the emergency nurse may be able to give advice about home management of orthopedic injuries, but this advice should always include a recommendation for examination by a physician.

Before giving advice about orthopedic injuries, the emergency nurse should obtain the following information:

- length of time since injury occurred
- mechanism of injury
- signs of injury (obvious deformity, edema, ecchymosis, pain, impaired circulation below site of injury, loss of sensation)

If any evidence of neurovascular impairment is present, the child should be evaluated by a physician immediately. The nurse can recommend the following care guidelines until medical evaluation is available for any orthopedic injury:

1. Keep the affected extremity elevated on pillows above the level of the heart to prevent or decrease swelling and/or pain.
2. Apply cold packs over the area of swelling and pain for 24–48 hours after injury.
3. Limit the child's activity and weight bearing to rest the affected extremity.
4. Give nonprescription analgesics (acetaminophen) for pain relief.

PRIORITY RATING

Emergent: Hemodynamically unstable child with severe blood loss, symptoms of shock (hypotension, tachycardia, cool pale skin, decreased level of consciousness) associated with long-bone, pelvic fractures ; open fractures; fractures resulting in neurovascular compromise in the affected extremity; amputations.

Urgent: Hemodynamically stable child with obvious angulation or deformity of extremity; moderate to severe edema, ecchymosis; moderate to severe pain; slight to moderate neurovascular compromise distal to injury.

Nonurgent: Hemodynamically stable child with mild to moderate pain, edema, ecchymosis at site of injury; little or no neurovascular compromise distal to site of injury; may be able to move or bear weight on extremity.

TREATMENT AND NURSING CARE

Nursing interventions in the treatment of orthopedic injuries are aimed at:

- relieving pain
- preventing complications such as further neurovascular injury and micro-embolization
- assisting with immobilization or reduction
- educating child and parents about home management of the injured extremity

Initial treatment should include:

- cold application
- immobilization of the joints distal and proximal to the injury, and elevation of the affected limb
- NPO until evaluation by a physician

Specific management for the various types of orthopedic injuries include the following:

1. fractures of the shoulder (proximal humerus). Usually associated with falls on an extended forearm. Immobilize in presenting position. Assist with reduction, application of immobilization device (examples: sling and swath dressing, sugar tong splint, spica cast, skeletal traction). Keep child NPO if open reduction is necessary for open fractures, epiphyseal injury.
2. fractures of the distal humerus (supracondylar fracture). Can cause Volkmann's ischemic contracture (neurovascular compromise distal to the

injury). Immobilize in present position, assist with closed reduction or prepare for open reduction in OR.

3. fractures of the radius/ulna. Commonly associated with falling on an extended arm. Immobilize, elevate extremity. Assist with closed reduction (traction-countertraction can be applied using suspended finger traps). Prepare for open reduction if closed reduction manipulations are unsuccessful.

4. wrist and hand fractures. The majority of children's hand fractures are treated with closed reduction and splinting. Open reduction may be anticipated if displaced intra-articular fractures are present. Immobilize hand/wrist in position of function. Prepare for closed reduction with possible anesthetization of finger by physician using a local finger block.

5. pelvic fractures. When pelvic fractures occur in a child, they are usually caused by a significant "high-velocity" force and are often associated with other life-threatening injuries to underlying vessels and organs. With pelvic fractures, compression of the ileac crests produces pain at the fracture site. Immediate management of pelvic fractures in the emergency department should include immobilization of the pelvis and assessment of ABCs. X-rays should be done only after stabilization is accomplished. Long-term treatment may be as simple as bedrest and not bearing weight, or as complex as open reduction and internal and/or external fixation.

6. femur fractures. Can be caused by direct high velocity forces that cause transverse fractures as well as indirect rotational forces that can produce spiral or oblique fractures. Femur fractures can result in severe neurovascular compromise and significant blood loss. Emergency nursing management should include elevation and immobilization of the affected extremity, cold pack application, and assessment of ABCs and neurovascular status. Long-term management measures include skin or skeletal traction, cast immobilization, and internal or external fixation.

7. tibia/fibula fractures. Occur as a result of sports injuries, falls, or indirect rotational trauma associated with bicycle spoke accidents. Emergency nursing management should be aimed at elevating and immobilizing the affected extremity, reducing pain, and assisting with closed reduction and cast or splint application. Open reduction may be necessary if the epiphysis is involved or if closed reduction manipulations are unsuccessful.

8. foot/ankle fractures. May also be associated with neurovascular compromise. Nondisplaced talus fractures can be treated with cast immobilization. Metatarsals are often injured by a falling object or when torque is applied to the foot. They are usually treated with elevation and a short leg cast. Initial emergency nursing management of these fractures should include elevation, cold pack application, and immobilization.

9. amputations. Care of the child should follow the ABCs of trauma resuscitation guidelines. The stump should be dressed with a snug sterile pressure dressing. Do not apply a tourniquet unless arterial bleeding cannot be controlled with direct pressure or elevation. A tourniquet should be applied only if ordered by a physician. Care of the amputated part should include wrapping the part in gauze slightly soaked with saline. The part should then be placed in a sealable plastic bag, and the bag should be placed in a container containing ice water. Both patient and body part should be transported together to a facility with capabilities for reimplantation.

10. subluxation. One of the most common cases of joint subluxation occurs with "nursemaid's elbow" or subluxation of the radial head. This type of injury is often seen when the child is lifted up by one hand so that the extended arm must support the entire body weight. Nursing care involves assisting with reduction by flexing the elbow and supinating the hand.

PARENT TEACHING

Since an increase in swelling can lead to neurovascular compromise, parents must be educated on measures to prevent this complication. Written discharge instructions should include the following guidelines:

- Observe for signs of impending neurovascular compromise: numbness; pale, cool skin below site of injury; pain. Notify physician or return to ED if these signs occur.
- Keep affected extremity elevated above the level of the heart.
- Never allow child to relieve itching by putting sharp objects such as knives or coat hangers down inside the cast (can tear the skin under the cast, cause secondary infections).
- Apply cold packs for 24–48 hours after injury to prevent or diminish swelling.
- Limit child's activity level pending further evaluation by a physician.
- For pain relief, give over-the-counter medications or analgesics as prescribed by the physician.
- Instruct parents on how to loosen and reapply compression bandages or splints if applicable.
- Teach child and parents correct technique for crutch walking; have child do return demonstration if able.

NURSING DOCUMENTATION

- primary, secondary assessment findings
- history data, including mechanism of injury
- diagnostic studies done
- nursing interventions, medical-nursing collaborative interventions, and patient response
- discharge instructions, including guidelines for follow-up care

NURSING DIAGNOSES

The following is a list of actual or potential nursing diagnoses that apply to the pediatric orthopedic trauma victim:

- alterations in comfort, pain related to pressure and/or fracture damage
- potential or actual alterations in tissue perfusion related to pressure and/or fracture damage
- fear related to hospitalization and procedures
- knowledge deficit of parents related to cast care and child safety

---

BIBLIOGRAPHY

Lovell, W., and R. Winter, eds. *Pediatric Orthopedics,* 2d ed. Philadelphia: J.B. Lippincott Co., 1986.

Menkes, J. "Pitfalls in Orthopedic Trauma: Part 1. The Upper Extremity." *Emergency Medicine* 21 (1989): 64–74, 79–80, 85–91.

O'Hara, M. "Emergency Care of the Patient with a Traumatic Amputation." *Journal of Emergency Nursing* 13 (1987): 272–77.

Rockwood, C., K. Wilkins, and R. King, eds. *Fractures in Children.* Philadelphia: J.B. Lippincott Co., 1984.

Sheehy, S., and J. Barber. *Emergency Nursing: Principles and Practices.* St. Louis: C.V. Mosby Co., 1985.

Chapter 24

Burns

Donna Ojanen Thomas

INTRODUCTION

Burn injuries are the third leading cause of accidental death in childhood. Most occur in the home and the majority are considered preventable. Nearly 52% of all burns occur in children between birth and 4 years of age and can be related to their developmental stage and total dependence on caretakers.[1]

Burns are classified by the American Burn Association (ABA) into four categories according to depth. These are described in Table 24-1.

PATHOPHYSIOLOGY

Burn injuries disrupt skin integrity and function. Local and systemic responses occur, depending on the extent of the burn injury. As a result of destruction and damage of tissue at the burn site, the following reactions occur:

Table 24-1 Classification of Burns by Depth

Type	Characteristics
Superficial partial thickness (first degree)	Involves only epidermis; results in pain and redness
Partial thickness (second degree)	Involves the epidermis and corium; produces pain, redness, and blisters
Deep partial thickness (third degree)	White and dry; reduced sensitivity to touch and pain; blanches with pressure
Full-thickness burns (fourth degree)	Tough, tannish brown surface; dry; does not blanch with pressure

1. loss of microbial barrier: increases chances of serious infection
2. loss of fluid barrier: increases fluid loss at site of injury
3. loss of temperature control: increases the risk of hypothermia

Systemic responses occur depending on the severity of the burn and result in burn shock. Burn shock results from a capillary leak that allows plasma to leak from the tissue. In burns greater than 15–30% of the body surface area (BSA), a generalized leak occurs throughout the body, not just at the site of the injury. This process occurs for 24 hours after the injury and then resolves.

Systemic responses include the following:

- cardiovascular. Cardiac output decreases up to 50% of normal due to decreases in circulating volume. This occurs because of the capillary leak into the interstitial space.
- renal. Renal blood flow decreases leading to decreased urine output. Tubular necrosis can occur due to myoglobin released by damaged muscle cells and hemoglobin released by hemolysis of red blood cells. Acute renal failure can occur if fluid resuscitation is inadequate.
- pulmonary. Pulmonary injury may occur from inhalation injuries, especially if the burn occurred in a closed place. Upper airway edema may follow administration of large amounts of fluid.

Other systemic responses affect the gastrointestinal system, resulting in ileus and possible ulcers due to increased secretions of stomach acids. In children the stress response may result in hypoglycemia because of inadequate glycogen stores.

The common causes of burn injuries in the different age groups include the following:

1. scalding. Scald burns caused by hot liquids usually occur among toddlers and preschool-aged children.
2. electrical. Electrical burns occur often in children less than 2 years of age, usually resulting from chewing on an electrical cord.
3. fire. Flame burns are most common in school-aged children and adolescents, resulting from playing with matches or flammable liquids.
4. sunburn. Sunburn occurs in all age groups, but typically in toddlers and preschoolers; it can be superficial partial thickness or partial thickness (first or second degree).

TRIAGE ASSESSMENT

The triage assessment occurs simultaneously with the initial treatment of the child and includes the following:

- determination of type of burn
- estimation of the extent of the burn, usually based on body surface area (Lund and Browder chart commonly used; Exhibit 24-1)
- estimation of the severity of the burn (American Burn Association classification according to criteria listed in Exhibit 24-2)
- possible referral to a burn unit after stabilization

The American College of Surgeons recommends that all children with burns classified as major be transferred to a burn center. Children with electrical burns, inhalation injuries, or significant burns around the face as well as children with lesser burn injuries who have pre-existing conditions should also be transferred.

TRIAGE HISTORY

- mechanism and time of burn injury
- pre-existing conditions, current medications
- possibility of smoke inhalation
- possibility of child abuse

The possibility of child abuse needs to be considered if the story doesn't fit the extent or mechanism of injury. Types of findings that are commonly found with child abuse include:

- circumferential burns of the feet
- circumferential burns of the buttocks
- cigarette burns
- extensive scalding injuries
- existing areas of scarring that may be the result of old, inflicted burns

TELEPHONE TRIAGE GUIDELINES

Generally, all burns should be evaluated by a physician since it is difficult to assess the extent of the burn and the family situation over the phone. The nurse's telephone advice can, however, be guided by the location and extent of the burn, age of the child, mechanism of the injury, and the possibility of other injuries.

Any child with a burn injury that involves the eyes, face, ears, hands, feet, or perineum should be seen by a physician as soon as possible despite how minor it seems. Children with electrical burns need to be evaluated immediately.

Exhibit 24-1 The Lund and Browder Chart

RELATIVE PERCENTAGES OF AREAS AFFECTED BY GROWTH

	Age					
Area	0	1	5	10	15	Adult
A = 1/2 of Head	9 1/2	8 1/2	6 1/2	5 1/2	4 1/2	3 1/2
B = 1/2 of One Thigh	2 3/4	3 1/4	4	4 1/4	4 1/2	4 3/4
C = 1/2 of One Leg	2 1/2	2 1/2	2 3/4	3	3 1/4	3 1/2

% BURN BY AREAS

Probable 3rd° { Head_____Neck_____Body_____Up. Arm_____Forearm_____Hands_____
Burn   Genitals_____Buttocks_____Thighs_____Legs_____Feet_____

Total Burn { Head_____Neck_____Body_____Up. Arm_____Forearm_____Hands_____
                Genitals_____Buttocks_____Thighs_____Legs_____Feet_____

Sum of All Areas   Probable 3rd° _____ Total Burn_____

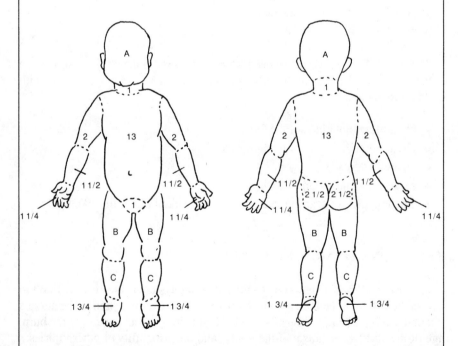

Source: Reprinted with permission from *Surgery, Gynecology, and Obstetrics*, Vol. 79, p. 356, © 1947. Drawing courtesy of Chris Gustauson.

Exhibit 24-2 Classification of the Severity of Burns in Children

---

MINOR BURN INJURY
10% BSA* in children
2% BSA, full-thickness injury without cosmetic or functional risk to eyes, ears, face, hands, feet, or perineum

MODERATE BURN INJURY
10–20% BSA mixed partial and full thickness in children under 10
10% or less BSA full thickness that does not present serious threat of functional or cosmetic impairment of the eyes, ears, face, hands, feet, or perineum

MAJOR BURN INJURY
20% BSA in children
10% or greater BSA full-thickness injury
All burns to face, eyes, ears, hands, feet, or perineum likely to result in functional or cosmetic impairment
All burn injuries complicated by inhalation injury or major trauma

*BSA = body surface area.

When giving advice about minor burns, the nurse should inform the family to watch for signs and symptoms of infection in the area and to avoid putting substances like butter on the injury. The nurse should not recommend that other ointments be used; if there is a question about this, the child should be evaluated by a physician.

PRIORITY RATING

Emergent: All major burn injuries as classified by the ABA, and those associated with major trauma, respiratory distress, or child abuse.

Urgent: Electrical burns, moderate burn injuries, child is awake and in minimal pain. Airway is not affected.

Nonurgent: Minor burn injury. Child is awake, alert, in little or no pain.

TREATMENT AND NURSING CARE

Moderate to Severe Burns

1. Stop the burning process (usually done by prehospital care providers).
   - Flames: Smother with blankets or water; remove smoldering clothes.

- Scalds: Cool.
- Chemical burns: Dilute with copious amounts of water.
- Tar, asphalt: Cool; leave material in place.

2. Assess and support airway and breathing. The burned child should be treated as a trauma victim. Inhalation injury should be suspected based on the mechanism of injury and signs and symptoms and treated. Table 24-2 lists signs and symptoms of smoke inhalation.

- Provide supplemental oxygen.
- Prepare for intubation—may need to be done early even if respiratory distress does not appear severe, especially if circumferential injuries of the chest are present.
- Obtain vital signs (temperature, pulse, respirations, and blood pressure). Weigh child, if possible, or estimate weight.

3. Assess and support circulation.

- Insert IV line; may need a cutdown or central line. Fluid replacement is the main objective in burn resuscitation. Fluids are commonly given based on the Parkland formula shown in Exhibit 24-3.
- Insert Foley catheter to measure urine output. Children should have 1–2 ml/kg/h of urine.
- Insert NG tube to decompress stomach and prevent aspiration.
- Attach cardiac monitor—especially important in electrical injuries to detect dysrhythmias.
- Remove watches, rings, and clothing that might restrict circulation to the extremities.

Table 24-2 Signs and Symptoms of Inhalation Injury

Type of Inhalation Injury	Signs/Symptoms
1. Carbon monoxide: replaces oxygen on hemoglobin molecules; suspect when burn occurs in a closed space	Headache, confusion, coma
2. Upper airway injury: burn to face, nose, mouth	Signs and symptoms of respiratory distress; requires *early* intubation due to increased pharyngeal edema.
3. Pulmonary injury: chemical injury to lungs (not common in pediatrics)	Signs and symptoms may be absent for 48–72 h; presents as hypoxemia and respiratory distress syndrome (RDS)

Exhibit 24-3 The Parkland Formula for Fluid Resuscitation

---

4 cc of lactated Ringer's per percent of TBSA* burn/wt in kg:
1/2 given in the first 8 h after the burn occurred (not after admission)
1/4 given in the second 8 h after the burn occurred
1/4 given in the third 8 h after the burn occurred

Note: The Parkland formula is one formula that is used. Formulas only provide a starting guideline for therapy. Ongoing monitoring of the response of the child is of the utmost importance in guiding fluid resuscitation.

*TBSA = total body surface area.

- Keep child warm; hypothermia is often a problem due to increased heat loss from the injury.
4. Assess for other injuries.
   - Perform complete primary and secondary assessment as described in Chapter 21.
   - Consider head injuries. An unconscious child should be considered to be unconscious from an etiology other than the burn injury (carbon monoxide poisoning, head trauma, etc.).
   - Consider orthopedic trauma commonly associated with burns.
5. Initiate diagnostic studies as ordered.
   - complete blood count with differential
   - blood chemistries: BUN, creatinine, electrolytes, glucose, albumin, and globulin levels, coagulation studies
   - arterial blood gases (ABGs) (carboxyhemoglobin if concerned about smoke inhalation)
   - urinalysis (hemoglobin and myoglobin)
   - 12-lead electrocardiogram (ECG) for electrical burns
   - x-rays as indicated
6. Give medications as ordered. All medications except tetanus should be given intravenously because fluid shifts cause unpredictable absorption.
   - Pain management: morphine or meperidine hydrochloride (Demerol) is commonly ordered. May need to consult with burn center for recommendations.
   - Tetanus prophylaxis (see Chapter 3)
7. Prevent infection.
   - Wear gloves, cap, masks.
   - Use sterile technique for all procedures.

8. Care for the burn wound.
   - Wash with mild soap and water.
   - Cover with clean sheet and blankets.
   - Don't apply ointments.
9. Support the child and family.
   - Involve parents and explain all procedures.
   - Talk to the child according to developmental level, age.
   - Prepare for admission and/or transfer to the burn unit.

Minor Burns

1. Assess and support ABCs.
2. Assess for associated injuries.
3. Provide wound care:
   - Clean with bland soap and water.
   - Remove blisters and devitalized tissue.
   - Shave hair adjacent to wound in a 2-inch perimeter of unburned area around wound. Never shave eyebrows.
   - Apply bland ointment such as bacitracin.
   - Leave open or wrap lightly with Kerlex; don't use an occlusive or compression dressing.
   - Provide instructions for follow-up care.
   - Encourage active range of motion.

PARENT TEACHING

Prevention should always be a part of nursing care, especially in the child who has a minor burn and will go home. Preventive teaching is based on the age and the developmental level of the child. The nurse should be aware of the different types of burns that are common for each age group. Prevention is discussed in detail in Chapter 3.

NURSING DOCUMENTATION

- initial assessment and history, including type and extent of burn
- interventions and response to interventions; fluids, monitoring, pain management

- vital signs every 15 min until stable
- follow-up care if child is being discharged

A complete copy of the child's record should be sent to the burn unit if the child is referred.

NURSING DIAGNOSES

- ineffective airway clearance related to edema and/or smoke inhalation
- ineffective breathing patterns related to edema caused by burns to the chest
- fluid volume deficit related to burn shock
- impaired skin integrity related to burn
- potential for infection related to loss of skin barrier
- hypothermia related to increased heat loss due to impaired skin integrity
- fear related to ED procedures and burn injury
- alteration in comfort, pain related to burn
- alteration in family process related to child's injury (i.e., guilt feelings of parents)

NOTE

1. Mary K. East, et al., "Epidemiology of Burns in Children," in *Burns in Children: Pediatrics Burn Management,* ed. Hugo F. Carvajal and Donald H. Parks (Chicago: Year Book Medical Publishers, 1988), 3.

BIBLIOGRAPHY

American College of Surgeons Committee on Trauma. *Advanced Trauma Life Support Course,* student manual. Chicago: American College of Surgeons, 1984.

Carvajal, H., and D. Parks, eds. *Burns in Children: Pediatric Burn Management.* Chicago: Year Book Medical Publishers, 1988.

Cohen, C. "Burn Injuries in Children." *Pediatric Annals* 16 (1987): 328–29.

Ludwig, S. *Pediatric Emergencies.* New York: Churchill Livingstone, 1985.

Parish, R. "Smoke Inhalation and Carbon Monoxide Poisoning in Children." *Pediatric Emergency Care* 2 (1986): 36–39.

Saffle, J. "Emergency Care of the Burn Patient." Unpublished handout, 1988.

Sheehy, S., J. Marvin, and C. Jimmerson. *Manual of Clinical Trauma Care.* St. Louis: C.V. Mosby Co., 1989.

Surveyer, J., and J. Halpern. "Age Related Burn Injuries and Their Prevention." *Pediatric Nursing* (Sept./Oct. 1981): 29–34.

Part VIII

Poisoning and Overdose

Chapter 25

Poisoning: An Overview

Louis V. Melini

INTRODUCTION

Poisoning is frequently seen in an emergency department and 63% of all exposures occur in children below the age of 5 years.[1] Poisoning can involve ingested, inhaled, or absorbed substances. Referrals may come from the emergency medical services (EMS), or the local poison control center (PCC), or children may be brought directly from home by their parents. Children arrive in various states of toxicity, which must be taken into account when treatment is initiated.

From 1955 to 1985, the death rate per 100,000 population almost doubled from 0.9 to 1.7.[2] Opiates and related narcotic deaths in the 25- to 44-year-old age group have accounted for most of the increase in the total. The death rate for the 0- to 4-year age group has fallen from 1.9 in 1955 to 0.3 in 1985,[3] possibly related to the development of childproof containers.

PATHOPHYSIOLOGY

The effects of a substance vary with its type. Specific toxins act on specific organs or body systems.[4]

1. cellular level: cyanide
2. brain: narcotics, hypnotic sedatives, major tranquilizers
3. autonomic nervous system: organophosphates
4. lungs: mineral or seal oil, paraquat
5. gastrointestinal tract: caustics and corrosives
6. liver: acetaminophen
7. blood: heavy metals

The age of the child will influence the effects of the poison in terms of absorption, distribution, metabolism, and excretion. These factors need to be considered when treatment is given.

The causes of poisoning in children vary with the age group, but are usually the following:

- less than 1 year old: unintentional parental misuse of a drug, or child abuse
- toddlers: often a result of curiosity and the tendency to explore with the mouth
- preadolescent, adolescent, and teenage: poisoning may be intentional, such as a suicide attempt

Although the majority of poisonings occur in the home, incidents may occur anywhere medications and toxic substances are stored.

TRIAGE ASSESSMENT

- airway, breathing, circulation (the ABCs)
- vital signs: temperature, pulse, respiration, blood pressure (TPR, BP)
- level of consciousness
- perfusion (capillary refill time)
- pupils
- unusual odors, any spills on clothes
- burns in or around mouth

Table 25-1 lists signs and symptoms associated with various drug groups.

TRIAGE HISTORY

The history is very important in determining the presence of poisoning but should not delay needed treatment. The following information should be obtained:

- source of exposure
- symptoms present
- nature of toxin (check container if available)
- other toxins or medications kept in home
- time since exposure
- amount involved
- treatment given prior to admission to ED
- assessment of intent; accidental, therapeutic, suicide attempt

Table 25-1 Signs and Symptoms of Various Drug Intoxications

Signs/Symptoms	*Drug or Drug Classification*
Hyperthermia	Aspirin
	Acetaminophen
	Amphetamines
	Atropine
	β-Blockers
	Organophosphates
	Anticholinergics
	Withdrawal from alcohol or narcotics
Hypothermia	Alcohol
	Anesthetics
	Barbiturates
	Carbon monoxide
	Phenothiazines
	Narcotics
	Tricyclic antidepressants
Tachycardia	Amphetamines
	Phencyclidine (PCP)
	Sympathomimetics
	Thyroid replacement drugs
	Narcotic withdrawal
Bradycardia	Digitalis
	β-Blockers
	Calcium channel blockers
	Clonidine
Depressed respirations	Sedative hypnotics and narcotics
	Alcohol
Increased respirations	Pulmonary aspiration of hydrocarbons
	Smoke inhalation resulting in pulmonary edema
	Ethylene glycol, methanol, salicylates, which all result in metabolic acidosis
	Theophylline
	Amphetamines
	Phenothiazines
Hypertension	Amphetamines
	PCP
	Sympathomimetics
	Thyroid replacement drugs
	Narcotic or sedative withdrawal
	Nicotine
	Tricyclic antidepressants

continues

Table 25-1 continued

Signs/Symptoms	Drug or Drug Classification
Hypotension	β-blockers Sedative, hypnotic, or narcotic drugs Tricyclic antidepressants
Seizures	Tricyclic antidepressants Narcotics, sedatives Lidocaine Cocaine Caffeine Aminophylline Pesticides
Psychotic reactions	Hallucinogens (PCP, LSD) Sympathomimetics Heavy metals
Small pupils (miosis)	Narcotics Barbiturates Cholinergics Clonidine
Large pupils (mydriasis)	Anticholinergics: also produce urinary retention, dry mucous membranes and flushed skin
Salivation, lacrimation, urination, defecation, gastrointestinal cramps, emesis (SLUDGE)	Cholinergics
Sweating, salivation, miosis, muscle fasciculation, bronchospasm, bradycardia (SMB2)	Organophosphates and carbamates

Source: American Academy of Pediatrics and American College of Emergency Physicians, *Advanced Pediatric Life Support* (Elk Grove Village, Ill.: American Academy of Pediatrics; and Dallas: American College of Emergency Physicians, 1989), 133; J. Arena, *Poisoning: Toxicology, Symptoms, Treatments,* 4th ed. (Springfield, Ill.: Charles C Thomas, Publisher, 1986), 15–19; R. Barkin and P. Rosen, *Emergency Pediatrics,* 2d ed. (St. Louis: C.V. Mosby Co., 1986), 268.

TELEPHONE TRIAGE GUIDELINES

Questions should be asked of the parents as listed under "Triage History." The parents should be advised to call the local poison control center (PCC) if the nurse is uncertain about the toxicity of the product. The nurse may call the PCC, keeping the parents on the line while this is done, especially if the parents are very upset.

The parents may be told to call the EMS for assistance if the child is symptomatic (seizures, coma, respiratory distress). The child should be seen in the ED immediately if a fast-acting or potentially toxic poison is involved. Children less than 1 year old should be seen as soon as possible. The parents can be instructed to give ipecac (discussed later in this chapter) unless contraindicated.

Poisoning should be suspected in a child with the following symptoms or history:[5]

- abrupt onset of illness without any explanation, especially a convulsion or decreased level of consciousness without fever
- illness involving multiple organ systems
- unusual odor from the child's mouth
- unexplained hematemesis

PRIORITY RATING

Emergent: Child with a known ingestion who is comatose or has an altered level of consciousness or is experiencing seizure activity or respiratory difficulty. Child who has ingested a potentially toxic amount of a potent drug (especially narcotics, tricyclic antidepressants) who may be currently asymptomatic but has the potential for deteriorating rapidly. Child who has ingested an unknown poison; considered emergent until ingestion (type, amount, time) is known.

Nonurgent: Child known to have ingested a nontoxic substance as listed in Exhibit 25-1.

TREATMENT AND NURSING CARE

The principles of management for the poisoned child include:

1. Initial stabilization. This may include the following:
   - support of the ABCs; supplemental oxygen, intubation, mechanical ventilation
   - IV line
   - cardiac monitor, oxygen saturation monitor

Exhibit 25-1 A Partial Listing of Frequently Ingested Nontoxic Products

Antibiotics	Felt tip markers
Antacids	Glues
Baby product cosmetics	Hair products
Ball point pen ink	Incense
Bubble baths	Laxatives
Calamine lotion (without topical	Makeup
diphenhydramine hydrochloride, or	Matches
Benedryl)	Paint
Candles	Petroleum jelly
Chalk	Rubber cement
Clay	Shampoo (liquid)
Colognes	Shaving cream
Contraceptives (oral)	Soaps
Cosmetics	Suntan lotions
Crayons	Teething rings
Deodorant	Toothpaste
Fabric softeners	Zinc oxide

Source: Committee on Accident and Poison Prevention: American Academy of Pediatrics, *Handbook of Common Poisonings in Children,* 2d ed. (Evanston, Ill.: American Academy of Pediatrics, 1983), 18–19.

2. Identifying the poison.
   - history
   - physical examination
   - laboratory diagnosis
3. Preventing or decreasing absorption of the poison. Three methods of preventing or decreasing absorption of ingested poisoning are as follows:
   - inducing emesis with syrup of ipecac
   - administering gastric lavage
   - administering activated charcoal

These three methods are compared in Table 25-2.

4. Hastening elimination of the poison. Cathartics are sometimes used in conjunction with charcoal to hasten elimination from the gastrointestinal tract. Other methods include hemodialysis and ion trapping (changing the pH of the urine so that the drug is excreted more readily). This method is used in salicylate poisoning.
5. Providing symptomatic care.
   - frequent monitoring of vital signs
   - frequent observation of neurological status
   - arranging for hospital admission if appropriate

Table 25-2 Preventing or Decreasing Absorption of Poisons: Comparison of Ipecac, Gastric Lavage, and Activated Charcoal

Description	Dose/How Given	Indications/Contraindications	Comments/Nursing Considerations
Ipecac syrup	< 1 yr: 10 mL 1–8 yr: 15 mL > 8 yr: 30 mL Given PO, vomiting should occur in 20 min. Dose may be repeated after 20 min if vomiting does not occur.	Given to induce vomiting in the conscious child when the ingestion is known. Contraindicated in: • Children less than 6 months of age • Children with a decreased level of consciousness or the potential to develop a decreased LOC • Ingestions of corrosives, petroleum distillates, or tricyclic antidepressants	Ipecac should only be given after the child has been assessed, the drug is known, and the amount and time of the ingestion have been considered. Give with 4–8 oz water. (Studies have not shown that large amounts of oral fluids hasten vomiting time.) Because of the danger of aspiration, ipecac should never be given to a child with a decreased level of consciousness or when the potential exists for a decrease in consciousness, such as with tricyclic antidepressant ingestions. Gastric lavage should be done if vomiting does not occur after two doses of ipecac. Overdose of ipecac may result in cardiotoxicity.

continues

Table 25-2 continued

Description	Dose/How Given	Indications/Contraindications	Comments/Nursing Considerations
Gastric lavage	Insertion of a large-bore orogastric (OG) or nasogastric (NG) tube into the stomach and instilling normal saline in an attempt to remove the poison. Saline may be instilled by continuous infusion or by intermittent instillation. 15 mL/kg is the recommended amount of lavage fluid to use.	Recommended when the risk of aspiration is high (if the airway is protected), in the unconscious child, or when the potential for seizures exists. Contraindicated in: • Caustic or corrosive ingestions • Uncontrolled convulsions • Coma, unless endotracheal tube is inserted • Significant dysrhythmias (due to vagal stimulation) • Certain petroleum distillate hydrocarbons due to risk of aspiration pneumonia	The child who is unconscious should be intubated prior to lavage. If the child is not intubated, place on left side with head lower than hips to prevent aspiration.
Activated charcoal	1–2 g/kg mixed with 100 mL water. Sorbitol may be used to increase intestinal passage of charcoal. Given orally or by NG tube.	Used for substances rapidly absorbed by charcoal. Charcoal does not absorb iron, boric acid, caustics, corrosives, cyanide, lead, and common electrolytes. Contraindications: • Ingestion of caustics or corrosives • Child with absent bowel sounds • When oral antidotes will be given	Difficult to administer due to appearance and taste; usually must be given via NG tube. Repeated doses of charcoal with sorbitol may result in electrolyte imbalances. Aspiration of charcoal is a serious side effect. Administer charcoal slowly to prevent overdistention of the stomach and vomiting.

Note: In many institutions, giving ipecac as the initial treatment has been replaced by performing gastric lavage in some circumstances. The effectiveness of early administration of activated charcoal is being evaluated. Administering ipecac will delay the administration of activated charcoal due to ipecac's emetic effects. Performing lavage allows activated charcoal to be given sooner. These procedures should be performed based on the ingested substance, time of ingestion, and condition of the child.

6. Giving appropriate antidote. Antidotes specific to every poison are not available. Some antidotes that may be used in the ED include:

- *N*-acetylcysteine: acetaminophen overdose (see Chapter 26)
- Naloxone: narcotic overdoses
- Deferoxamine: iron overdoses
- Diphenhydramine: phenothiazine overdose
- Glucagon: β-blocker overdose

The local poison control center should always be contacted for information on treating specific poisonings.

Although all cases of poisoning in children follow the same general guidelines, specific treatment may vary depending on the drug ingested. Chapter 26 discusses specific treatments for some common poisonings seen in children.

PARENT TEACHING

- Store all cleaning solutions out of the reach of children. Put safety locks on all cabinets.
- Keep all medications out of the reach of children. Do not store any medications in a purse.
- Keep all medications and cleaning products in original containers.
- Do not refer to medicine as candy.
- Check to be sure that household plants are not poisonous.
- Check garage and basements to be sure all paints, solvents, and fertilizers are out of the reach of children.
- Have syrup of ipecac available.
- Know the number for the local poison control center.

Many emergency departments have a policy that requires a public health nurse to inspect the home of any child who has been seen for a poisoning incident. The nurse should consider the possibility of child abuse in repeated cases, and when the ingestion occurs in a child over the age of 5 years or under the age of 1 year.

NURSING DOCUMENTATION

- history (parameters as listed in "Triage Assessment" section)
- signs and symptoms
- interventions and child's response to emesis or lavage
- vital signs

- referral for psychiatric evaluation for suicide attempt (psychiatric evaluation should be done in the ED on all children who have attempted suicide)
- disposition of child, discharge instructions

NURSING DIAGNOSES

- ineffective breathing patterns related to depression of central nervous system
- potential for aspiration related to lavage and administration of charcoal
- potential for injury related to ingestion
- alteration in comfort related to ED procedures (e.g., lavage and emesis)
- anxiety of parent and child related to child's condition and procedures
- knowledge deficit (of parent) related to preventive measures
- altered parenting/family processes related to suicide attempt or child abuse

---

NOTES

1. Jay Schauben, Howard Mofenson, and Thomas Caraccio, "Problems in the Management of Intoxications," in *Problems in Pediatric Emergency Medicine*, ed. Robert C. Luten (New York: Churchill Livingstone, 1988): 245, 250, 252–53.

2. American Safety Council, *Accident Facts* (Chicago: American Safety Council, 1988).

3. Ibid.

4. American Academy of Pediatrics and the American College of Emergency Physicians, *Advanced Pediatric Life Support* (Elk Grove Village, Ill.: The American Academy of Pediatrics; and Dallas: The American College of Emergency Physicians, 1989), 131.

5. Schauben, Mofenson, and Caraccio, "Problems in the Management of Intoxications," 245, 250, 252–253.

BIBLIOGRAPHY

Arena, J.M., and R.H. Drew, eds. *Poisoning: Toxicology, Symptoms, Treatment*, 4th ed. Springfield, Ill.: Charles C. Thomas, Pub., 1986.

Arnold, M. "Ipecac: When Prevention Fails." *American Journal of Diseases of Children* 142 (1988): 595.

Banner, W., and J. Veltri. "The Case for Ipecac Syrup." *American Journal of Diseases in Children* 142 (1988): 596.

Dreisbach, R., and W. Robertson. *Handbook of Poisoning*, 12th ed. Norwalk, Conn.: Appleton & Lange, 1987.

Dymoski, J., and D. Vehara. "Common Household Poisonings." *Pediatric Emergency Care* 3 (1987): 261–65.

Fazen, L., F. Lovejoy, and R. Crone. "Acute Poisoning in a Children's Hospital: A Two Year Experience." *Pediatrics* 77 (1986): 144–51.

Gernsheimer, J., and R. Roberge. "The Comatose Overdose." *Hospital Physican* (January 1985): 28–45.

Grbeich, P., P. Lacouture, and F. Lovejoy. "Effect of Fluid Volume on Ipecac Induced Emesis." *Journal of Pediatrics* 110 (1987): 970–72.

Litovitz, T., et al. "Ipecac Administration in Children Younger than One Year." *Pediatrics* 76 (1985): 761–64.

McClung, H., et al. "Intentional Ipecac Poisoning in Children." *American Journal of Diseases of Children* 142 (1988): 637–39.

Newton, M., et al. "Descriptive Outline of Major Poisoning Treatment Modes." *Journal of Emergency Nursing* 13 (1987): 102–06.

Rosenstein, B., and P. Fosarelli. *Pediatric Pearls: The Handbook of Practical Pediatrics.* Chicago: Year Book Medical Publishers, 1989.

Steele, P., and D. Spyker. "Poisonings." *Pediatric Clinics of North America* 32 (1985): 77–85.

Wong, D. "Dispelling Some Myths About Ipecac." *American Journal of Nursing* 88 (1988): 952.

Chapter 26

Common Ingestions

Louis V. Melini

INTRODUCTION

This chapter discusses specific treatment for some common poisonings seen in children brought to the emergency department. The following poisonings are discussed:

1. acetaminophen
2. corrosives
3. hydrocarbons
4. iron
5. salicylates
6. tricyclic antidepressants

Initial triage assessment and stabilization of airway, breathing, and circulation (the ABCs) are discussed in the previous chapter.

ACETAMINOPHEN

Acetaminophen is one of the most commonly used drugs for analgesia and antipyresis in children. Ingestions occur most frequently in children under age 6, but may be associated with suicide attempts in the adolescent and preadolescent child. An ingestion greater than 140 mg/kg is considered toxic.

Signs and Symptoms

1. Stage 1 (first 24 hours after ingestion): Nausea, vomiting, diaphoresis occur.

239

2. Stage 2 (second 24 hours after ingestion): Patient may be asymptomatic; liver enzymes may be elevated.

3. Stage 3 (48–95 hours after ingestion): Abnormal liver enzymes are present; death can occur from hepatic failure.

4. Stage 4 (7–8 days after ingestion): Hepatic abnormalities resolve in survivors.

Treatment and Nursing Care

Treatment is often based on estimated amount of drug ingested. Drug levels can be obtained to estimate toxicity. They need to be obtained 4 hours after the ingestion occurred.

1. If estimated dose taken is 70–140 mg/kg
   - induce vomiting with ipecac; check emesis for pill fragments
   - give charcoal and cathartic via NG tube
   Hepatotoxicity is rare with this dose.

2. If dose taken is greater than 140 mg/kg
   - induce emesis or lavage
   - don't give charcoal unless ingestion occurred within 2 hours of ED admission or other drugs are involved
   - Obtain drug levels
   - N-Acetylcysteine (NAC) may be ordered to be given orally depending on blood levels. NAC acts to detoxify acetaminophen metabolites, preventing liver damage associated with toxic doses of acetaminophen. Activated charcoal absorbs the NAC.

CORROSIVES

Corrosives include chemicals such as drain cleaners, dishwasher detergents, and household cleaning products often containing oxalic acid. Corrosives can be ingested, inhaled, or spilled on the skin or in the eyes.

Signs and Symptoms

1. Ingestions
   - burning pain in mouth, pharynx and abdomen
   - vomiting and diarrhea

- burns around the mouth
- edema to the glottis (can result in asphyxia)

2. Inhalation
   - coughing and choking
   - headache or dizziness
   - respiratory distress

3. Skin or eye contact
   - severe pain
   - brownish or yellow stains, burns
   - conjunctival edema and destruction of the cornea
   - pain, photophobia, tearing

Treatment and Nursing Care

1. Ingestions
   - Do not induce vomiting or do gastric lavage.
   - Dilute with large quantities of water or milk.
   - Provide pain relief if appropriate.
   - Prepare child for admission; esophagoscopy may be necessary.

2. Inhalation
   - Maintain airway; provide supplemental oxygen and be prepared for emergency airway management.
   - Observe for signs and symptoms of pulmonary edema and shock.

3. Skin or eye contact
   - Dilute with copious amounts of water for at least 15 minutes.
   - Obtain ophthalmology consult as soon as possible for eye contact.
   - Treat thermal burns of the skin. Consult with regional burn center if necessary.

HYDROCARBONS

Hydrocarbons are carbon compounds that are liquid at room temperature and include solvents, fuels, and petroleum distillates. The major concern is aspiration and the development of chemical pneumonitis, but CNS symptoms can develop.

Signs and Symptoms

- nausea and vomiting
- cough and pulmonary irritation
- CNS depression
- dizziness and weakness (may indicate chronic poisoning by inhalation)

Treatment and Nursing Care

- Provide respiratory support as necessary.
- Induce vomiting for compounds that may have CNS toxicity (see Chapter 25) unless the child has a decreased level of consciousness.
- Induce vomiting for compounds that are unlikely to cause systemic symptoms (gasoline, kerosene, charcoal lighter fluid) only when large amounts have been ingested and spontaneous vomiting has not occurred.
- Obtain chest x-ray in symptomatic children and prepare child for possible admission to the hospital.
- Observe asymptomatic children in the ED for 4–6 hours for the development of respiratory symptoms.
- Activated charcoal is not useful in absorbing hydrocarbons.

IRON

Ingestion of iron often occurs with ingestion of children's chewable multivitamins. The ingestion of 20–60 mg/kg of iron is considered mild to moderate, while ingestions greater than 60 mg/kg are considered severe. Serum iron levels drawn within 4 hours of ingestion help to determine toxicity. An iron level of greater than 300 μg/dL indicates that intoxication is likely; the lethal range is greater than 500 μg/dL.

Signs and Symptoms

1. Phase 1 (1/2–1 hour after ingestion)
   - vomiting and bloody diarrhea
   - metabolic acidosis
   - shock
   - coma

2. Phase 2 (6–24 hours after ingestion)—relative improvement of symptoms
3. Phase 3 (24–48 hours after ingestion)
   - delayed profound shock
   - acidosis
   - pulmonary edema
   - hepatic failure
   - coma
4. Phase 4 (1–2 months after ingestion)
   - gastric scarring
   - pyloric stenosis

Treatment and Nursing Care

- Induce vomiting if child is awake.
- Perform gastric lavage if child has depressed level of consciousness (may not be as effective as inducing vomiting due to size of pill fragments).
- Do not use activated charcoal because it will not bind with iron.
- Treat for shock.
- Administer deferoxamine (chelation therapy) as ordered, IV or IM, for severe toxicity.
- Prepare for admission to the hospital.

SALICYLATES

Salicylates are commonly found in many analgesics, such as in children's chewable aspirin, and oil of wintergreen. A dose of 500 mg/kg can be potentially lethal, while a dose of 300–500 mg/kg is considered serious. The incidence of salicylate poisoning has decreased probably due to childproof caps. Accidental intoxication may occur when a parent is unaware that a medication contains salicylates and gives additional doses of another salicylate-containing medication.

Signs and Symptoms

- nausea
- hyperventilation
- hyperglycemia (hypoglycemia in the young child)

- tinnitus
- oliguria
- disorientation, convulsions, coma
- bleeding (less common)

Treatment and Nursing Care

- Induce vomiting or perform gastric lavage.
- Obtain salicylate blood levels.
- Administer activated charcoal.
- Intravenous fluids for alkalinization of the blood may be ordered for moderate to severe ingestions.
- Observe for other signs and symptoms such as bleeding and seizures; treat as necessary.

TRICYCLIC ANTIDEPRESSANTS

Accidental ingestion of these drugs is becoming a problem in pediatrics. These drugs are often available in the household for therapy of depression or to treat enuresis. Toxic effects vary but have been noted after ingestion of one tablet in a child. The toxicity is related to anticholinergic properties; 30 mg/kg should be considered a potentially lethal dose in a child.

Signs and Symptoms

The following three categories of signs and symptoms suggest tricyclic ingestion:

1. Anticholinergic signs
   - fever
   - dry mouth
   - dysrhythmias (prolongation of the QRS complex occurs in some cases of severe overdoses)
   - flushing
   - dilated pupils
   - confusion and excitation
   - hypotension
   - seizures

2. Acute alteration of mental status
3. Sinus tachycardia

Treatment and Nursing Care

1. Begin gastric lavage.
   - Do not induce vomiting even if child is alert because mental status can deteriorate rapidly.
   - Perform intubation to protect the airway in the unconscious child prior to lavage.
2. Administer sodium bicarbonate.
   - Goal is a serum pH of 7.45–7.5.
   - Alkalinization increases protein binding and decreases circulating toxin.
3. Treat persistent dysrhythmias.
4. Treat hypotension.
5. Treat seizures.
6. Prepare for admission to the intensive care unit for further treatment.

INTENTIONAL POISONING (SUICIDE ATTEMPTS)

Although the majority of suicide attempts are made by people between the ages of 15 and 24 years, ingestions by children more than 5 years of age may indicate a suicide attempt. The nurse needs to be aware of the following factors that put children and adolescents at risk for suicide attempts:

- chronic physical illness
- history of depression
- family problems (divorce, alcoholism, or abuse)
- substance abuse
- history of previous attempts

Nursing care includes stabilization and the following:

- psychiatric evaluation
- safety (don't leave patient unattended)
- admission to the hospital or referral to outpatient program depending on the child's condition

BIBLIOGRAPHY

American Academy of Pediatrics and the American College of Emergency Physicians. *Advanced Pediatric Life Support.* Elk Grove Village, Ill.: The American Academy of Pediatrics; and Dallas: The American College of Emergency Physicians, 1989.

Arena, J. *Poisoning: Toxicology, Symptoms, Treatment,* 4th ed. Springfield, Ill.: Charles C Thomas, Pub., 1986.

Banner, W., and T. Tong. "Iron Poisoning." *Pediatric Clinics of North America* 33 (1986): 393–407.

Braden, N., J. Jackson, and P. Walson. "Tricyclic Antidepressant Overdose." *Pediatric Clinics of North America* 33 (1986): 287–97.

Dreisbach, R. and W. Robertson. *Handbook of Poisoning,* 12th ed. Norwalk, Conn.: Appleton & Lange, 1987.

Kelley, S., ed. *Pediatric Emergency Nursing.* Norwalk, Conn.: Appleton & Lange, 1988.

Rosenstein, B., and P. Fosarelli. *Pediatric Pearls: The Handbook of Practical Pediatrics.* Chicago: Year Book Medical Publishers, 1989.

Rothstein, F. "Caustic Injuries to the Esophagus in Children." *Pediatric Clinics of North America* 33 (1986): 665–74.

Rumack, B. "Acetaminophen Overdose in Children and Adolescents." *Pediatric Clinics of North America* 33 (1986): 691–701.

Snodgrass, W. "Salicylate Toxicity." *Pediatric Clinics of North America* 33 (1986): 381–91.

Temple, A. "Poisoning." In *Emergency Management of Pediatric Trauma,* edited by T. Mayer, 444–58. Philadelphia: W.B. Saunders Co., 1985.

Woodward, G. "Tricyclic Ingestions." Unpublished handout, 1989.

Part IX

Hematological Problems

Chapter 27

Hemophilia

Debra Ann Mills

INTRODUCTION

Hemophilia is a sex-linked recessive congenital disorder affecting 1 of every 10,000 males. This disorder is characterized by a deficiency or absence of blood-clotting factors that results in prolonged bleeding. The two most common types of hemophilia are as follows:

1. hemophilia A (classic hemophilia): deficiency of factor VIII or antihemophiliac factor (AHF), the protein needed for clot formation
2. hemophilia B (Christmas disease): deficiency of plasma thromboplastic component (PTC) or factor IX

Von Willebrand's disease is another type of bleeding disorder often included as a type of hemophilia characterized by moderate to severe factor VIII deficiency and absence of the factor that allows platelets to adhere to the walls of a ruptured vessel. It is caused by an autosomal dominant gene and can affect females as well as males. The clinical manifestations of hemophilia A and B are the same.

PATHOPHYSIOLOGY

When one of the clotting factors is inactive or defective, clotting time is prolonged. The clot formed is soft, mushy, and ineffective. Bleeding is prolonged due to the ineffective clot formation.

The severity of hemophilia is proportionate to the degree of factor deficiency and can be mild, moderate, or severe as listed in Table 27-1. Hemophilia is seldom diagnosed during infancy unless severe bleeding occurs following traumatic birth, severing of the umbilical cord, or during circumcision. Diagnosis is usually made

Table 27-1 Classification of Hemophilia

Severity of Hemophilia	% of Factor VIII or IX Present	Characteristics
Normal	50–150%	30% required for surgical hemostasis
Mild	5–50%	Excessive bleeding only after severe trauma, surgery, dental procedures
Moderate	2–5%	Occasional spontaneous hemorrhages following minor trauma. If joint injury repeated, dysfunction can occur. Partial thromboplastin times (PTT) prolonged
Severe	<1%	Frequent spontaneous hemorrhages, especially into joints and muscles. All coagulation tests abnormal.

Source: C. Miller, The Inheritance of Hemophilia (The National Hemophilia Foundation, 1986).

on the basis of prolonged bleeding episodes or a family history of hemophilia. Exhibit 27-1 lists common types of symptoms seen in the child with hemophilia.

TRIAGE ASSESSMENT

- airway, breathing, circulation (ABCs)
- level of consciousness (LOC)
- area of hemorrhage (estimate blood loss as necessary)
- vital signs: temperature, pulse, respirations, blood pressure
- presence of petechiae, ecchymoses, and/or hematoma, swelling, limited range of motion
- hydration status

TRIAGE HISTORY

- past medical history (may be helpful to get old medical records if available)
- time and mechanism of injury
- home care given

Exhibit 27-1 Clinical Manifestations of Hemophilia

JOINT BLEEDING (HEMARTHROSES)
Most common complication, often occurring in the absence of trauma.
Large joints (knees and elbows) often involved.
Bleeding into hip can cause aseptic necrosis to femoral head due to impeded blood flow.
Signs and symptoms include pain, immobility and swelling.

MUSCLE BLEEDING
Usually superficial.
Nerve function can be impaired with substantial blood loss.
Extensive hemorrhage most common in retroperitoneal or thigh bleeds.

SUBCUTANEOUS BLEEDING
May cause discoloration, but is rarely dangerous.
Pressure on the airway from subcutaneous bleed in neck may be life-threatening.

ORAL BLEEDING
Common in young children.
Common manifestation of von Willebrand's disease (epistaxis also common with this disease).
Airway compromise may occur from extensive bleeding of the tongue.

GASTROINTESTINAL BLEEDING
Rarely severe.

URINARY TRACT BLEEDING
Painless hematuria is common manifestation of renal bleeding.
If bleeding is persistent, anemia may occur.

INTRACRANIAL HEMORRHAGE
Most serious complication.
All hemophiliac children with head trauma need to be evaluated carefully for signs and symptoms of intracranial bleeding.

Source: J. Bender and A. Cohen, "Disorders of Coagulation," in *Textbook of Pediatric Emergency Medicine,* 2d ed., eds. G. Fleisher and S. Ludwig (Baltimore: Williams & Wilkins, 1988), 540–46.

- medications child is taking
- last factor replacement or 1-deamino-8-D-arginine vasopressin (DDAVP) or ε-aminocaproic acid (EACA) administration

TELEPHONE TRIAGE GUIDELINES

Any child who is unconscious or is experiencing any change in LOC, or who has difficulty breathing, tachycardia, or uncontrolled, active hemorrhaging should be considered an emergency and evaluated as soon as possible.

For suspected joint bleeding (hemarthrosis) the nurse should inquire about the location and intensity of the bleeding (pain and limitation of joint movement), home therapy (application of pressure and cold, elevation of extremity, and factor replacement), and response to therapy. If the child is alert and without signs and symptoms of shock, the parents can be instructed to call their physician but told that they may come to the emergency department for evaluation.

PRIORITY RATING

Emergent: Active hemorrhaging from a wound or artery, signs and symptoms of shock, head injury, bleeding in the neck (possibility of obstructed airway), abdominal or chest wall injuries.

Urgent: Moderate hemorrhaging, evidenced by hemarthrosis, severe pain, and/or limited motion.

Nonurgent: Factor VIII replacement therapy given at home, bleeding episode controlled, follow-up needed.

TREATMENT AND NURSING CARE

Treatment is aimed at controlling bleeding and preventing permanent disability. Nursing care of the child with an acute bleeding episode includes the following:

1. initial assessment and stabilization; the ABCs
   - Manage shock.
   - Control bleeding.
   - Check vital signs.
   - Assess for associated injuries or illnesses.
2. care of the affected area
   - Elevate and apply pressure to the affected area to allow clot formation.
   - Apply ice packs to promote vasoconstriction.
   - Immobilize and align affected extremity.
3. diagnostic studies
   - Initiate coagulation studies as ordered to determine percentage of factor activity present (not routinely done in the ED on children who are frequent patients for replacement therapy).
   - Arrange for x-rays as ordered depending on history and mechanism of injury.
4. administration of replacement therapy. The common types of replacement therapy and nursing implications are discussed in Table 27-2.

Table 27-2 Replacement Products Used in Hemophilia and Other Bleeding Disorders

Product	Uses	Comments/Nursing Implications
1. Fresh frozen plasma (contains both factor VIII and IX activity)	Newborn or infant with inherited but undefined bleeding disorder. Generally used in patients with mild or moderate factor IX deficiency.	Low concentration of factor VIII and IX (1 U/ml) restricts use in older children due to large volumes that must be given. Use microaggregate filter when administering. Prior to administration, obtain baseline vital signs. Do not mix any blood products with other medications.
2. Cryoprecipitate. Contains 60–125 units of factor VIII/bag)	Children with factor VIII deficiency. Smaller children who require less volume. Von Willebrand's disease.	Risk of post-transfusion hepatitis is low. Use microaggregate filter.
3. Factor VIII concentrates (Hemofil, Koate) contain 280–300 units of Factor VIII/bottle	Factor VIII deficiency—especially for major bleeding. Usual initial dose for minor bleeding is 20 U/kg.	All concentrates are heat treated to prevent transmission of HIV—higher risk of post-transfusion hepatitis because product is made from large pool of donors.
Factor IX concentrates (Konyne) contain 400–600 units of factor IX per bottle	Factor IX deficiency. Children with factor VIII deficiency with inhibitor (antibodies to factor VIII)	Concentrates must be mixed and drawn up through a special filter needle. May be given IV push. Convenient—many children can learn to administer at home. All concentrates are expensive. Much smaller volumes are needed than with fresh-frozen plasma or cryoprecipitate.
4. Adjunct therapies DDAVP (1-deamino-8-D-arginine vasopressin). Increases activity of factor VIII—does not increase synthesis of factor VIII	Minor bleeding episodes in children with mild hemophilia. Type I von Willebrand's disease.	All children do not respond to this therapy. Usual dose is 0.3 μg/kg IV over 30 min. Side effects include facial flushing and headaches. Second doses are not as effective.
EACA (Amicar), ε-aminocaproic acid—inhibits fibrinolysis	Oral bleeding in children older than 1 year. Usually used as an adjunct to other therapies.	Available in IV preparations/syrup or tablet form: usual dosage is 50 mg/kg every 6 h for 7 days. Do not administer IV push; must be given slowly when given by IV.

5. pain management
   - Immobilize and apply cold.
   - Give acetaminophen (aspirin products should be avoided because they interfere with platelet function).
   - Demerol may be needed for severe pain, but should not be used routinely.
6. infection control. Because of the numerous blood transfusions that children with hemophilia may have received, they are at increased risk for acquired immunodeficiency syndrome (AIDS) and hepatitis B. The nurse should maintain body substance isolation precautions as recommended by the Centers for Disease Control.
   - Wear gloves when starting intravenous infusion and when handling any secretions.
   - Wear mask and goggles during procedures that may result in splashing of body fluids (suctioning, laceration repair).

These guidelines should be followed routinely on all children when the nurse may come in contact with body fluids. Although hemophiliacs account for only a small percentage of pediatric AIDS victims, nurses should take the necessary precautions and look for signs of HIV infection. See Exhibit 27-2.

PARENT/PATIENT TEACHING

- Explain all procedures and tests.
- Allow participation of parent and child as appropriate.
- Teach accident prevention.
- Discuss recognition of signs of bleeding.
- Teach prevention of joint dysfunction.
- Teach avoidance of aspirin-containing products.
- Give Medic Alert bracelet.

Parents of children with hemophilia seen in the ED usually have routine medical care and are well versed in the disease. Local support groups may be available, or the parents can be given the following addresses for more information:

National Hemophilia Foundation
19 W. 34th Street
New York, NY 10011

NURSING DOCUMENTATION

- general assessment including level of consciousness, activity level, color, vital signs, and associated signs and symptoms
- condition upon arrival including presence of cold packs, immobilization devices, elevation of extremity
- diagnostic tests done
- therapeutic management
- response to therapy
- teaching on follow-up care and bleeding control

Exhibit 27-2 Pediatric AIDS

HIV TRANSMISSION
infants and children
- born to an HIV-positive mother (80%)
- received contaminated blood products (15%)
- hemophiliac (5%)
adolescents
- sexual activity
- sharing needles
- sexual abuse

SIGNS AND SYMPTOMS SUGGESTIVE OF HIV INFECTION
lymphadenopathy
hepatomegaly and/or splenomegaly
failure to thrive
bacteremia
oral thrush
opportunistic infections: *Pneumocystis carinii* pneumonia
recurrent fevers
chronic or recurrent diarrhea
wasting syndrome
developmental delay
acquired microcephaly
spastic paresis

Note: Although children with AIDS may be more prevalent in areas of the country with high numbers of IV drug users, it is very important to maintain universal precautions (gloves, masks, gowns, eye protection) when dealing with all children in the ED.

Source: E. Crain and L. Berstein, "Pediatric HIV Infection for the Emergency Physician: Epidemiology and Overview," *Pediatric Emergency Care* 6 (1990): 214–18.

NURSING DIAGNOSES

- alteration in comfort and/or pain related to injury
- potential for injury and bleeding
- impaired physical mobility due to bleeding into joints
- potential for ineffective coping and family dysfunction related to child's chronic condition
- knowledge deficit about hemophilia and its complications
- potential for infection of the nursing staff related to HIV or hepatitis
- fear of child related to ED procedures

BIBLIOGRAPHY

Aledort, L.M. *Current Management in the Treatment of Hemophilia: A Physician's Manual.* New York: National Hemophilia Foundation, 1986.

Behrman, R.E., and V.C. Vaughan, III, eds. *Nelson Textbook of Pediatrics,* 13th ed. Philadelphia: W.B. Saunders, 1987.

Bender, J., and A. Cohen. "Disorders of Coagulation." In *Textbook of Pediatric Emergency Medicine,* 2nd ed., edited by G. Fleisher and S. Ludwig, 540–46. Baltimore: Williams & Wilkins Co., 1988.

Eckert, E.F. *Your Child and Hemophilia.* New York: National Hemophilia Foundation, 1985.

Graf, J.W., and T.E. Cone, Jr., eds. *Manual of Pediatric Therapies,* 2d ed. Boston: Department of Medicine, Children's Hospital, 1986.

Kelley, S. "Hemophilia." In *Pediatric Emergency Nursing,* edited by S. Kelley, 301–04. Norwalk, Conn.: Appleton & Lange, 1988.

Landier, W.C., M.L. Barrell, and E.J. Styffe. "How to Administer Blood Products in Children." *Maternal Child Nursing.* (May/June 1987): 178–84.

Lanzkowsky, P. "Inherited Coagulation Factor Disorders." In *Manual of Pediatric Hematology,* edited by P. Lanzkowsky, 196–201. New York: Churchill Livingstone, 1989.

Miller, C. *The Inheritance of Hemophilia.* New York: National Hemophilia Foundation, 1986.

Sergis-Davenport, E., and J.W. Varni. "Overview of Hemophilia." *Issues in Comprehensive Pediatric Nursing,* (Sept./Oct. 1983): 317–18.

Whaley, L., and D. Wong. "Hemophilia." In *Nursing Care of Infants and Children,* edited by L. Whaley and D. Wong, 1541–46. St. Louis: C.V. Mosby Co., 1987.

Chapter 28

Sickle Cell Disease

Laurel S. Campbell

INTRODUCTION

Sickle cell anemia is a pathological process involving a gene in the hemoglobin that causes an increased susceptibility to hemoglobin aggregation and deformed red blood cells. These red blood cells form a "sickle" shape that does not pass freely through the capillary circulation, resulting in red blood cell stasis and occlusion in the circulation. This process has an approximate genetic frequency of 8% in black Americans.[1]

PATHOPHYSIOLOGY

Sickling in red blood cells results from the presence of sickling hemoglobin rather than normal hemoglobin. This abnormal hemoglobin causes the red blood cell to lose its ability to move through the circulation of a capillary without being destroyed. Vasocclusive crises, ischemia, chronic hemolytic anemia, infarction, and multisystem compromise occur as a result of the hemolysis and thrombosis of the sickled cells.

Vasocclusive crises are thought to be precipitated by factors such as stress, infection, cold exposure, and dehydration.[2] Microvascular obstruction by sickled cells leads to statis, ischemia, and acidosis. Clinically, these events cause deep, aching pain in the abdomen, chest, back, and extremities; low-grade fever; and tenderness, edema, and erythema of the hands and feet, especially in infants and small children. Chronic vasocclusion may result in progressive optic atrophy and blindness, progressive renal insufficiency, respiratory insufficiency, congestive heart failure, recurrent ischemic leg ulceration, arthropathy, and priapism (penile engorgement).

Potentially life-threatening complications associated with sickle cell disease include the following:

- aplastic crisis. The bone marrow of a child recovering from an infectious disease temporarily stops producing red cells, resulting in a profound anemia.
- splenic sequestration. A large volume of blood pools in the spleen and results in severe hypovolemia and shock. This occurs in 1–2% of children with sickle cell disease, usually before the age of 5 years, and is uncommon in older children and adolescents.[3]

Sickle cell disease is genetically determined. The most severe form, sickle cell anemia, occurs when the sickling gene is inherited from both parents. The sickle cell trait occurs when a sickle cell gene is inherited from one parent. Patients with sickle cell trait are generally asymptomatic.

TRIAGE ASSESSMENT

- airway, breathing, circulation (ABCs), level of consciousness
- vital signs: temperature, pulse, blood pressure, respiratory rate
- evidence of edema, erythema (abdominal, peripheral)
- signs of dehydration, congestive heart failure

TRIAGE HISTORY

- age of child
- precipitating events (high altitude, stress, infection, cold exposure, dehydration)
- viral precipitants (vomiting, diarrhea, fever, upper respiratory congestion)
- known presence of sickle cell disease or trait
- treatment done in the past to avert/treat crisis
- measures taken at home
- present history: activity level, present medications, allergies

TELEPHONE TRIAGE GUIDELINES

Since a differential diagnosis of the disease process in the child with an acute onset of pain could include osteomyelitis, appendicitis, pneumonia, or many other pathophysiological states, telephone triage must ascertain specific data:

- fever: low-grade; higher than 102° F, relieved by antipyretics
- pain: location, severity; measures taken to relieve the pain
- respirations: nonlabored; tachypnea, dyspnea

Parents may choose to try palliative measures at home with bedrest, analgesics, warm packs over painful areas, and PO fluids if the pain is mild and is relieved with over-the-counter analgesics and if the child is afebrile. A physician should always be consulted before the nurse recommends these measures.

The child should be evaluated by a physician if the pain is unrelieved, fever persists, respirations are labored, or if the child is lethargic, pale, or diaphoretic.

PRIORITY RATING

Emergent: Hemodynamically unstable child with signs of splenic sequestration (hypovolemic shock, altered level of consciousness); sepsis (fever > 102° F, meningeal signs, tachypnea, tachycardia, hypotension); or vasocclusive crisis (severe pain, tenderness unrelieved by acetylsalicylic acid (ASA) or acetaminophen) with hypoxia ($PaO_2 < 70$), respiratory distress.

Urgent: Hemodynamically stable child with mild-to-moderate pain in abdomen, chest, back, or extremities; signs of infection (lethargy, tachypnea, tachycardia, fever < 102° F); mild respiratory distress ($PaO_2 > 70$).

Nonurgent: Hemodynamically stable child with mild pain relieved with ASA or acetaminophen; no fever or respiratory distress.

TREATMENT AND NURSING CARE

Treatment of the child in sickle cell crisis is directed at providing stabilization and support, relieving pain, and determining the precipitant factor causing the crisis. Nursing care of the child in sickle cell crisis should begin with primary and secondary assessment measures:

1. airway: signs of respiratory distress
   - retractions
   - tachypnea
   - cyanosis
2. breathing
   - apnea
   - tachypnea

3. circulation: signs of hypovolemia
   - tachycardia
   - hypotension
   - low urinary output
   - dry mucous membranes
   - sunken anterior fontanelle
4. extremities
   - erythema
   - edema
   - pain
5. sources of infection
   - adventitious breath sounds
   - upper respiratory congestion
   - cloudy urine
   - hematuria
   - frequency of urination

Nursing care based on assessment findings includes the following interventions:

1. cooling measures, use of antipyretics
2. rehydration
   - oral or IV fluids as ordered
   - IV volume expanders (lactated Ringer's; 0.9% normal saline) for initial rehydration
3. pain management
   - Use therapeutic conversation as a distraction technique concurrently with prescribed analgesia.
   - Provide a comfortable environment.
   - Position extremities on pillows for comfort.
   - Use warm packs over affected extremities (cold packs may stimulate vasoconstriction and further ischemia).
4. treatment of priapism (penile engorgement) if necessary
   - Use cold packs and analgesia. (Do not apply ice or cold packs directly to penile tissue.)
   - Urological consultation may be necessary.

Diagnostic studies that might assist in the diagnosis of the precipitant as well as provide information on the patient's hemodynamic and metabolic state can include the following:

- complete blood count (CBC) with differential
- specimen cultures (urine, blood, spinal fluid, sputum)
- reticulocyte count
- arterial blood gases
- chest, extremity x-rays

PARENT TEACHING

Parents of children with sickle cell disease should be knowledgeable about many aspects of the disease, including the following:

- genetic transmission of the disease (sickle cell trait or sickle cell disease)
- precipitant factors that could lead to sickle cell crisis (stress, infection, dehydration, high altitude, cold exposure)
- signs and symptoms of impending and actual crisis
- pain relief and fever control measures that can be instituted at home (if fever is low grade and pain mild)
- parameters that necessitate bringing the child to the ED for evaluation and treatment

Parents can also be referred to the following organizations for more information:

National Sickle Disease Program
National Institutes of Health
Sickle Cell Disease Branch
Room 4a-27, Bldg. 31
Bethesda, MD 20014

or

National Association for Sickle Cell Disease, Inc.
945 S. Western Avenue
Suite 206
Los Angeles, CA 90006

NURSING DOCUMENTATION

- primary and secondary assessment findings
- history data, including measures taken at home to relieve symptoms

- diagnostic studies done
- nursing interventions, medical-nursing collaborative interventions, and patient response
- patient/parent teaching done, including discharge instructions and guidelines for follow-up care

NURSING DIAGNOSES

- alteration in comfort related to vasocclusion
- alterations in temperature related to infectious process
- fluid volume deficit (actual or potential) related to inadequate intake, increased fluid losses
- knowledge deficit (parent and child) related to crisis-provoking events
- fear related to age, illness, pain, and ED personnel and surroundings

---

NOTES

1. Daniel Esposito, "Sickle Cell Anemia," in *Emergency Medicine: A Comprehensive Study Guide,* ed. Judith Tintinalli (New York: McGraw-Hill, 1988), 533–34.

2. Glenn C. Hamilton, "Anemia and White Blood Cell Disorders," in *Emergency Medicine: Concepts and Clinical Practice,* ed. Peter Rosen (St. Louis: C.V. Mosby Co., 1987), 1635–38.

3. Oswaldo L. Castro, et al., "Managing Sickle Cell Emergencies," *Patient Care* 19 (1985): 92–141.

BIBLIOGRAPHY

Castro, O., B. Lubin, H. Pearson, and E. Vichinsky. "Managing Sickle Cell Emergencies." *Patient Care* 19 (1985): 91–141.

Esposito, D. "Sickle Cell Anemia." In *Emergency Medicine: A Comprehensive Study Guide,* edited by J. Tintinatti, 533–34. New York: McGraw-Hill, 1988.

Hamilton, G. "Anemia and White Blood Cell Disorders." In *Emergency Medicine: Concepts and Clinical Practice,* edited by P. Rosen, 1635–38. St. Louis: C.V. Mosby Co., 1987.

Hathaway, G. "The Child with Sickle Cell Anemia: Implications and Management." *Nurse Practitioner* 9 (1984): 16–22.

Part X

Psychosocial Problems

Chapter 29

Sudden Infant Death Syndrome

Donna Ojanen Thomas

INTRODUCTION

Sudden infant death syndrome (SIDS) is the sudden death of an infant under 1 year of age, which remains unexplained after a complete postmortem examination, including an investigation of the death scene and a review of the case history.[1] SIDS is the major cause of death in infants more than 1 month of age and less than 1 year. Seven to ten thousand infants die yearly of SIDS, 91% before the age of 6 months, with the peak incidence occurring at 10 weeks of age. The majority of SIDS cases occur during the winter months.

PATHOPHYSIOLOGY

After years of research, the pathophysiology is still unclear. Autopsy findings are consistent, usually showing minor lung changes such as:

- pulmonary edema
- pulmonary congestion
- pulmonary inflammation
- intrathoracic petechiae

The autopsy also shows evidence of a mild respiratory or gastrointestinal infection, but does not demonstrate cause for sudden death.

Many theories about the cause of SIDS have been studied. In biblical times, SIDS was thought to be caused by "overlying": death resulting from a mother rolling on her infant during sleep. Theories that have been researched over the years as causes for SIDS include infections, electrolyte imbalances, hypoglycemia, cow's milk allergies, diphtheria-pertussis-tetanus (DPT) vaccination, and abnormal placenta. None of these has been proven to cause SIDS.

Research has also focused on elevated levels of fetal hemoglobin,[2] altered cardiac function,[3] and prolonged cerebral hypoxia.[4] The National Institutes of Health (NIH) has recommended that research be directed to the following areas:[5]

- anatomy and maturation of the CNS during prenatal development
- infectious agents and immunologic function
- behavioral patterns because some infants demonstrated behavioral changes such as listlessness shortly before death

NIH has also recommended the establishment of a registry of SIDS deaths. For more information on theories and current research, the reader is referred to the bibliography at the end of this chapter.

Known risk factors for the mother that may increase the risk of SIDS include the following:

- age less than 20 years
- multiple births
- poor prenatal care and home births
- smoking
- narcotic use
- prior infant deaths
- low socioeconomic status

Risk factors for the infant include the following:

- prematurity
- low birth weight
- low Apgar score at birth
- infant of multiple birth
- males

TRIAGE ASSESSMENT

Often the triage nurse will receive a call from prehospital care providers who describe a pulseless, apneic baby not known to be ill. The child may have a pink, frothy discharge from the nose and mouth. The paramedics usually will have begun cardiopulmonary resuscitation and the child will be transported to the hospital. Depending on local protocols, the decision not to resuscitate may be made in the home. Upon arrival at the ED the infant is usually pale or mottled, and lifeless. Pooling of blood in dependent parts may resemble bruising. Usually the child is unable to be resuscitated in the ED and is pronounced dead shortly after arrival. Nursing care then becomes focused on the family.

TRIAGE HISTORY

The parent's history may include the following:

- healthy when put to bed
- recent visit to private physician for minor illness—usually respiratory
- found pale and lifeless

Although child abuse needs to be considered, care must be taken to not imply that the parents are guilty of causing the death. Child abuse is usually ruled out by the history, physical exam, and autopsy.

PRIORITY RATING

Emergent: Obviously, any child who presents in full cardiac arrest or a child who has a history of apnea is treated as emergent.

TREATMENT AND NURSING CARE

Because the baby is usually pronounced dead soon after arrival in the ED, the parents and family of the baby become the patients. A nurse or social worker should remain with the family and keep them informed of what is being done. The family should be taken to a quiet room where they can have some privacy. An ED nurse or social worker should do the following:

- Update the family on resuscitative efforts without providing false hope.
- Allow the family to see the baby during the resuscitative efforts. This is controversial, but it allows the family to see that everything possible is being done and may provide comfort later.
- Tell the family as soon as possible after the child has been declared dead.

The following are suggestions for helping a family whose child has died of SIDS and can be used as guidelines for any sudden death that occurs in the ED:

1. Say you are sorry.
2. Give the family time to hold and say goodbye to the baby. This will make the death more real to them.
3. Ask the family if they would like the baby baptized and contact the appropriate clergy.
4. Provide mementos of the baby. A lock of hair may be appreciated by the family.
5. Answer any questions concerning the resuscitation or autopsy. Many families are concerned that an autopsy means that a viewing will not be possible.
6. Provide the family with the coroner's telephone number. They will have questions and will be anxious to receive the report.
7. Give family information about a local SIDS support group. Call the group and report the infant's death to them so that they can contact the family.
8. Help the family deal with siblings.
9. Help the mother obtain information about stopping lactation, if appropriate.
10. Walk to the car with the family when they leave. It is hard for them to leave their baby. You may need to arrange for someone to take them home.
11. Don't tell them you know how they feel.
12. Don't imply that they are guilty in any way.
13. Don't tell them they can always have another baby.

The grief reactions of the parents may vary but often include extreme guilt, especially if they were not at home when the infant was found. There are four tasks of grieving:[6]

1. acceptance. The parents must accept the reality of the death.
2. pain of the loss. The parents will experience grief in a variety of ways, depending on the culture.
3. adjustment. The parents must adjust to the environment without their child.
4. reinvestment. The parents must reinvest emotional energy into other activities and relationships.

Nursing interventions in the emergency department are usually focused on the first two tasks. The family must be provided with follow-up care to help them with the third and fourth tasks.

PARENT TEACHING

The parents should be allowed to express their feelings of grief and be reassured that the feelings are normal. The nurse needs to assess parental beliefs about the cause of death. Some common beliefs of parents concerning the cause of death include the following:[7]

- suffocation
- choking
- unsuspected illness
- death caused by sibling
- hemorrhage
- freezing
- reaction to medications
- crying to death

The nurse can help the family by explaining that there was nothing anyone could have done to prevent the death and that they are not at fault. Parents will remember everything that was said to them and the nurse can make a difference by being supportive and compassionate.

Parent teaching at the time of the child's death may not be effective because of the grief reaction. The parents should be referred to a local SIDS chapter. An ED nurse should call the family a few weeks after the death to offer any help and to reinforce teaching. Many emergency departments have programs that involve a home visit to the family. The parents can also write to the National SIDS Clearing House or the National Center for Prevention of SIDS at the following addresses:

National SIDS Clearing House
8201 Greensboro Drive, Suite 600
McLean, Virginia 22102
(703) 821-8955

National Center for the Prevention of Sudden Infant Death Syndrome
330 North Charles Street
Baltimore, Maryland 21201
(800) 638-SIDS

NURSING DOCUMENTATION

- history, prehospital care given, and infant's condition upon arrival to the ED
- interventions and response to interventions

- time of death
- disposition of the body (in suspected SIDS cases an autopsy is required)
- family support given, including social worker involved and referral to SIDS chapter

SIDS babies are candidates for some organ donations, such as heart valves. The family should be approached about this in a sensitive manner according to hospital protocols.

NURSING DIAGNOSES

- grief related to the death of the infant
- alteration in family processes related to sudden death
- post-trauma response related to death
- knowledge deficit of parents related to SIDS
- potential for ineffective family coping

NOTES

1. J. Zylke, "Sudden Infant Death Syndrome: Resurgent Research Offers Hope," *Journal of the American Medical Association* 262 (1989): 1565–66.

2. Gary Giulian, Enid Gilbert, and Richard Moss, "Elevated Fetal Hemoglobin Levels in Sudden Infant Death Syndrome," *New England Journal of Medicine* 316 (1987): 1122–26.

3. Dror Sadeh et al., "Altered Cardiac Repolarization in Some Victims of Sudden Infant Death Syndrome," *New England Journal of Medicine* 317 (1987): 1501–05.

4. Torleiv O. Rognum, et al., "Elevated Levels of Hypoxanthine in Vitreous Humor Indicate Prolonged Cerebral Hypoxia in Victims of Sudden Infant Death Syndrome," *Pediatrics* 82 (1988): 615–18.

5. Zylke, "Sudden Infant Death Syndrome," 1565–66.

6. W.J. Worden, *Grief Counseling and Grief Therapy: A Handbook for the Mental Health Practitioner* (New York: Springer Publishing Co., Inc., 1982), 11–15.

7. Abraham B. Bergman, et al., *Sudden Unexpected Death in Infants* (New York: MSS Information Corp., 1974), 93.

BIBLIOGRAPHY

Buschbacher, V., and R. Delcampo. "Parents' Response to Sudden Infant Death Syndrome." *Journal of Pediatric Health Care* 1 (1987): 85–90.

Christoffel, K. "Should Child Abuse and Neglect Be Considered When a Child Dies Unexpectedly?" *American Journal of Diseases of Childhood* 139 (1985): 875–80.

Guntheroth, W. *Crib Death: The Sudden Infant Death Syndrome,* 2d ed. Mount Kisco, N.Y.: Futura Publishing Co., 1989.

Herbst, J., et al. "New Findings Shed Light on SIDS." *Patient Care* (May 15, 1988): 61–88.

Hoffman, J., et al. "Diphtheria-Tetanus-Pertussis Immunization and Sudden Infant Death: Results of Development Cooperative Epidemiological Study of Sudden Infant Death Syndrome Risk Factors." *Pediatrics* 79 (1987): 598–611.

Jezierski, M. "Infant Death: Guidelines for Support of Parents in the Emergency Department." *Journal of Emergency Nursing* 15 (1989): 475–76.

Merritt, T., and M. Valdes-Dapena. "SIDS Research Update." *Pediatric Annals* 13 (1984): 193–207.

Peterson, D., E. Sabotta, and J. Daling. "Infant Mortality Among Subsequent Siblings of Infants Who Died of Sudden Infant Death Syndrome." *Journal of Pediatrics* 108 (1986): 911–14.

Savitt, T. "Social and Medical History of Crib Death." *Journal of the Florida Medical Association* (August 1979): 853–59.

Swoiskin, S. "Sudden Infant Death: Nursing Care for the Survivors." *Journal of Pediatric Nursing* 1 (1986): 33–39.

Woolsey, S. "Support After Sudden Infant Death." *American Journal of Nursing* 88 (1988): 1348–52.

Zebal, B., and S. Friedman. "Sudden Infant Death Syndrome and Infantile Apnea: Introduction." *Pediatric Annals* 13 (1984): 188–89.

Chapter 30

Child Abuse and Neglect

Marilyn K. Johnson

INTRODUCTION

Child abuse was defined by Congress in 1974 (Public Law 93-247). The definition states, "Child abuse and neglect means the physical or mental injury, sexual abuse, negligent treatment, or maltreatment of a child under the age of 18 by a person who is responsible for the child's welfare under circumstances which indicate that the child's health or welfare is harmed or threatened thereby."[1] The four types of child abuse can be further defined as follows:

1. physical abuse: any injury inflicted by a parent or caretaker
2. neglect: acts of omission or failure to meet basic needs of the child
3. emotional abuse: failure of parent to provide a nurturing environment conducive to growth, including verbal abuse, threats, and criticism
4. sexual abuse (see Chapter 31)

PATHOPHYSIOLOGY

Multiple dynamics can create situations that result in the maltreatment of children. Maltreatment results in injury, psychological impairment, or neglect. Exhibit 30-1 lists some factors that may contribute to child abuse.

Any caretaker has the potential to abuse a child at some time. While most child abusers are psychologically normal, a small number are pathological. Live-in significant others are at a high risk of abusing children.

Exhibit 30-1 Parental Factors That May Contribute to Child Abuse

---

1. Unrealistic expectations of a child for the level of the child's development
2. Lack of parenting skills (poor parent models; immaturity; lack of knowledge)
3. Social isolation (low self-esteem)
4. Rigid religious practices and beliefs
5. Drug or alcohol impairments (chronic and/or acute)
6. Environmental factors (monetary, cultural, living conditions, work, legal, major loss or crisis)
7. Unmet emotional needs (caregiver looks to child to fulfill needs—role reversal; parents themselves were abused)
8. Devaluation of child and other dependents
9. Child is different (handicapped physically or mentally, temperamentally difficult, hyperactive, or a foster child)
10. Family conflict

Source: S. Bittner and E. Newberger, "Pediatric Understanding of Child Abuse and Neglect" in *Pediatrics in Review,* Vol. 2 (Elk Grove Village, Ill.: American Academy of Pediatrics, 1981), 197–207.

TRIAGE ASSESSMENT

The triage exam is based on the chief complaint and, as always, the nurse should assess airway, breathing, and circulation (the ABCs) first. During the triage exam and history, a few "red flags" should be looked for that may alert the nurse to child abuse. These include:

- unexplained or nonwitnessed injuries
- conflicting stories or history inconsistent with injury
- passive, withdrawn behavior of the child
- lack of concern by parents or caretakers
- delay in seeking medical care without reasonable home care or effort to treat
- "gut feeling" of the nurse that a problem exists

TRIAGE HISTORY

- pre-existing conditions (blood dyscrasias, bone disorders, genetic illnesses, etc.)
- medications/immunization history
- activity level of the child: diminished or hyperactive
- when injury happened, and reason or explanation for what happened; reason for delay in seeking medical attention, if this is the case

- demeanor and interaction between parent/caretaker and child
- home care or effort to treat

TELEPHONE TRIAGE GUIDELINES

If suspicion of child abuse and neglect exists, the nurse should not provoke anxiety in the caller. Instead, encourage the caller to bring the child to the emergency department for an evaluation. Concerned family members may call for advice on how to report cases of child abuse. They should be given the appropriate phone numbers and advised of reporting laws.

Parents who fear they will abuse their child may call, seeking help. The ED nurse should keep a list of community support groups or hot lines available, or refer the family to available psychiatric services within the hospital.

PRIORITY RATING

Emergent: Any child with an airway, breathing, or circulatory impairment. Child with altered level of consciousness. Fractures with deformities of long bones (open or closed) or multiple fractures. Trunk injuries accompanied by pain, pallor, impairment of breathing. Compromising attitude of the caretaker, placing the child at risk.

Urgent: Child exhibiting symptoms of suspected child abuse or neglect with a fracture or a medical component. Open or closed wounds that do not match the mechanism of injury. Multiple bruises at varying ages of healing. Failure to thrive.

Nonurgent: Child in no acute distress physically or emotionally and in no danger of the caretaker leaving with the child before evaluation and treatment.

TREATMENT AND NURSING CARE

After the child is taken to a room, the nurse will be able to do a more thorough physical assessment and evaluation. The assessment is related to the chief complaint, but the nurse should look at the entire child. Findings listed in Exhibit 30-2 may indicate possible child abuse.

Other injuries and conditions that may be found after the complete physical exam and diagnostic workup that are indicative of child abuse include the following:

1. Burns
   - cigarette burns
   - circumferential burns

Exhibit 30-2 Clues to the Diagnosis of Child Abuse

SIGNS AND SYMPTOMS NOTED IN THE PHYSICAL EXAM

1. Bruises in various stages of healing
2. Linear or circumferential marks placed by forceful blow on the skin (belt, whips, cords, or other implements)
3. Pressure bruises (pinch marks, choke marks, hand or finger print marks, paddling)
4. Unusual marks (gag marks, circumferential marks on extremities, fork or implement puncture wounds, demarcations outlining blunt instruments)
5. Human bite marks (over 3 cm between incisors indicates permanent teeth)
6. Inflicted burns (cigarette, forced contact with electrical or heat-producing devices, scalding injuries, circumferential or "stocking" burns or dunking burns from forced immersion)

Source: B. Schmitt, "The Visual Diagnosis of Non-Accidental Trauma and Failure to Thrive" (Revision of a lecture handout delivered in the Department of Pediatrics, University of Colorado Medical Center, Boulder, Colo., 1978).

- scald burns
- submersion burns

2. Head injuries
   - subdural hematomas (in infants, subdurals are caused by child abuse until proven otherwise)
   - subgaleal hematoma, scalp bruises, or traumatic alopecia (healthy hair at varying lengths or petechial spots on scalp)
   - black eyes
   - subarachnoid hemorrhages

3. Shaken baby syndrome
   - no skull fracture
   - no scalp swelling or bruising
   - retinal hemorrhages
   - long-bone fractures in 25% of cases

4. Abdominal injuries (often no evidence of bleeding, but child may present in hypovolemic shock)
   - ruptured liver or spleen
   - intestinal perforation
   - intramural hematoma of duodenum or proximal jejunum
   - ruptured blood vessel
   - pancreatic injury
   - kidney injury

5. Fractures
  - unusual fractures (ribs, scapula, sternum)
  - metaphysis chip fractures or bucket handle fractures
  - subperiosteal bleeding and calcification
  - fractures at different stages of healing
  - repeated fractures at the same site
6. Failure to thrive
  - 20% or more below the ideal weight for height, or actual weight that is 10% or more below the ideal weight combined with a poor weight gain
  - deprivational behavior
  - ravenous appetite
  - failure to gain weight in the home or poor weight gain
  - psychosocial dwarfism (growth failure between the ages of 3 and 12 without disease)
7. Münchausen syndrome by proxy
  - frequent visits to various emergency departments or other medical settings
  - falsification of medical history and symptoms by parents
  - illness caused by deliberate poisoning

During the assessment, the ED nurse needs to be aware of ethnic practices that may be mistaken for child abuse. Table 30-1 lists practices that exist in different cultures.

The decision of whether or not abuse has taken place should be made by the department of social services (DSS); health care providers can only suspect harm and do not have to prove it.

Other imitators of child abuse and neglect are the following:

- failure to thrive; short stature; normal leanness; organic, skeletal, or endocrine disorders
- bruising: clotting disorders; leukemia; idiopathic thrombocytopenic purpura; hemophilia; Wiskott-Aldrich syndrome
- Ehlers-Danlos syndrome: bruise and scar easily and have poor healing properties
- unusual but realistic mechanism of injury due to sport injury, falls, play, or accident
- sudden infant death syndrome (SIDS)
- mongolian spots: birthmark which does not blanch when depressed
- phytophotodermatitis: increased melanin production caused by rubbing skin with lime, lemon, fig, celery, or parsnip.

Table 30-1 Cultural Practices That May Be Mistaken for Child Abuse

Ethnic Group	Practice
East African tribes	Cuts to face and charcoal rubbed into the wounds produce scarring for tribal identification.
Vietnamese	In cao gio (coin rubbing), heated metal coins or implements and oil are rubbed on the child's body creating bruises and occasional burns. Used to reduce fever, chills, and headaches.
Chinese	In cupping, an application of a heated cup to the chest is used to draw out congestion. Pinching, a folk medicine practice, leaves marks and bruises on the skin.
Asians	Moxibustion causes "therapeutic" wounds on the trunks and abdomens of refugee children who are treated by folk medicine practitioners.
Hispanics	In an attempt to cure a child suffering from diarrhea, vomiting, and sunken fontanelle (mollera caida), the child is held upside down with the top of the head in water and shaken. Subdural hematomas and retinal hemorrhaging may result.

Source: B. Schmitt, "The Child with Non-Accidental Trauma" in *The Battered Child,* 4th ed., eds. R. Helfer and C. Kempe. (Chicago: University of Chicago Press, 1987).

- maculae ceruleae: bluish spots on skin primarily in pubic area when infected with lice; goes away with lice treatment
- mutiple petechiae and purpura of the face: discoloration caused by vigorous crying, retching, or coughing because of increased vena cava pressure

Nursing care is specific to the type of injury, but nurses should always

- notify appropriate authorities (department of social services and/or police agency as directed by state and local law)
- enlist help of hospital child protection team or medical social workers
- support child and family and maintain confidentiality
- assist in documentation and collection of evidence
- maintain objectivity with the family (i.e., be the advocate of the child and the family, allow the investigative process to determine who injured the child)
- arrange for 35mm quality pictures to be taken for bruises or other visual injury

PARENT TEACHING

The nurse needs to remain supportive, nonjudgmental, and objective throughout the visit. If the child is allowed to return home with the parents, the nurse should

- assist in understanding the medical needs and follow-up care
- teach about appropriate feeding, clothing, and discipline
- refer to community agencies for crisis nurseries, parenting classes, and other support groups
- encourage the following of directions of the DSS worker or law enforcement officer
- reinforce support and the fact that by law the report had to be made

If the child is removed to a shelter agency, be certain the legal caretakers are aware of the follow-up care needed.

NURSING DOCUMENTATION

- assessment, including description and mechanism of injury (where, when, how, reason for delay in seeking medical attention)
- quotes of statements made by the child and caretakers, relating to cause of the injury or parenting behavior
- description of interaction of the child and caretakers (overprotectiveness; apathy; inappropriate response to pain; unusual fear or complacency)
- past medical history, especially of previous injury
- general appearance of child: hygiene, clothing, etc.
- agency involved: DSS, police, social workers, etc.
- disposition of child and follow-up planned

NURSING DIAGNOSES

- alteration in parenting
- potential for injury of child related to abuse or neglect
- altered growth and development of child related to physical or emotional injuries or neglect
- knowledge deficit of caretaker related to normal childhood growth and development
- fear of child and parents related to possible separation
- ineffective coping of parent to demands of parenting

NOTE

1. R.L. Mindlen, "Child Abuse and Neglect: The Role of the Pediatrician and the Academy," *Pediatrics* 54 (1974): 393.

BIBLIOGRAPHY

Bittner, S., and E. Newberger. "Pediatric Understanding of Child Abuse and Neglect." *Pediatrics in Review* 2 (1981): 197–207.

Bross, D., et al. *The New Child Protection Team Handbook*. New York: Garland Publishing, 1988.

Council on Scientific Affairs. "AMA Diagnostic and Treatment Guidelines Concerning Child Abuse and Neglect." *Journal of the American Medical Association* 254 (1985): 796–800.

Helfer, R., and C. Kempe. *The Battered Child*, 4th ed. Chicago: University of Chicago Press, 1987.

Keil, M. "Child Abuse." In *Pediatric Trauma Nursing*, edited by C. Joy, 211–29. Gaithersburg, Md.: Aspen Publishers, Inc., 1989.

Kelley, S. "Child Abuse and Neglect." In *Pediatric Emergency Nursing*, edited by S. Kelley, 1–26. Norwalk, Conn.: Appleton & Lange, 1988.

Kelley, S. "Physical Abuse of Children: Recognition and Reporting." *Journal of Emergency Nursing* 14 (1988): 82–89.

Kessler, D., and M. New. "Emerging Trends in Child Abuse and Neglect." *Pediatric Annals* 18 (1989): 471–75.

Schmitt, B.D. "The Visual Diagnosis of Non-Accidental Trauma and Failure to Thrive." Handout from lecture, Department of Pediatrics, University of Colorado Medical Center, 1978.

U.S. Department of Health and Human Services. *The Nurse's Role*. No. (DHHS) 79-30202. Washington, D.C.: U.S. Department of Health and Human Services, 1979.

Wissow, L. *Child Advocacy for the Clinician. An Approach to Child Abuse and Neglect*. Baltimore: Williams & Wilkins Co., 1988.

Chapter 31

Sexual Abuse

Marilyn K. Johnson

INTRODUCTION

Sexual abuse is defined as the use of a child for sexual gratification and/or financial benefit by an adult, significantly older child, or adolescent. Sexual activity between an adult and a child is considered maltreatment. There are three types of sexual abuse against both male and female children.

1. Nontouching
   - verbal abuse (obscene phone calls, frank discussions of sexual acts)
   - exhibitionism
   - voyeurism
   - visual or auditory witnessing of sexual activity
2. Touching
   - fondling: genital stimulation
   - oral stimulation
   - intercourse
3. Violent acts
   - rape
   - physical injury
   - murder

Those who may sexually abuse a child include the following:

1. family members (incest): fathers, mothers, sisters, brothers, aunts, uncles, grandparents
2. trusted adults: close friends, neighbors, teachers, babysitters, or other significant people in the child's life

3. strangers: those with no emotional ties to the child have a higher incidence of violence

CAUSES OF SEXUAL ABUSE

Many theories exist about the causes of sexual abuse, but one thing that is known is that children who are victims of these crimes may suffer deep psychological harm if not treated. Even with treatment, the trauma is revisited many times throughout the life cycle.

Many offenders were themselves abused as children. Sexual abuse tends to be habitual. Within the family system, the involvement frequently increases as the child grows and develops. Confusion is common because the progression of the involvement is frequently pleasurable and not painful. Coercion, threats, and lies often accompany the abuse.

TRIAGE ASSESSMENT

Although children may present in the ED with sexual maltreatment as the chief complaint, often the diagnosis can be suspected based on some other, less obvious complaint. Some complaints that might lead the triage nurse to suspect sexual abuse are the following:

- repeated urinary tract infections
- difficulty walking or sitting (due to anal or genital pain)
- vaginal discharge or pruritus
- bruises or bleeding of the genitalia, perineum, or perianal area

If possible when sexual abuse is given as the chief complaint, the nurse should assign a higher priority to the care, especially if the event occurred within 72 hours. The triage nurse should pursue only sufficient questions to establish a concern.

TELEPHONE TRIAGE GUIDELINES

If the question of sexual abuse is posed, the caller should be urged to go to a medical facility that can perform a sensitive and forensically acceptable rape examination. In most cases, it is not urgent. The nurse should not ask the parent for further information other than that necessary to clarify the urgency of the concern. The caller should be told that it is required that he or she report the incident or suspicions to the department of social services and the police to protect the child from further harm. If the nurse feels this might inhibit the caller from seeking medical assistance, the nurse can delay informing the caller of the reporting requirement until the child and family are in the medical setting.

PRIORITY RATING

Emergent: Child with airway, breathing, or circulatory impairment; or acute abdominal, rectal, or perineal injuries. Child in danger of immediate physical or emotional harm. Child with suicide gesture or overdose.

Urgent: Child with hematuria, abdominal pain, emotional distress (of parents as well), or bleeding or bruising of the genitalia.

Nonurgent: Majority of sexual abuse cases come under this heading. Most cases of sexual abuse are not accompanied with overt physical signs and symptoms. The victims and the families frequently are in emotional crisis and need support and guidance.

TREATMENT AND NURSING CARE

Treatment and nursing care are specific to any injuries. Treatment of the sexually abused child is aimed at assisting in the collection of evidence and supporting the family and child throughout the experience. Usually certain hospitals, especially in urban areas, are designated to handle sexual abuse cases. If the child will be transported to another facility, the nurse should

- treat any physical injuries and document care given
- document any comments made by the parents and child, but not ask specific questions about the alleged incident
- collect, label, and document any evidence (clothing in a porous paper bag, lab or x-ray studies) and send to the receiving agency
- notify the proper authorities (police, DSS). The medical role is to report suspicions to the investigating agencies, not to have proof of the allegation.
- arrange for transfer according to hospital policy. Transfer may need to be done by ambulance or by the police.
- maintain an empathetic and calm demeanor. Be sensitive to the needs of the child and parent.
- assure the transfer with a police escort as necessary if the child will not need ambulance service

At the receiving hospital (one that is capable of completing a forensic rape exam), the nurse should

- take parent and child to a private room to maintain confidentiality, arrange for support personnel, and establish a comfortable, trusting environment
- assess any injuries and assist in appropriate intervention
- notify appropriate people to do the questioning (DSS, caseworker, police agency, hospital crisis worker) and the exam (nurse, physician)
- ask questions that are simple, direct, and open-ended. The nurse should not use terminology that may prompt child's responses, put thoughts in the child's mind, or lead the child's statements. Anatomically correct dolls should only be used by those trained in their use.
- allow the child to maintain a sense of control throughout the exam; give choices where possible (i.e., "What color gown would you like to wear?" rather than "Do you want to. . . ."). The consent of the child to the exam is very important.
- document terminology child uses for parts and functions of the body

A complete physical exam may have to be delayed and performed under another setting depending on the urgency of the injuries. Performing the exam under general anesthesia is rarely necessary.

THE PEDIATRIC RAPE EXAM

The Interview

During the interview, the physican and/or crisis workers will interview the parent and child separately, and obtain proper consents for the procedure (state laws vary on how this must be done). Parents may request the exam but the proper authorities must be notified. Only the authorities (usually the police) can authorize an exam at public expense. If the exam is requested by the authorities (police, DSS), the exam may be done with or without parental consent. If the parents do not consent to the exam, the child will need to be placed in protective custody, and the exam will be done at public expense. The child should be allowed to remain dressed during the interview to clearly separate it from the physical exam.

The procedure will be explained to the parent and child at a level that the child can understand, without alarming the child. A patient history will be taken from the caretaker and the victim, which includes the following:

- chief complaint in child's words
- place where incident took place
- name, age, relationship of the perpetrator if known
- the act described by the patient
- hygiene or activity since the assault took place if the assault happened within 72 hours
- symptoms: physical, emotional, and behavioral
- past medical history including gynecological information
- prior history of abuse, if known

The Physical Examination

Hospitals that perform rape exams generally have a packet that contains all of the necessary equipment and forms needed to document and collect evidence. These are listed in Exhibit 31-1. Once the packet has been opened and items removed, someone must be in attendance at all times who can verify that the chain of evidence was not tampered with. The physical exam, done by the ED physician, includes the following:

- general physical exam including vital signs, weight, and percentiles per nomogram (for all children under age 6 years).
- examination of the external genitalia, including inner thighs
- vaginal exam (if indicated by history and trauma is present). May need to consider using general anesthesia in some cases if a large amount of trauma is present or delaying the exam if the child is extremely upset and uncooperative. Frequently, a vulvar inspection without instruments is all that is needed on younger children. The hymenal opening should be documented in millimeters as well as the appearance of the perihymenal mucous membrane (erythema, disruptions, scars, hyperpigmentation, etc.).
- rectal and anal exam, including notation of anal tone and presence of fissures, hemorrhoids, scars, tags, or pigment changes
- inspection for any injuries or foreign bodies
- presence of herpes viral infection of genital or anal area, or genital warts, which are suggestive of sexual abuse
- inspection for semen, which fluoresces light brownish yellow with Wood's lamp
- Tanner's classification of sexual maturity; child's developmental level

Exhibit 31-1 The Rape Collection Kit

Contents
Use a manila envelope 9-3/4 in. by 13 in. to collect evidence. (Seal after evidence is collected.)
All specimens (tubes, containers, envelopes) must be labeled with:
1. specimen (location)
2. patient name and ID #
3. date and time
4. examining physician's initials

Blood Samples
Take three blood samples for the following tests:
1. blood and semen typing
2. alcohol and drug analysis
3. pregnancy in pubescent girls

Fingernail Scrapings
Use spatulas provided, obtain scrapings, and place in appropriate envelopes (left and right).

Saliva Sample
Use filter paper gauze pad or swabs. *Do not allow the pad to be touched by anyone but the patient.*

Pubic Hair Combings (in pubescent children)
Use comb provided, place hairs and debris in envelope.

Pubic Hair Clippings (in pubescent children)
Cut sample of pubic hair (10–12) and place in envelope.

Dry Smears and Swabs
Cotton swab collection is done from the vagina, mouth (particularly around the gums and under tongue), rectum, and any semen stains. After the smears are on slides, the swabs are placed in dry tubes.

Vaginal Wash
Use 3–5 cc saline, wash the vaginal vault, and place washings in vial.

Debris/Other Potential Evidence
Collect any foreign debris or foreign matter (internal or external) and place in envelopes or tubes provided. Note collection site.

Use only designated containers provided to preserve the forensic evidence. Once the kit is opened, someone must be in attendance to monitor that the chain of evidence is not broken or tampered with. After the exam, the evidence is refrigerated until delivery to the forensic evidence collection laboratory. In many states, the state medical examiner's office is designated to be the agency lab.
After all evidence is collected and secured with the evidence seal, refrigerate but do not freeze.

Evidence Collection

- clothing—placed in porous bag
- dried and moist secretions, stains suggestive of blood or ejaculate, and foreign material from the body including head, hair, and scalp
- saliva sample and collection of secretions around mouth and gingival swabs for acid phosphotase
- fingernail scrapings
- hair samples from the head and pubic area
- vaginal specimens with dry and wet mounts for girls
- penile swabs from the urethral meatus, glans, and shaft for boys
- *Neisseria gonorrhoeae* (gonococcal), *Treponema pallidum (*syphilitic), *Chlamydia,* and *Trichomonas* cultures
- seminal fluid, lubricants, fecal matter, or blood from anus and rectal area

Clinical Tests

- HIV screening
- blood serology
- blood alcohol if indicated; only Betadine swabs for preparing the skin
- urine or serum tests for pregnancy and drugs, if indicated
- venereal disease cultures
- cultures for *Chlamydia,* hanging drop *Trichomonas,* and other sexually transmitted organisms
- DNA fingerprinting and profiling: future possibilities
- typing of blood and seminal fluid specimens

Findings suggestive but not conclusive for sexual abuse are as follows:

- genital warts
- AIDS
- multiple anal fissures or rectal prolapse without medical cause
- sexually transmitted diseases: gonorrhea, syphilis, *Trichomonas, Chlamydia*
- vulvar hemangioma: congenital abnormality can also appear on the lips that looks like circular burns
- vaginal "beads" or particulate matter from a rupture of a hyperabsorbent diaper
- herpes II: can be autoinoculation
- herpes I can occur genitally

Treatment

- STD (sexually transmitted disease) prophylaxis (Exhibit 31-2)
- treatment of all injuries
- tetanus vaccination if indicated
- psychologic/psychiatric therapy
- pregnancy prevention

Medical Documentation

The entire exam should be documented by the physician on the proper forms. The location, size, and appearance of erythema, abrasions, bruises, contusions, induration, lacerations, fractures, bites, burns, stains, or other concerns should be indicated on diagrams usually provided with the documentation forms.

PARENT TEACHING

- written instructions for physical care and referrals
- referral to therapist for emotional support

Exhibit 31-2 Medications Used for Prophylaxis in Sexual Abuse Involving Children*

Pregnancy Prophylaxis for Pubertal Females not Using Contraception When Penetration or Ejaculation Has Taken Place
Single day treatment with oral contraceptives

Treatment for Suspected Gonorrhea Infections
Amoxicillin, 50 mg/kg in one dose: for a child whose weight is < 40 kg
Amoxicillin, 3.0 g PO in one dose: for children whose weight is > 40 kg
Probenecid, 25 mg/kg—weight < 40 kg. Single dose
       1 g PO—weight > 40 kg. Single dose
For penicillin-allergic children, spectinomycin or tetracycline may be used.

Treatment for Chlamydial Infections
Tetracycline
Erythromycin

*All children with a history of sexual contact should be treated.

Source: S. Ludwig, "Sexual Abuse" in *Textbook of Pediatric Emergency Medicine,* eds. G. Fleisher and S. Ludwig. (Baltimore: Williams & Wilkins Co., 1988), 1155–56.

- care for any injuries present
- instructions for any medications given

NURSING DOCUMENTATION

- signs and symptoms
- any comments made by child or parents
- names of support personnel involved: crisis worker, police, DSS
- exam done; time, by whom
- disposition and follow-up of child
- any prophylactic medications given
- parent and patient teaching

NURSING DIAGNOSES

- rape trauma syndrome related to experience
- alteration in parenting related to sexual abuse
- potential for infection by sexually transmitted disease
- ineffective family coping related to incident
- anxiety of child related to rape experience and feelings of guilt

BIBLIOGRAPHY

Kelley, S. "Child Abuse and Neglect." In *Pediatric Emergency Nursing,* edited by S. Kelley, 27–51. Norwalk, Conn.: Appleton & Lange, 1988.

Kelley, S. "Interviewing the Sexually Abused Child: Principles and Techniques." *Journal of Emergency Nursing* 11 (1985): 234–41.

Krugman, R., and D. Jones. "Incest and Other Forms of Sexual Abuse." In *The Battered Child,* 4th ed., edited by R. Helfer and C. Kempe, 286–300. Chicago: University of Chicago Press, 1987.

Ludwig, S. "Sexual Abuse." In *Textbook of Pediatric Emergency Medicine,* edited by G. Fleisher and S. Ludwig, 1142–57. Baltimore: Williams & Wilkins Co., 1988.

Muchlinski, E., C. Boonstra, and J. Johnson. "Planning and Implementing a Pediatric Sexual Assault Evidentiary Examination Program." *Journal of Emergency Nursing* 15 (1989): 249–55.

Schetky, D., and A. Green. *Child Sexual Abuse: A Handbook for Health Care and Legal Professionals.* New York: Brunner/Mazel Publishers, 1988.

Sgroi, S. *Handbook of Clinical Intervention in Child Sexual Abuse.* Lexington, Mass.: D.C. Heath and Co., 1985.

Strickland, S. "Sexual Abuse Assessment." *Pediatric Annals* 18 (1989): 495–99.

Part XI

Common Pediatric Complaints

Chapter 32

Fever

Donna Ojanen Thomas

INTRODUCTION

Fever is typically described as an elevation in normal body temperature, which is generally 36–37.2° C (97–99° F) orally, and 1° higher rectally. Fever is one of the most common chief complaints of parents who bring their child to the emergency department.

PATHOPHYSIOLOGY

Body temperature is regulated by the hypothalamus, which establishes a set point based on blood temperatures. This set point can be raised by infections or malignancies and can be lowered by antipyretics. Other factors, such as excessive heat production and heat stroke, may raise the temperature even though the set point is normal. The benefits of fever in helping to fight infection remain controversial.

Physiological and behavioral effects of fever in the child include the following:

- increased basal metabolism, which results in increased heart rate, respiratory rate, and oxygen demand
- increased fluid and caloric requirements. Caloric requirements are increased by 12% for each degree Centigrade of fever.[1]
- increased likelihood of dehydration because of increased insensible water loss, increased fluid requirements, and decreased intake
- lowered seizure threshhold and increased chances of febrile seizure in some children
- lethargy and increased irritability

293

The majority of fevers in children are caused by a viral illness. However, if the fever is 40° C (104° F), an increased likelihood of bacterial infection exists, especially in children less than 2 years of age.[2]

Possible causes of fever are listed in Exhibit 32-1.

Exhibit 32-1 Possible Causes of Fever in Children

BACTERIAL INFECTIONS
Bacteremia
Cellulitis
Meningitis
Osteomyelitis
Otitis media
Pneumonia
Pyelonephritis
Shigellosis
Urinary tract infections

COLLAGEN VASCULAR DISEASES
Henoch-Schönlein purpura
Juvenile rheumatoid arthritis
Lupus erythematosus
Rheumatic fever

DRUG INTOXICATION (ACCIDENTAL OR INTENTIONAL)
Amphetamines
Atropine
Phenothiazines
PCP
Salicylates

MALIGNANCIES
Hodgkin's lymphoma
Leukemia
Neuroblastoma
Sarcoma

VIRAL ILLNESSES
Aseptic meningitis
Croup
Cytomegalovirus
Gastroenteritis
Upper respiratory infections

TRIAGE ASSESSMENT

- airway, breathing, circulation (ABCs)
- level of consciousness
- associated signs and symptoms of illness
- hydration status
- vital signs: temperature, pulse, respiration, blood pressure

TRIAGE HISTORY

- history of present illness, height of fever, response to antipyretics
- pre-existing conditions and medications child may be taking
- hydration status. Check anterior fontanelles, if open.
- other signs and symptoms, including rashes
- activity level of the child
- prior exposure to illness
- recent immunizations
- time and amount of last antipyretic

TELEPHONE TRIAGE GUIDELINES

Any child less than 3 months of age with a fever needs to be evaluated as soon as possible by a physician. Care must be taken in all cases to ask about related signs and symptoms. A child who has a decreased level of consciousness or has a rash that sounds as if it might be a petechial rash (pinpoint bruising that does not blanch with pressure) should be seen immediately. Parents should be told that they may come to the ED at any time for evaluation of their child. The nurse should not try to diagnose over the phone but may give symptomatic advice for fever control if the child has no other signs and symptoms. Parents should also be instructed to contact their own physician for further information.

PRIORITY RATING

Emergent: Child is experiencing seizure activity, has petechial or purpuric rash, or has decreased level of consciousness, or signs and symptoms of shock.
Urgent: Fever in a child less than 3 months of age with or without other symptoms.

Nonurgent: Fever in a child greater than 3 months of age who is alert, active, and playful, and without other symptoms.

TREATMENT AND NURSING CARE

Treatment is aimed at finding the cause of the fever and ruling out serious bacterial infection. Fever in children under 3 months of age is of greater concern because these children localize infections poorly and may have no other symptoms of illness. Therefore, these children are treated more aggressively and given higher priority in the ED.

Nursing care of the child with a fever involves the following:

1. initial assessment
2. history (as listed under "Triage History")
3. cooling measures
   - antipyretics: 15 mg/kg acetaminophen. Aspirin should not be used due to its association with Reye's syndrome. Pediatric ibuprofen preparations are also being used. The dose is 10 mg/kg.
   - sponging with tepid water if the child's temperature is above 40° C (104° F). Care must be taken to prevent shivering, as this will raise the body temperature as the body attempts to conserve heat. Parents should be discouraged from giving alcohol sponge baths, as alcohol intoxication can occur by inhalation of fumes and absorption through the skin.
4. fluids: administered intravenously or orally depending on the condition of the child and hydration status.

Children less than 3 months old, and those who exhibit signs and symptoms of serious illness, will usually have a complete "septic workup," which may include the following:

- CBC with differential
- spinal tap
- blood and urine cultures
- electrolytes
- blood glucose
- chest x-ray

Further treatment will depend on the results of the diagnostic studies and the diagnosis. Infants less than 3 months of age are often admitted for observation and/or

IV antibiotics due to the increased possibility of a serious infection in this age group. Specific nursing interventions based on diagnoses are discussed in other chapters.

Once the fever is reduced, the child will be more comfortable. Children with high fevers often look very ill; they are tachypneic, tachycardic, and often listless. Some of these symptoms may disappear once the fever is decreased.

Specific diagnostic tests will be done depending on the history, appearance of the child, the height of the fever, and if no obvious focus for the fever is found. If no focus is found, a CBC may be done and, depending on the white blood cell count, additional studies may be done.

PARENT TEACHING

The nurse should discuss the following topics with parents:

1. diagnostic tests. Many parents fear spinal taps and will need explanations and reassurance about this test. They need to understand that the insertion site for the spinal needle is below the level of the spinal cord and that the risk of paralysis is negligible. They also need to know how to call back to receive culture results if cultures have been done.
2. fever control. Avoid use of aspirin.
3. antibiotic therapy, if indicated
4. follow-up instructions. Discharge instructions should include conditions that would require the child to be re-evaluated.

NURSING DOCUMENTATION

- general assessment including level of consciousness and activity, color, skin turgor, rashes, and associated signs and symptoms
- temperature on arrival, antipyretics given, temperature on discharge or after antipyretics
- diagnostic tests done
- teaching on follow-up care and fever control

NURSING DIAGNOSES

- alteration in temperature (hyperthermia)
- potential fluid volume deficit related to decreased intake or increased output
- alteration in comfort related to fever

- fear of child relating to ED procedures and environment
- knowledge deficit of caregivers related to fever control
- potential for injury due to possibility of seizures

NOTES

1. Robert W. Winters, "Fluid Therapy: Maintenance Requirements," in *Principles of Pediatric Fluid Therapy*, ed., Robert W. Winters (Boston: Little, Brown, and Co., 1982), 75.

2. Paul L. McCarthy, "Controversies in Pediatrics: What Tests Are Indicated for the Child with Fever," *Pediatrics in Review* 1 (1979): 51–56.

BIBLIOGRAPHY

Baker, D., P. Fosareli, and R. Carpenter. "Childhood Fever: Correlation of Diagnosis with Temperature Response to Acetaminophen." *Pediatrics* 80 (1987): 315–18.

Barkin, R.M. "Fever in Children under 2 years of Age." In *Emergency Pediatrics,* edited by R. Barkin and P. Rosen, 192–97. St. Louis: C.V. Mosby Co., 1990.

Dubois, E. "Why Are Fever Temperatures over 106 Degrees F. Rare?" *American Journal of Medical Science* 217 (1949): 361–68.

Kresch, M.J. "Axillary Temperature as a Screening Test for Fever in Children." *Journal of Pediatrics* 104 (1984): 597–99.

Levin, R., B. Nahlen, and D. Kent. "Diagnosis of the Child with Fever in the Emergency Department." *Journal of Emergency Nursing* 14 (1988): 359–64.

Lewin, T. "Coma from Alcohol Sponging." *Journal of the American College of Emergency Physicians* 6 (1977): 165–67.

Lorin, M. "Fever: Pathogenesis and Treatment." In *Textbook of Pediatric Infectious Diseases,* edited by R. Feigin and J. Cherry, 148–54. Philadelphia: W.B. Saunders Co., 1987.

McNally, J.M. "Fever: Management and Measurement." In *The Emergently Ill Child,* edited by R. Barkin, 32–36. Gaithersburg, Md.: Aspen Publishers, Inc., 1987.

Schmitt, B. "Fever Phobia." *American Journal of Diseases of Childhood* 145 (1980): 176–81.

Younger, S., and B. Brown. "Fever Management: Rational or Ritual?" *Pediatric Nursing* (Jan./Feb. 1985): 26–29.

Chapter 33

Diseases Associated with Rashes

Laurel S. Campbell

INTRODUCTION

One of the most difficult triage decisions to be made by the ED nurse involves evaluation of the many different pediatric rashes. A life-threatening illness may be represented by a petechial or purpuric rash. A rash could also be a symptom of one of the many infectious diseases that should be isolated to prevent spread to other patients.

PATHOPHYSIOLOGY

Rashes can either be caused by or be a symptom of a variety of pathophysiological disorders:

- bacterial infections
- viral infections
- loss of vascular integrity
- thrombocytopenia
- disorders of platelet function
- deficiencies of clotting factors
- allergic reactions
- parasitic infections

Several types of rashes exist, most of which can be grouped according to three general classifications:[1]

1. Primary lesions: lesions that may arise from previously normal skin
   - macule: small, flat, circumscribed

- papule: palpable elevated solid mass up to 0.5 cm
- nodule: 0.5–2 cm, deeper and firmer than a papule
- wheal: a slightly irregular area of skin elevation, which may be discolored
- vesicle: circumscribed superficial lesion, filled with serous fluid
- pustule: circumscribed superficial lesions, filled with pus
2. Secondary lesions: lesions that result from changes in primary lesions
- erosion: loss of the superficial epidermis, moist surface area
- crust: a lesion composed of dried residue (serum, pus, or blood)
- scale: flakes of exfoliated epidermis
3. Hemorrhagic lesions: lesions that occur as a result of bleeding under the skin
- petechiae: small pinpoint (1–2 mm) lesions that do not blanch under pressure
- purpura: larger ecchymotic lesions that do not blanch under pressure

Tables 33-1, 33-2, and 33-3 list the probable causes for a variety of childhood rashes.

TRIAGE ASSESSMENT

The initial assessment of a child with a rash should include a quick head-to-toe survey to assess the type and extent of the rash. The triage nurse should also assess for the presence of the following signs, which may also serve as clinical indicators of the pathophysiological process involved. Children with suspected communicable diseases should be isolated from other waiting patients.

- respiratory distress, tachypnea
- circulatory compromise: cool pale skin, mucous membranes, extremities
- fever
- joint or extremity pain
- toxic appearance: lethargy, irritability
- appearance of rash: flat, raised, scaly, vesicular; color; distribution
- tongue, oral mucous membranes appearance
- conjunctivitis, cough, coryza

TRIAGE HISTORY

- exposure to possible allergens/irritants (e.g., new pets, foods, detergents, or drugs)

Table 33-1 Diseases Associated with Maculopapular Rashes

Disease	Type of Rash	Incubation Period	Duration	Cause
Rubella (German measles, 3-day measles)	Macular, pink to red. First appears on head and spreads downward.	14–21 days; contagious from 7 days before to 5 days after rash appears.	3–4 days	Viral; can cause joint pain. Fever is uncommon.
Rubeola (measles, "red measles")	Preceded for 2–3 days by cough, coryza, and conjunctivitis. Koplik's spots appear on buccal mucosa (pinpoint white lesions on a red base) 12–24 h before rash. Rash consists of reddish macules and begins on face and spreads downward. Within 1–2 days, rash is confluent.	10–20 days; contagious from 4 days before to 5 days after rash appears.	10–15 days	Viral
Roseola	Maculopapular, small, pink, widely disseminated, and nonpruritic. Onset follows 3–4 days of fever.	Unknown	1–2 days	Probably viral
Erythema infectiosum (fifth disease)	Macular; facial distribution ("slapped cheeks" appearance). Lacy rash is found on flexor surfaces of arms and legs.	6–14 days	Acute phase = 3–4 days; may recur for several weeks if exposed to strong sunlight.	Viral (parvovirus B19)
Scarlet fever	Fine, raised generalized maculopapular rash ("sandpaper rash"). May be absent around mouth and face. Red "strawberry" tongue, bright red lines found in axilla and antecubital fossae (Pastia's lines). May peel after 5 days.	1–7 days. Contagious during incubation period.	Up to 3 weeks, until treated	Bacterial: Group A strep toxin

continues

Table 33-1 continued

Disease	Type of Rash	Incubation Period	Duration	Cause
Rocky Mountain spotted fever	Systemic signs for 1–3 days, consists of fever, headache, vomiting, and myalgias. Rash consists of pink macules on peripheral extremities that become papular after 1–2 days.	2–10 days	Until treated	Tick-introduced *Rickettsia*
Scabies	Initial: linear, threadlike grey to brown lesions between fingers and toes, and on ankles and axillae. Advanced: pruritic red papules.	Up to 30–60 days	Until treated	Parasitic mite that burrows under the skin
Contact dermatitis	Red maculopapular lesions; sharp demarcation exists between involved and uninvolved areas of skin. May develop into a secondary lesion (e.g., vesicles or wheals)	Lesions develop within a few minutes to a few hours after contact with allergen.	Until treated; may gradually disappear without treatment.	Irritating agents such as soaps, detergents, and rough sheets

Table 33-2 Diseases Associated with Secondary Lesions

Disease	Type of Rash	Incubation Period	Duration	Cause
Varicella (chickenpox)	Rash begins as small red macules and then progresses to papules and then vesicles. After the vesicles rupture, a dry crust forms over the lesion. May have all types of lesions present at the same time.	14–21 days; contagious from 1 day before eruption of lesions until 6–7 days after all lesions are crusted over.	5–20 days	Viral; scratching may cause a secondary bacterial infection.
Tinea corporis (ringworm)	Round or oval, red scaly patch that spreads peripherally and clears centrally.	N/A	Until treated	Fungus acquired through direct or indirect contact.
Impetigo	Rash begins as vesicular lesions, advances to yellow crusts on a red base. Usually seen on feet, hands, and around the mouth. May cause cellulitis.	N/A	Until treated	Bacterial (staph or strep)
Candida (Monilia)	Oral: white patches on mucous membranes; will not scrape off. Skin: red lesions with serous drainage, white crust (usually in diaper area).	N/A	Until treated	Yeast infection, which proliferates in warm, moist environments.
Kawasaki syndrome	Rash begins as red maculopapular lesions, commonly in the perineum area. Progresses to confluent pruritic wheals. Desquamation of lesions occurs within 2–7 days	Unknown	6–8 weeks	Unknown

Table 33-3 Diseases Associated with Hemorrhagic Lesions

Rash Type	Appearance	Disease(s)
Petechiae	Small (1–2 mm) pinpoint reddish purple macular lesions that do not blanch with pressure.	Platelet disorders Leukemia Meningococcemia Bacterial meningitis
Purpura (ecchymoses)	Larger ecchymotic lesions that are macular and do not blanch with pressure.	Henoch-Schönlein purpura Idiopathic thrombocytic purpura Hemophilia Trauma Viral infections

- exposure to other children wtih a similar rash
- immunization status including date of last injection
- current medications including over-the-counter drugs, antipyretics
- duration of symptoms
- presence of other symptoms such as fever, vomiting, sore throat, diarrhea, cough, lethargy, and/or itchiness

Tables 33-1 and 33-2 list possible symptoms that might occur in addition to rashes in selected diseases.

TELEPHONE TRIAGE GUIDELINES

The ED nurse should ask questions related to the triage assessment and history listed earlier in this chapter. Assessing rashes over the telephone is extremely difficult. A child with the following signs and symptoms should be evaluated immediately:

- acutely ill appearance
- petechial or purpuric rash (as described by caller)
- respiratory distress
- extreme discomfort (itching, pain, etc.)
- anxious parents

If the child does not appear to be acutely ill based on the parent's description, symptomatic treatment (for itching, preventing secondary infections) can be recommended, but the parent should be instructed to call the pediatrician. If the child has a hivelike rash with itchiness and is on an antibiotic, the antibiotic should be discontinued until the child can be evaluated.

If the parents want confirmation of a disease (e.g., chickenpox, measles, or scarlet fever), they should be told to call their pediatrician or come to the ED. They should be instructed on the possible contagiousness of the condition.

A chart that describes and pictures the various types of rashes caused by common pediatric conditions is useful at the triage area. The nurse's decisions should always be guided by how the child looks and acts, as well as by the type of rash.

PRIORITY RATING

The order in which patients are seen is determined by their clinical appearance as well as their need for isolation to prevent cross-contamination to other patients.

Emergent: Child with widespread ecchymotic or petechial rash with signs of sepsis, meningitis, circulatory compromise, or collapse (e.g., unstable airway, irritability, shock, decreased level of consciousness, fever > 102° F).

Urgent: Hemodynamically stable child with prodromal symptoms (fever < 102° F, cough, coryza, conjunctivitis, sore throat, joint pain), progressing or receding rash.

Nonurgent: Hemodynamically stable child with nontoxic rash (e.g., diaper dermatitis, candidiasis, mild contact dermatitis) with no other symptoms.

TREATMENT AND NURSING CARE/PARENT TEACHING

A rash that is a sign of life-threatening illness usually does not require treatment for the rash itself; however, supportive measures should be initiated in the emergency department setting (see Chapters 10 and 18). Table 33-4 lists medical and nursing interventions for common pediatric diseases accompanied by a rash, as well as parent teaching guidelines for each disease.

NURSING DOCUMENTATION

- history, including medications
- signs and symptoms of illness
- description of rash
- vital signs
- interventions and child's response
- follow-up care

Table 33-4 Medical and Nursing Interventions for Diseases Accompanied by Rashes

Disease/Rash	Treatment/Parent Teaching
Rubella	Fever control, PO fluids, supportive measures, analgesics for discomfort; isolate from pregnant females.
Rubeola	Fever control, respiratory isolation if hospitalized until fifth day of rash; bedrest, quiet activities; clean eyes with saline to remove secretions, use cool-mist vaporizer.
Roseola	Fever control, anticonvulsants for child with history of febrile seizures, seizure precautions.
Scarlet fever	Antibiotics, fever control, PO fluids, bedrest, soft diet, analgesics for sore throat, avoid irritating liquids; stress need for compliance with antibiotics (e.g., penicillin, erythromycin).
Rocky Mountain spotted fever	Antibiotics (e.g., tetracycline, chloramphenicol), fever control, supportive measures (usually hospitalized); inspect children frequently for ticks if they play in wooded areas.
Scabies	1% lindane (Kwell) shampoo/bath, also treat close contacts; wash linens in hot water; hospital personnel should wear gloves when in contact with child.
Candidiasis	Anticandidal ointment topically with each diaper change; teach parents good hygiene; oral antifungal agent if GI infection possible.
Contact dermatitis	Prevent further exposure to irritants; supportive measures.
Varicella	Supportive measures (e.g., PO and topical antihistamines), fever control (no aspirin); avoid scratching, keep fingernails short (use mittens on hands if necessary); after bath apply calamine or diphenhydramine lotion; teach parents about communicability period.
Tinea corporis	Oral griseofulvin, topical antifungal medications; may have been infected by a pet; prevent scratching.
Impetigo	Topical antibiotic ointment, systemic antibiotics (penicillin); avoid scratching (keep fingernails short; use mittens on hands if necessary).
Erythema infectiosum (fifth disease)	Rash should subside but may reappear if skin is irritated; analgesics for arthralgias.

NURSING DIAGNOSES

- potential alteration in body temperature (e.g., hyperthermia) related to infectious process
- alterations in oral mucous membranes related to infectious process
- actual or potential impairment of skin integrity related to primary and secondary lesions
- impaired tissue integrity related to secondary infectious process
- impaired physical mobility related to dressings, intravenous lines, hospitalization
- potential for infection of staff and other patients

NOTE

1. Barbara Bates, *A Guide to Physical Examination* (Philadelphia: J.B. Lippincott Co., 1979), 48–50.

BIBLIOGRAPHY

Brown, J. *Pediatric Telephone Medicine: Principles, Triage and Advice*. Philadelphia: J.B. Lippincott Co., 1989, 80–84.

Cohen, A.R. "Rash: Purpura." In *Textbook of Pediatric Emergency Medicine*, edited by G. Fleisher and S. Ludwig, 248–57. Baltimore: Williams & Wilkins Co., 1988.

Honig, P.J. "Rash: Vesiculobullous." In *Pediatric Emergency Medicine*, edited by G. Fleisher and S. Ludwig, 259–67. Baltimore: Williams & Wilkins Co., 1988.

Jaffe, D., and A.T. Davis. "Rash: Maculopapular." In *Textbook of Pediatric Emergency Medicine*, edited by G. Fleisher and S. Ludwig, 239–47. Baltimore: Williams & Wilkins Co., 1988.

Lynch, P. "Vascular Reactions." In *Pediatric Dermatology*, edited by L. Schachner and R. Hansen, 959–1014. New York: Churchill Livingstone Inc., 1988.

Urbach, A., R. McGregor, J. Malatack, J.C. Gartner, and B. Zitelli. "Kawasaki Disease and Perineal Rash." *American Journal of Diseases in Children* 142 (1988): 1174–76.

Whaley, L.F., and D.L. Wong. *Nursing Care of Infants and Children*. St. Louis: C.V. Mosby Co., 1987.

Chapter 34

Ear, Eye, Nose, and Throat Problems

Donna Ojanen Thomas

INTRODUCTION

Complaints relating to the ear, eye, nose, and throat (EENT) are common in the pediatric population. Ear pain caused by otitis media is one of the most common situations encountered both in the physician's office and in the ED. Therefore, otitis media is discussed in detail in this chapter. Other common EENT complaints that may be seen in the ED, along with their causes and treatment, are listed in Table 34-1.

OTITIS MEDIA

Otitis media, which is defined as an inflammation of the inner ear, is the most common cause of ear pain. Otitis externa, an infection of the ear canal, is the second most common cause. Otitis media can be classified into two types, depending on the etiology of the infection, signs and symptoms, and the otoscopic examination.

1. Acute suppurative otitis media: An inflammation of the middle ear usually caused by bacteria, often associated with a purulent drainage. Bacterial causes include the following:
   - *Streptococcus pneumoniae* (most common)
   - *Haemophilus influenzae*
   - *Branhamella catarrhalis*
   - *Staphylococcus aureus*
   - group A beta *Streptococcus*

   The actual bacterial or viral cause is not identified unless fluid from the inner ear is cultured. This is not done routinely. Diagnosis is usually based on the otoscopic exam of the eardrum. Signs and symptoms of acute suppurative otitis media include:

Table 34-1 Other Common EENT Conditions

Condition	Causes	Signs and Symptoms	Treatment and Nursing Care
Foreign body in the ear	Roaches Paper Toy parts Earring parts Hair beads Eraser tips	Pain and discomfort Hearing loss	Assist physician with removal of object. Insects: kill with alcohol prior to removal. Irrigation: use water pic on low setting or connect large (18-gauge) butterfly catheter to irrigation syringe and cut off needle, leaving tubing. Do not irrigate if tympanic membrane is perforated. Do not irrigate if vegetable matter is in ear as the material will absorb liquid and swell, making removal difficult. Mechanical removal includes using forceps and superglue. To use superglue, attach a small drop of cyanoacrylate glue on blunt end of swab so that only the tip is covered. Apply a small amount of superior and posterior traction on the auricle. Hold stick loosely and introduce into ear canal. Glue will adhere to object and then object can be removed.
Foreign body in the nose	Beads Toy parts Paper Food	Foul odor Discharge	Have child blow nose forcefully. Apply suction—may need to use vasoconstrictive drugs such as topical epinephrine or cocaine to reduce swelling. Then remove object with forceps. (Cocaine should be used with caution as intoxication can occur.) In cases of nasal and aural foreign objects, if attempts to remove object are unsuccessful, an ear, nose, and throat specialist should be consulted. *Parent Teaching* Keep small objects away from children. Teach children *not* to put objects in ears or nose.

Conjunctivitis	Inflammation of the conjunctiva caused by: Bacteria, Virus, Allergy, Chemical (due to make-up, eyedrops, or aerosols)	Conjunctival redness, Pain (usually with foreign body), Vision changes	Assist with the following when needed: Fluorescein stain of the eye to look for abrasion or foreign body. Removal of foreign body. Antibiotic drops or ointment. (Antihistamines may be prescribed for allergic conjunctivitis.) *Parent Teaching* Clean discharge from eye with warm water. Use of antibiotics. Prevent spread of infection. Call physician if eyelids become swollen or red, vision becomes blurred, or if not better in 72 h.
Chalazion	Inflammation of the meibomian gland on eyelid from retained secretions	Painful red nodule	Hot compresses. May need referral to ophthalmologist if not better.
Hordeolum (stye)	Infection of the hair follicle of the eyelash	Reddened macule at base of eyelash	Treatment the same as for chalazion.
Periorbital cellulitis	Bacterial infection of the periorbital region often resulting from a pre-existing break in the skin caused by animal or insect bites, chickenpox, or abrasions	Edema and "violet" color around the eye, No change in vision, Fever, May have pain with eye movement	Antibiotics as ordered. Child may be admitted for intravenous antibiotics if condition warrants. Periorbital cellulitis is an urgent condition. Complications include: Bacteremia with secondary focus, Infection of underlying bone, Spread of infection to orbit. If child is discharged, encourage follow-up as planned, and instruct to take antibiotics as directed.

continues

Table 34-1 continued

Condition	Causes	Signs and Symptoms	Treatment and Nursing Care
Epistaxis (most cases originate in anterior septum)	Trauma Foreign body Nose picking Upper respiratory infection Consistent exposure to dry air Polyps/neoplasms Bleeding disorders Aspirin ingestion Leukemia Anticoagulants	Active bleeding from one or both nostrils Vomiting coffee ground-like substance Persistent bleeding will lead to symptoms of shock	Obtain vital signs. Examine nose to determine bleeding site. To stop acute bleeding apply constant pressure over anterior nares for 15 min (with patient sitting forward). Vasoconstrictive drugs may be necessary if this is not successful. Cautery with silver nitrate may be necessary (should not be done in children with bleeding disorders). If bleeding cannot be controlled or is thought to originate in the posterior septum, an ear, nose, and throat specialist should be consulted.
Sore throat	*Common Causes* Infectious pharyngitis Respiratory viruses Group A streptococci Epstein-Barr virus Irritative pharyngitis *Emergent Causes* Epiglottitis (see Chapter 11) Peritonsillar abscess Retropharyngeal abscess Severe tonsillar hypertrophy	Pain Redness with or without exudate Swelling Difficulty swallowing Respiratory distress In addition to the above, children with streptococcal pharyngitis may have: Vomiting Abdominal pain Headache Fever Rash	Assess for presence of respiratory distress. If present, consult physician immediately (see Chapter 11). If not in respiratory distress, obtain throat culture for streptococci. *Parent Teaching* Acetaminophen. Antibiotics if ordered for streptococcal infection. Symptomatic family members should be cultured. Have child gargle with warm water. Children may return to school 24 h after antibiotics for *Streptococcus* have been started.

- deep, boring, constant ear pain
- fever (usually present)
- pain not exacerbated by pulling on pinna of ear
- changes in behavior (infants): fussy, irritable, tendency to rub, hold, or pull affected ear, changes in feeding habits

  2. Otitis media with effusion: An inflammation of the middle ear associated with a collection of fluid in the inner-ear space, usually caused by a virus, but possibly a complication of acute suppurative otitis media. The child may be asymptomatic or exhibit any or all of the following symptoms:

- feeling of fullness in the middle ear
- tinnitis or vertigo
- hearing loss

PATHOPHYSIOLOGY OF OTITIS MEDIA

The pathophysiology of otitis media is most commonly related to a dysfunctioning eustachian tube. The eustachian tube normally functions to

- protect the middle ear from nasopharyngeal secretions
- provide drainage into the nasopharynx of secretions produced in the middle ear
- permit equilibration of air pressure with atmospheric pressure

Eustachian tube obstruction results in negative middle-ear pressure and, if not relieved, in a middle-ear effusion. The fluid becomes trapped by the sustained negative pressure. Contamination of the inner-ear space with pharyngeal secretions may also occur by reflux.

Functional obstruction of the eustachian tube in infants and young children is common because they have less cartilaginous support than older children and adults. This makes the eustachian tube more susceptible to collapse and obstruction.

OTITIS EXTERNA

Otitis externa is an infection of the auditory canal that can be localized or diffuse, and is usually associated with prolonged exposure to water such as in swimming ("swimmer's ear"). Common causes include the following:

- *Pseudomonas aeruginosa* (most common)
- *Candida aspergillus*
- allergic reactions to ear drops
- complication of acute suppurative otitis media

The signs and symptoms differ from those of otitis media and include the following:

- constant pain, exacerbated by pulling on or touching the ear or chewing
- foul-smelling, purulent discharge
- redness, itchiness, and edema around the external auditory canal

TRIAGE ASSESSMENT OF THE CHILD WITH EAR PAIN

Although the majority of children with ear pain have otitis media or externa, other causes of ear pain need to be considered. Other causes include the following:

- foreign bodies in the ear canal; the second most common cause after inflammation and infection.
- tumors (uncommon)
- dental inflammation or erupting teeth
- pharyngitis
- sinusitis
- cervical lymphadenitis

The triage assessment focuses on signs and symptoms and appearance of the child, including the following:

- vital signs, especially presence of fever
- general appearance: symptoms of upper respiratory infection
- presence of drainage or odor from the ear canal
- presence of pain on manipulation of the ear
- presence of hearing deficits
- behavioral signs such as irritability and pulling at ears

TRIAGE HISTORY

- history of present illness
- changes in behavior or feeding habits

- previous ear infections
- trauma to ear or ear canal
- possibility of foreign body in ear
- measures taken to relieve ear pain
- pre-existing conditions: increased incidence of otitis media in children with unrepaired cleft palates or other craniofacial malformations

TELEPHONE TRIAGE GUIDELINES

Ear pain is rarely an emergency condition, but the child who is in acute pain needs some relief, as do the parents. The nurse should ask the following questions:

- age of the child
- duration of pain
- type of pain: is it affected by moving the outer ear?
- discharge present
- other symptoms
- general appearance

A child with acute ear pain that has lasted more than 1 hour should be told to come to the emergency department or see a physician. If the pain is not acute, simple measures such as acetaminophen or external heat may be helpful. The parent should be discouraged from putting ointments or oil in the ear canal until a physician is seen. Any child that appears acutely ill, or an infant less than 2 months of age who is fussy and has a fever, should also be seen as soon as possible.

The child with possible external otitis or with draining ears should be referred to a pediatrician for examination.

PRIORITY RATING

Emergent: Any child who appears acutely ill.

Urgent: Any child in acute pain and/or with a fever greater than 40° C (104° F).

Nonurgent: Child who is awake, alert, and afebrile, history of chronic otitis, or child who needs ears checked after antibiotic therapy.

TREATMENT AND NURSING CARE OF THE CHILD WITH OTITIS MEDIA OR EXTERNA

- General assessment. Check airway, breathing, circulation (ABCs).
- Control fever. Give acetaminophen 15 mg/kg if indicated.
- Assist with otoscopic exam.
- Remove earwax, if necessary. Liquid stool softener such as docusate sodium (Colace) instilled in the ear and left in for 15 minutes prior to irrigation with warm water is usually effective and nonirritating.
- Manage pain. Anesthetic drops containing antipyrine and benzocaine (Auralgan) can be ordered to relieve pain. This can often be done immediately if there will be a delay in examination of the child.
- Assist with other diagnostic tests. Laboratory studies can be done depending on the child's signs and symptoms.
- Give medications as ordered.
  - Amoxicillin 50 mg/kg/day given every 8 hours is the usual drug of choice.[1]
  - Combination antibiotic/corticosteroid drops (Cortisporin) 4 drops 4 times/day.[2]
  - Decongestants may be prescribed as they may help upper respiratory signs and symptoms.

Although amoxicillin is the drug of choice for otitis media, antibiotics are prescribed according to the child's age, allergies, and type of infection. Antibiotic drops are prescribed for cases of otitis externa.

PARENT TEACHING

- Continue all antibiotics until gone.
- Observe for possible side effects of antibiotics.
- Make follow-up appointment.
- Control fever and administer topical anesthetic, if appropriate.
- Keep child upright after feeding; don't prop up bottle.
- Provide comfort measures: hot packs or a heating pad in an older child.
- Return if fever is persistent or if child appears acutely ill or is not getting better.
- Keep water out of ear canal if otitis externa has been diagnosed.
- Instill 2–3 drops of 1:1 white vinegar/ 70% ethyl alcohol in ears as prophylaxis against otitis externa before and after swimming.[3]
- Observe for hearing loss.

NURSING DOCUMENTATION

- general appearance and level of consciousness
- vital signs
- duration of signs and symptoms
- past history of infections and antibiotic use
- interventions and child's response
- antibiotic given and follow-up instructions
- condition on discharge

NURSING DIAGNOSES

- alteration in comfort, pain related to ear infection
- alteration in body temperature (e.g., hyperthermia) related to infectious process
- fear of child related to ED and procedures
- knowledge deficit of parents regarding disease treatment and preventive measures

---

NOTES

1. Gary Fleisher, "Infectious Disease Emergencies," in *Textbook of Pediatric Emergency Medicine*, ed. Gary Fleisher and Steven Ludwig (Baltimore: Williams & Wilkins Co., 1988), 415, 474.

2. Barton Schmitt and Stephen Berman, "Ear, Nose, and Throat," in *Current Pediatric Diagnosis and Treatment*, ed. C. Kempe et al. (Norwalk, Conn.: Appleton & Lange, 1987), 318.

3. Ibid.

BIBLIOGRAPHY

Baker, M. "Foreign Bodies of the Ears and Nose in Childhood." *Pediatric Emergency Care* 3 (1987): 67–70.

Barkin, R., and P. Rosen. "Ear, Nose and Throat Disorders." In *Emergency Pediatrics*, edited by R. Barkin and P. Rosen, 479–97. St. Louis: C.V. Mosby Co., 1990.

Bluestone, C., and J. Klein. *Otitis Media in Infants and Children.* Philadelphia: W.B. Saunders Co., 1988.

Fleisher, G. "Sore Throat." In *Textbook of Pediatric Emergency Medicine*, edited by G. Fleisher and S. Ludwig, 294–99. Baltimore: Williams & Wilkins Co., 1988.

Hoffet, H. *Pediatric Infectious Disease*, 3d ed. Philadelphia: J.B. Lippincott Co., 1989, 82–88.

Klein, J., and C. Bluestone. "Acute Otitis Media." *Pediatric Infectious Disease* 1 (1982): 66–73.

Marchant, C., and P. Shurin. "Therapy of Otitis Media." *Pediatric Clinics of North America* 30 (1983): 281–95.

Potsic, W. "Earache." In *Textbook of Pediatric Emergency Medicine,* edited by G. Fleisher and S. Ludwig, 153–55. Baltimore: Williams & Wilkins Co., 1988.

Pride, H., and R. Schwab. "A New Technique for Removing Foreign Bodies of the External Auditory Canal." *Pediatric Emergency Care* 5 (1989): 135–36.

Schmitt, B., and S. Berman. "Ear, Nose and Throat." In *Current Pediatric Diagnosis and Treatment,* edited by C. Kempe et al., 308–22. Norwalk, Conn.: Appleton & Lange, 1987.

Sprague, J. "Eye Disorders." In *Emergency Pediatrics,* edited by R. Barkin and P. Rosen, 510–13. St. Louis: C.V. Mosby Co., 1990.

Whaley, L., and D. Wong. *Essentials of Pediatric Nursing,* 3d ed. St. Louis: C.V. Mosby Co., 1989, 702–04.

Williams, R. "Otitis Media and Otitis Externa." In *Primary Pediatric Care,* edited by R. Hockelman, 1401–04. St. Louis: C.V. Mosby Co., 1987.

Chapter 35

Genitourinary and Gynecological Problems

Jeanette H. Walker

URINARY TRACT INFECTIONS

INTRODUCTION

Urinary tract infections (UTIs) are the most frequently encountered genitourinary problem in children. A UTI is an infection that may involve the urethra or the bladder in the lower genitourinary (GU) tract or the ureter or kidney in the upper GU tract. Because the source of the infection is difficult to localize, the term UTI is applied to a growth of 100,000 organisms/mL anywhere in the urinary tract.[1]

PATHOPHYSIOLOGY

Most UTIs are a result of organisms moving upward through the urethra to the bladder, except in neonatal sepsis, where infection results from bacteremia. In most cases these infections are unlikely to cause complications. Recurrent infections, however, may cause distortion of the ureter as it crosses the bladder wall, resulting in incompetence of the vesicoureteral valve. Bacteria progress upward through the ureter into the kidney. A kidney infection may result, causing scarring and loss of renal tissue. Congenital anomalies and functional abnormalities are frequently associated with UTI.

A UTI is usually caused by a bacteria, but is occasionally the result of a virus. The most common organisms are the *Escherichia coli* and other gram-negative organisms including *Proteus mirabilis, Pseudomonas, Klebsiella, Staphylococcus aureus,* and *Haemophilus influenzae.* These organisms are commonly found in the anal, perianal, and perineal area.

Males have a higher incidence of UTI than females during infancy due to the higher incidence of anatomic defects. Beyond infancy, the short urethra and the close proximity of the urethra to the rectum are thought to account for the higher incidence in the female.

TRIAGE ASSESSMENT

- airway, breathing, circulation (ABCs)
- level of consciousness
- hydration status
- vital signs: temperature, pulse, respirations and blood pressure
- signs and symptoms of UTI

Signs and symptoms of UTI are related to the child's age and the area of infection. In a child less than 2 years old, signs and symptoms are nonspecific. Some signs and symptoms in the child are listed in Exhibit 35-1.

Exhibit 35-1 Signs and Symptoms of Urinary Tract Infection in the Child

GENERAL*
Failure to thrive
Vomiting
Diarrhea
Fever
Abdominal pain and distention
Strong-smelling urine
Chronic diaper rash
Hematuria

SYMPTOMS OF LOWER URINARY TRACT INFECTION
Frequency
Urgency
Painful urination
Incontinence in a toilet-trained child
Lower abdominal pain
Hematuria

SYMPTOMS OF UPPER URINARY TRACT INFECTION
Fever
Chills
Malaise
Flank pain
Anorexia
Nausea and vomiting

*These symptoms may be the only presenting symptoms in the child less than 2 years of age.

TRIAGE HISTORY

- previous history of urinary problems and/or anomalies
- history of current illness
- oral intake
- medications child may be taking, especially antibiotic therapy

TELEPHONE TRIAGE GUIDELINES

Any child with localized symptoms (hematuria, urgency, frequency, pain on urination, or incontinence) should be evaluated by a physician as soon as possible. Children under 2 years of age with a history of fever, irritability, vomiting, diarrhea, or strong-smelling urine should be examined to rule out UTI or another type of infection.

PRIORITY RATING

Emergent: Child with signs and symptoms of UTI, but who also has a decreased level of consciousness and looks acutely ill.

Urgent: A child with a history which is suggestive of UTI should be seen as soon as possible to have a urine culture and antibiotics started.

TREATMENT AND NURSING CARE

The primary goal in the medical management of a UTI is preservation of renal function through:

- identification of the organism responsible
- eradication of the organism with antibiotic therapy
- prevention of recurrent infections
- recognition and correction of anomalies

Nursing care of the child with a suspected UTI includes the following:

- antipyretics as needed for fever control
- collection of clean voided or catheterized urine specimen for analysis and culture. Exhibit 35-2 describes the method for obtaining a clean voided urine specimen in an infant.

Exhibit 35-2 Collection of a Clean Voided Specimen Using a Urine Collection Bag

---

EQUIPMENT
Washcloth
Sterile gauze sponges
Betadine solution
Gloves
Pediatric or infant collection bag
Diaper

PROCEDURE
Put on gloves.
Remove stool and protective ointments or powders with washcloth.
Clean perineal area with Betadine on sterile sponges.
  • Separate the labia and clean toward the anus in girls.
  • Retract the foreskin in boys and clean well.
Allow Betadine to dry.
Remove Betadine with moist sponge and dry with a sterile sponge.
Apply urine bag evenly. Place the fold of the bag first in the posterior perineal crease in girls.
Put on diaper to prevent the child from pulling off the bag.
Remove urine from bag with a sterile syringe.

- fluids: Encourage oral intake. Child may need intravenous replacement depending on hydration status.
- antibiotic therapy as ordered. Most symptomatic children are started on antibiotics prior to sensitivity results. Table 35-1 lists common antibiotics used to treat UTI.

PARENT TEACHING

The nurse should discuss the following topics with parents:

- antibiotic therapy
- importance of increased fluid intake
- follow-up. Repeat urine cultures are often done.
- reinfection. If it occurs, a referral to a urologist may be necessary.
- prevention
  1. Clean from front to back (girls) after voiding or defecating.
  2. Avoid tight clothing or diapers.
  3. See physician for perineal itching.

Table 35-1 Drugs Commonly Used in the Treatment of UTI

Drug	Dose* (Oral)	Nursing Implications/ Parent Teaching
Trimethoprim (TMP)	Based on TMP component	Increase fluid intake to prevent crystalluria.
Sulfamethoxazole (SMZ) (Septra, Bactrim)	< 40 kg: 8–10 mg/kg/day every 12 h > 40 kg: 320 mg/day every 12 h	Discontinue if skin rash appears; avoid use in neonates.
Amoxicillin	20–40 mg/kg per day every 8 h	May cause diarrhea, but has fewer gastrointestinal side effects than ampicillin.
Amoxicillin-Clavulanic acid	20–40 mg/kg per day every 8 h	β-Lactamase inhibitor extends activity of amoxicillin, but causes more diarrhea than amoxicillin.
Nitrofurantoin (Macrodantin)	5–7 mg/kg/24 h every 6 h	Give with meals or with milk.

*Doses from Peter C. Rowe, *The Harriet Lane Handbook,* 11th ed. (Chicago: Year Book Medical Publishers, Inc., 1987).

4. Teach the child to urinate regularly.
5. Avoid the use of detergents or bubble bath when bathing child.

NURSING DOCUMENTATION

- patient assessment: signs and symptoms present
- vital signs
- child's response to interventions
- method of collecting urine and urinalysis results
- teaching and follow-up instructions given

GENITOURINARY PROBLEMS IN MALES

Table 35-2 lists problems seen in the ED specific to male children.

Table 35-2 Genitourinary Problems in the Male Child

Condition	Definition/Causes Signs and Symptoms	Treatment/Nursing Care
Disorders occurring in the uncircumsized male		
Balanitis	Inflammation of the glans and foreskin of the penis associated with poor hygiene or trauma. Signs and symptoms include crustiness, swelling, and redness of the foreskin.	Clean area with soap and water. Antibiotics. Circumcision may be necessary. Teach parents proper hygiene. Observe for acute urinary obstruction.
Phimosis	Inability to retract foreskin over glans due to repeated infection or poor hygiene (retraction usually possible by age 4 years).	Circumcision may be necessary. Teach proper hygiene.
Paraphimosis	Foreskin retracted behind glans and cannot be drawn back into normal position, resulting in swelling or venous congestion.	Pain medication as ordered. Apply ice to area to reduce swelling. Manual reduction by physician. Teach parents proper hygiene of foreskin.
Penile trauma Direct injury	Often caused by toilet seat in small children learning to use toilet.	Significant injury is rare. Instruct parents to use warm soaks and observe for increased pain, swelling, or bleeding. Urologic consult may be necessary if laceration or bleeding at urethral meatus is present.
Zipper injury	Penile skin or foreskin caught in zipper, resulting in entrapment.	Assist physician in cutting median bar of zipper with wire cutters. May need local anesthetic. Instruct parents to use warm soaks for swelling.

continues

Table 35-2 continued

Condition	Definition/Causes Signs and Symptoms	Treatment/Nursing Care
Strangulation	Constriction of the penis by hair or fiber thread resulting in edema; causes constriction and decreased blood flow.	Cool compresses to reduce swelling. Removal of hair or thread (may require general anesthesia). May require urological consult. Constriction of the penis has been reported as a form of sexual abuse.
Testicular torsion	Twisting of the spermatic cord, leading to venous and arterial congestion. Symptoms include sudden onset of pain and swelling.	Testicular torsion is a life-threatening emergency and should be considered in all cases of scrotal pain. Evaluate immediately. Give nothing by mouth. Prepare for surgery. Analgesia as ordered. Doppler exam may be done and shows decreased blood flow.
Epididymitis	Infection of the epididymis (usually seen in males after puberty), associated with a history of trauma, lifting, or heavy exercise. Signs and symptoms include fever, tenderness, and swelling of epididymis.	Rule out testicular torsion. Antibiotics as ordered. Bedrest and scrotal support. Consider referral to urologist.
Inguinal hernia	Visceral contents are forced into the scrotum due to a defect that creates an open pouch. Most common surgical procedure in children. Can affect females, but 90% affect males. Signs and symptoms include history of crying and scrotal swelling.	Manual reduction is attempted by surgeon (often in ED). If manual reduction is unsuccessful, the hernia is termed incarcerated. Surgery is necessary to prevent compromises of blood supply to contents. Elective surgery may be done if manual reduction is successful, since recurrence is common.

Source: S. Kelley, "Genitourinary and Gynecologic Disorders," in *Pediatric Emergency Nursing,* ed. S. Kelley. (Norwalk, Conn.: Appleton & Lange, 1988), 400–15; H. Snyder, "Urologic Emergencies," in *Textbook of Pediatric Emergency Medicine,* ed. by G. Fleisher and S. Ludwig (Baltimore: Williams & Wilkins, 1988), 1032–40.

GYNECOLOGICAL PROBLEMS

Three gynecological conditions commonly seen in children in the ED are vaginal bleeding, vulvar bleeding, and vulvovaginitis. Adolescent pregnancy and pelvic inflammatory diseases are becoming more prevalent but are not discussed here as they are covered in many comprehensive textbooks. Sexual abuse is discussed in Chapter 31.

Table 35-3 discusses causes and treatment for gynecological complaints seen in the ED.

NURSING DIAGNOSES FOR THE CHILD WITH A GENITOURINARY OR GYNECOLOGICAL PROBLEM

- alteration in body temperature (e.g., hyperthermia) related to infection
- actual or potential fluid volume deficit related to decreased intake or increased output
- potential for infection
- altered patterns of urinary elimination
- alteration in comfort, pain related to condition
- knowledge deficit of condition and preventive measures

Table 35-3 Common Gynecological Problems Seen in the ED

Problem	Causes	Treatment and Nursing Care
Vaginal bleeding	Sexual abuse (Chapter 31) Trauma Foreign body Urethral prolapse Hematuria Rectal bleeding Pinworms Neonatal hormonal bleeding Precocious puberty Tumor Pregnancy Infections	Obtain history of menstrual cycle, trauma, and urinary complaints. Assess for injury. Assist physician with vaginal exam. Prepare child and family. Arrange for laboratory studies including hemoglobin, urinalysis, cultures, and pregnancy test. Conduct parent teaching including menstrual cycle, and refer for prenatal care if necessary. Consider sexual abuse (see Chapter 31). May need gynecological referral.
Vulvar bleeding	Trauma resulting in lacerations Urethral prolapse Pinworms	Evaluate for injury and urethral prolapse. May need gynecological referral. Treat as listed under "Vaginal bleeding."
Vulvovaginitis (most common gynecological problem in childhood)	Infection Trauma Allergic reactions related to soaps, bubble baths, and tight clothing	Apply antibiotic cream, depending on cause as instructed. Conduct parent teaching regarding sitz baths, improved hygiene, and avoiding contact with bubble baths and tight clothing.

Source: S. Kelley, "Genitourinary and Gynecologic Disorders," in *Pediatric Emergency Nursing,* ed. S. Kelley (Norwalk, Conn.: Appleton & Lange, 1988), 400–15.

NOTE

1. A. Wiesenthal, "Urinary Tract Infections: Assessment and Management," in *The Emergently Ill Child: Dilemmas in Assessment and Management,* ed. R. Barkin (Gaithersburg, Md.: Aspen Publishers, Inc., 1987), 73.

BIBLIOGRAPHY

Barkin, R. *The Emergently Ill Child: Dilemmas in Assessment and Management.* Gaithersburg, Md.: Aspen Publishers, Inc., 1987.

Barkin, R.M., and P. Rosen. *Emergency Pediatrics. A Guide to Ambulatory Care.* St. Louis: C.V. Mosby Co., 1990.

Bellman, A.B., and G.W. Kaplan. "Urinary Tract Infection." In *Genitourinary Problems in Pediatrics,* edited by A. Bellman and B. Kaplan, 37–66. Philadelphia: W.B. Saunders Co., 1981.

Hellerstein, S. *Urinary Tract Infections in Children.* Chicago: Year Book Medical Pubs Inc., 1982.

Kelley, S.J. "Genitourinary and Gynecological Disorders." In *Pediatric Emergency Nursing,* edited by S. Kelley, 400–15. Norwalk, Conn.: Appleton & Lange, 1988.

Snyder, H. "Urologic Emergencies." In *Textbook of Pediatric Emergency Medicine,* edited by G. Fleisher and S. Ludwig, 1032–40. Baltimore: Williams & Wilkins Co., 1988.

Stann, J.H. "Urinary Tract Infections in Children." *Pediatric Nursing* (1979): 49–52.

Thomas, C.K. "Childhood Urinary Tract Infections." *Pediatric Nursing* 8 (1982): 114–19.

Whaley, L.F., and D.L. Wong. "Urinary Tract Infection." In *Nursing Care of Infants and Children,* edited by L. Whaley and D. Wong, 1255–59. St. Louis: C.V. Mosby Co., 1987.

Chapter 36

Abdominal Pain

Donna Ojanen Thomas

INTRODUCTION

Although abdominal pain in children is frequently encountered in the ED, diagnosing the cause is often difficult. Evaluating a child with abdominal pain involves a thorough assessment and a complete history to determine if the pain results from a potentially life-threatening condition or one that is benign. Children less than 2 years old with abdominal pain are the most difficult to evaluate and may have pain resulting from a serious condition.

PATHOPHYSIOLOGY

Abdominal pain can originate in at least three neural pathways.[1]

1. visceral pain: generally a dull, aching sensation in the midabdominal, epigastric, or lower abdominal area
2. somatic pain: well localized and intense
3. referred pain: felt at a location distant from the diseased organ; can be sharp and localized or a vague ache

Some extra-abdominal illnesses such as tonsillitis, pneumonia, and viral syndromes are associated with abdominal pain although the pain can't be explained physiologically.

The causes of abdominal pain vary with the age of the child. Although acute gastroenteritis is a common cause in all age groups, other more serious conditions must be excluded.

Table 36-1 lists some causes of abdominal pain in different age groups.

Table 36-1 Some Causes of Abdominal Pain in Different Age Groups

Age	Causes
Infants (less than 2 years of age)	Colic (less than 3 months of age) Acute gastroenteritis Trauma (child abuse) Intussusception Intestinal anomalies Volvulus Perforated viscus Hirschsprung's disease Sickling syndromes
Preschool child (2–5 years of age)	Gastroenteritis Urinary tract infections Trauma Appendicitis Pneumonia Viral syndromes Constipation Sickling syndromes
School-aged child (greater than 5 years of age)	Gastroenteritis Trauma Appendicitis Urinary tract infections Functional pain Sickling syndromes Constipation
Adolescent	Same as for school-aged child, but genitourinary or gynecological problems need to be considered: • Pelvic inflammatory disease • Dysmenorrhea • Epididymitis • Testicular or ovarian torsion • Ectopic pregnancy

Source: R. Barkin and P. Rosen, "Acute Abdominal Pain," in *Emergency Pediatrics. A Guide to Ambulatory Care,* ed. R. Barkin and P. Rosen (St. Louis: C.V. Mosby Co., 1990), 154–56; R. Ruddy, "Abdominal Pain," in *Textbook of Pediatric Emergency Medicine,* eds. G. Fleisher and S. Ludwig (Baltimore: Williams & Wilkins, 1988), 71–72.

TRIAGE ASSESSMENT

- airway, breathing, circulation (ABCs); signs and symptoms of shock
- vital signs: temperature, pulse, respiration, and blood pressure
- general appearance of child: pain, difficulty in walking or moving
- hydration status
- pain: location, radiation, and type (constant or intermittent)
- presence of other signs and symptoms: vomiting, diarrhea, cough
- skin: color (pale, jaundiced, rashes)

TRIAGE HISTORY

- characteristics of pain
- history of trauma
- factors that alleviate or aggravate pain (positioning, eating, walking)
- history of associated symptoms
- stool patterns: diarrhea or constipation
- comfort measures done at home
- sexual activity if applicable
- past medical history: sickle cell disease, diabetes, prior abdominal surgery

The child with abdominal pain should be made NPO (give nothing by mouth) until a surgical condition is ruled out. Children with diabetic ketoacidosis may complain of abdominal pain. Children with a history of abdominal surgery may have an obstruction related to the previous condition.

TELEPHONE TRIAGE

Telephone triage for abdominal pain is difficult. The nurse needs to evaluate whether the child should be seen in the ED. Differentiating between gastroenteritis and an acute condition is extremely difficult over the telephone. The nurse can give advice based on the child's age. For infants, the nurse should ask questions concerning the following topics:[2]

- duration of pain. Colic is usually manifested by crying bouts that last 3 hours or more and occur at the same time of day several times a week.

- fever. An infant less than 3 months old should be evaluated as soon as possible.
- feeding patterns. Overfeeding may cause cramping and spitting up. Some foods may also cause abdominal pain.
- vomiting. Green-stained vomitus may indicate abdominal obstruction.
- diarrhea. Bloody diarrhea could be due to gastroenteritis, but could also be due to intussusception or another acute surgical condition. Red Jell-O water or beets may make stools look red. Nursing mothers who have cracked and bleeding nipples may also see blood in the baby's stools.
- frequency of pain
- history of trauma
- appearance of the baby. A baby who looks well between crying bouts may just have gas or colic; infants who are described as pale, or sweaty, or "not looking right" should be evaluated as soon as possible.

The nurse should tell the parents to bring the baby to the ED immediately if

- vomitus is bile stained
- diarrhea is present and is grossly bloody
- baby looks acutely ill
- parents are extremely worried

For the older child, the nurse should ask the same questions, as well as questions about other symptoms such as constipation, diarrhea, location and intensity of pain, and exposure to illness. The child needs to be evaluated immediately if

- pain is localized in the lower abdomen and has remained localized
- the child has bloody stools
- the child has green or bile-stained vomitus
- the child looks acutely ill

The nurse needs to be careful when giving any symptomatic advice without first checking with the ED physician. The nurse should tell the parent to bring the child to the ED at any time.

PRIORITY RATING

Emergent: Child with prolonged, severe pain; high temperature; crying and doubling over with pain; associated trauma; potential dehydration; tachypnea; grunting; acutely ill appearance.

Urgent: Child with history of abdominal pain, mild to moderate discomfort, and no history of trauma, who is well hydrated.

Nonurgent: Child with symptoms of gastroenteritis and no acute pain, who is well hydrated, alert, and active.

TREATMENT AND NURSING CARE

1. Stabilize child's condition as needed.
   - Do airway management: supplemental oxygen.
   - Give IV fluid: The child with a history of vomiting and diarrhea may need fluid replacement. Lactated Ringer's is the fluid of choice if the child shows signs and symptoms of dehydration and shock.
2. Do abdominal exam
   - Observe for signs and symptoms of trauma, abdominal distention.
   - Auscultate (do before palpation to avoid stimulating the bowel): Are bowel sounds present or absent?
   - Palpate. Check for presence of masses or rebound tenderness.
   - Arrange for rectal exam as indicated (done by physician).

   The following conditions should be considered during the abdominal exam:
   - obstruction. Involves intermittent, crampy pain, vomiting that is projectile or bilious, distended abdomen.
   - peritonitis. Child may look acutely ill, not want to move; has rebound tenderness.
   - abdominal mass. Discovered during palpation of abdomen, and may indicate appendicitis, intussusception.
   - signs and symptoms of abdominal trauma (Chapter 21).
3. Initiate diagnostic tests. The following may be ordered by the physician, depending on physical findings:
   - laboratory studies, including complete blood count with differential, throat, and blood cultures; electrolytes; glucose; BUN; amylase; urinalysis; pregnancy test; and vaginal cultures as indicated
   - radiologic tests: chest x-ray, abdominal film
4. Initiate surgical consultation. The ED physician may obtain surgical consultation depending on findings.
5. Initiate other procedures as appropriate.
   - Insert nasogastric tube to decompress the stomach.
   - Give enemas, as ordered, for constipation.
   - Give antibiotics as ordered by physician (for suspected peritonitis).

- Allow parents to remain with child as much as possible.
- Prepare child and family for possible surgery and admission.

PARENT TEACHING

1. Child's condition and needed treatment. If child is discharged
   - Give special instructions for diet.
   - Explain signs and symptoms that require child to be re-evaluated.
   - Discuss medications given.
   - Discuss symptomatic care.
   - Discuss any follow-up planned.
2. If child is admitted to the hospital
   - Explain all treatments.
   - Discuss surgical procedure (make sure parents understand explanation given by physician, and allow them to ask questions).
   - Explain hospital routine.
   - Assess need for additional support for the family.

NURSING DOCUMENTATION

- initial assessment: vital signs
- history of illness
- signs and symptoms: location and duration of pain, alleviating or aggravating factors
- interventions and child's response
- preparations for surgery: laboratory data, signed operative permit, NPO status
- disposition of child
- home care and follow-up if discharged

NURSING DIAGNOSES

- alteration in body temperature (e.g., fever)
- fluid volume deficit related to vomiting and/or diarrhea
- impaired skin integrity related to diarrhea

- alteration in elimination, constipation, or diarrhea
- alteration in gastrointestinal tissue perfusion
- alteration in comfort, pain (acute or chronic)
- alteration in comfort, related to nausea and vomiting
- knowledge deficit of parents about child's condition
- fear (child's) related to ED procedures and/or possible surgery

NOTES

1. Richard Ruddy, "Abdominal Pain," in *Textbook of Pediatric Emergency Medicine*, eds. G. Fleisher and S. Ludwig (Baltimore: Williams & Wilkins Co., 1988), 70.

2. Jeffrey Brown, ed., *Pediatric Telephone Medicine. Principles, Triage, and Advice* (Philadelphia: J.B. Lippincott Co., 1989), 37–45.

BIBLIOGRAPHY

Barkin, R., and P. Rosen. "Acute Abdominal Pain." In *Emergency Pediatrics: A Guide to Ambulatory Care,* edited by R. Barkin and P. Rosen, 154–56. St. Louis: C.V. Mosby Co., 1990.

Bourg, P., C. Sherer, and P. Rosen. *Standardized Nursing Care Plans for Emergency Departments,* edited by P. Bourg, C. Sherer, and P. Rosen, 3–11. St. Louis: C.V. Mosby Co., 1986.

Fraser, G. "Abdominal Pain." In *Handbook of Pediatric Emergencies,* edited by G. Baldwin, 150–58. Boston: Little, Brown, and Co., 1989.

Juster, F., and R. Ruddy. "Acute Abdominal Pain." In *Pediatric Emergency Medicine for the House Officer,* edited by S. Selbst and S. Torrey, 235–42. Baltimore: Williams & Wilkins Co., 1988.

Ruddy, R. "Abdominal Pain." In *Textbook of Pediatric Emergency Medicine,* edited by G. Fleisher and S. Ludwig, 70–77. Baltimore: Williams & Wilkins Co., 1988.

Sperhac, A. "Gastrointestinal Emergencies." In *Pediatric Emergency Nursing,* edited by S. Kelley, 349–88. Norwalk, Conn.: Appleton & Lange, 1988.

Index